# PC Assembly Language

## Step by Step

### by Alex Hoffman

**Abacus**

A Mico Application Book

First Printing 1990

Copyright © 1990            Abacus
                                     5370 52nd Street S.E.
                                     Grand Rapids, MI 49512

Copyright © 1989            Micro Application
                                     58 Rue du Faubourg Poissonniere
                                     75010 Paris

Every effort has been made to ensure complete and accurate information concerning the material presented in this book. However, Abacus can neither guarantee nor be held legally responsible for any mistakes in printing or faulty instructions contained in this book. The authors always appreciate receiving notice of any errors or misprints.

This book contains trade names and trademarks of many companies and products. Any mentions of these names or trademarks in this book are not intended to either convey endorsement or other associations with this book.

PC-DOS, IBM PC, XT, AT, PS/2, OS/2 and PC-BASIC are trademarks or registered trademarks of International Business Machines Corporation. MS-DOS and Microsoft Macro Assembler are trademarks or registered trademarks of Microsoft Corporation. Lotus 1-2-3 is a trademark or registered trademark of Lotus Development Corporation.

Edited by Scott Slaughter, Robbin Markley and Mike Bergsma.

```
                    Library of Congress Cataloging-in-Publication Data
Hoffman, Alex,
        PC Assembly language step-by-step / Alex Hoffman.
                p.  cm.
        "A Micro Application book."
        Includes index.
        ISBN 1-55755-096-4: $34.95
        1. Assembler language (Computer program language)  I. Title
QA76.73.A8H63 1990
005.265--dc20                                        90-21839
                                                        CIP
```

# Introduction

*Assembly Language Step-by-Step* introduces you to PC assembly language.

This is, quite simply, a self-teaching assembly language book. The companion diskette, which accompanies this book, contains a simulator called "SIM". It's a powerful learning tool. In fact, by using SIM, you'll execute the programs we discuss in this book and you'll discover how they work. SIM will describe, in detail, all the operations carried out by the 80x86 microprocessor.

After reviewing the basics of programming and how microcomputers work (with the emphasis on PCs), we'll study all the instructions of 80x86 assembly language. Each chapter presents a specific area of assembly language.

These instructions are presented progressively. They start with the simplest and move to the most complex. You'll quickly understand the purpose and relevance of each instruction by executing simulations with SIM. At the end of each chapter, specific exercises will let you review what you've learned. If you're completely lost or are uncertain of the answer, we provide the answers at the end of the book.

## Assembly language or machine language?

There is no significant distinction between machine language and assembly language for the beginning programmer. As you learn one, you learn the other as well. If you're confused by that statement, then *Assembly Language Step-by-Step* is for you.

## Hardware requirements

To make the most of this self-teaching method, you'll need an IBM PC, XT, AT or compatible with a 8088/86, 80286 or 80386 processor. Your system should include at least one floppy disk drive (preferably a hard drive) and 128K of RAM. The more memory available in your computer, the more free memory you'll have to work with SIM.

## Expertise

This book requires a working knowledge of the BASIC or other computer language. The more experience you have in programming, the more you'll understand machine language. However, *Assembly Language Step-by-Step* doesn't require previous experience programming in machine language.

## The format of *Assembly Language Step-by-Step*

Most books for teaching 80x86 machine language attempt to cover everything from floating decimal point math to printer drivers. We have chosen a different route. Instead of scaring you off by giving you something like algorithms for controlling elevators, this book intends to help you get over the first obstacles of programming in machine language.

*Assembly Language Step-by-Step* isn't an encyclopedia. It is, however, an easy introduction to programming in machine language. Even if you understand everything described in this book, we cannot guarantee a software company will hire you as a machine language programmer. However, if you learn and remember what we discuss in *Assembly Language Step-by-Step*, you'll be able to use machine language for your own applications.

### Chapters 1-4

The first four chapters discuss binary and hexadecimal numbers, basic computer concepts and boolean logic. If you're familiar with these subjects, you can skip these chapters. However, these are important subjects to understand for successfully writing in machine language.

### Chapters 5-9

These chapters introduce and discuss the SIM simulator.

### Chapters 10-31

The course in assembly language starts in earnest in Chapter 10 and ends at Chapter 31. Throughout these twenty-some chapters you'll work with programs in machine language that are more and more difficult. By this time, you'll have read and seen practically all the instructions of the 80x86.

### Chapters 32 and 33

Describe the complete process for developing a program from its conception to the final product. You'll also study about editing links. At that point, we use Version 4.0 of Microsoft assembly language.

### Appendices

Describe the commands of the SIM simulator, error messages, an ASCII table and a list of the complete 8088/80x86 instruction set.

# Table of Contents

# 1. What is Assembly Language?

You've probably heard many scary stories about machine or assembly language. So many in fact that you may wonder why anyone would want to learn such a difficult language. However, there are many advantages of programming in assembly language.

Although the most popular programming languages include Pascal, BASIC and Cobol, assembly language remains the best language to directly program the 80x86 processor (the 80x86 includes the 8088, 8086, 80286, 80386 and 80486). We'll provide a more formal definition in later chapters, but for now, we'll mention that the assembly language of the 80x86 is the primary language of IBM PCs and compatibles. These PCs execute instructions written in 80x86 assembly language. Other computer languages, such as BASIC and Pascal are actually only shortcuts for avoiding the difficulties inherent in using 80x86 assembly language.

At this point you might be wondering whether we're talking about learning machine language or assembly language. Actually, any distinction between machine language and assembly language is mostly a question of semantics. It's like knowing whether the 80x86 is an 8 bit, a 16 bit or a 32 bit processor.

By the time you finish reading this book, the relationship between machine language and assembly language will be clear. It's sufficient for now to understand that learning 80x86 machine language is the same as learning 80x86 assembly and vice versa.

Many new programmers believe that learning programming in assembly language is more difficult than learning an advanced language like BASIC or Pascal. For example, let's say we want a robot to build a fence around a garden. The following compares what a program for this type of operation would be like in both BASIC and assembly language:

**BASIC:**
> Put up a fence for the garden made of pine stakes each an inch in diameter and six feet long, placed in the ground every three yards.

**Assembly language:**
> Go to the lumber yard and buy 722 pine stakes that are each six feet long. Load them in the truck. Go home. Unload the truck. Start in the northeast corner of the garden. Make a hole two feet deep. Take a stake from the pile. Put the stake in the hole. Pour concrete into the hole. Move ahead three yards. If you're not at a corner of the garden, make a hole two feet deep. Take a stake from the pile, etc.

Although the assembly language example seems more complicated and requires more time to write, each of the individual steps such as "Make a hole two feet deep."; "Take a stake from the pile."; "Move ahead three yards", are easy to understand. The same applies to assembly language; although the result can be very complex, the individual steps (code) are actually very simple.

# 1.1    Why Assembly Language?

Programming in assembly language requires advancing in small steps to reach your goal. However, it requires more time to write, create, code and debug programs. Furthermore, almost everything that you can do in assembly language can be programmed using BASIC or Pascal.

There are at least three main reasons why people learn and program in assembly language:

1.      The program executes faster in assembly language than other languages.

2.      Assembly language provides more complete control over the progress of the program.

3.      Assembly language allows for smaller programs.

We'll discuss these reasons in the following section.

## 1.1.1    Fast execution

If you compare the execution speed of an identical program written in assembly language and in BASIC, you'll see the program executes much faster in assembly language. This difference can be hundreds of times faster. This difference applies to other languages besides BASIC. An assembly language program can execute twice as fast as the same program written in higher languages such as Pascal or C.

Of course, you don't always need fast execution speed. There are programs and applications (called *print bound programs* or *disk bound programs*) where fast execution speed is not as important as other considerations. When you use these applications, your computer spends most of its time waiting for keystroke, printing or performing a read/write to/from the hard drive to complete.

For example, if you were to write an accounting application in assembly language, you must write the program to anticipate extremely rapid keypresses. This type of program would cost several times more to develop and require more time than writing an identical application in BASIC.

On the other hand, there are times when speed is critical. For example, entertainment software, whether simple like Pacman or more complicated like Flight Simulator, might not respond quickly enough if written in BASIC. Graphics and animations on the screen require a lot from a computer; the computer must calculate the movement of thousands of numbers per second. If Pacman was written in BASIC, it would be so slow that the Pacman

minute to move from one side of the screen to the other. Therefore, entertainment software is usually written in assembly language because of the fast execution speed.

## 1.1.2    Few limitations

None of the high level languages are perfect for all applications. Most were created for a specific purpose. For example, BASIC was developed to provide new computer owners a simple and easy language to learn. In fact the name BASIC is an acronym for *Beginners All-Purpose Symbolic Instruction Code*. The strength of assembly language is that it's versatile and can be used for many applications. A good programer can bring out the full power of the PC by writing at least part of the program in assembly language.

## 1.1.3    Optimal size

Smaller program size is another advantage of programming in assembly language. However this is now less important than it has been in the past. In the early 1960's, 64K of RAM cost as much as the yearly income for most people so it was critical to reduce program size to a minimum. The cost of RAM chips are so inexpensive (and powerful) today that many computers have over 1 megabyte of RAM.

## 1.2   Hybrid Programs

There are cases when you may need to combine or write portions of a program in assembly language and portions in a higher language such as C or Pascal. This combination program is called a *hybrid program*. Dividing up tasks between an advanced language and assembly language is a technique currently used in most programs.

You can write part of the program with a higher level language such as C or Pascal. This part of the program may execute certain printer routines, data entry or other functions. Although this part of the program executes slower, it's also simple to write and faster to debug, if necessary.

However, other functions, such as sorting data, will execute much faster when written in assembly language. A BASIC sort program or routine is extremely slow. It requires at least two minutes (possibly as many as ten minutes, depending on the program) to sort a list of 3000 numbers in ascending order. Sorting methods range from the simplest (easy to read) to the most complex.

A time period of two minutes is important for users of business applications and 10 minutes is an eternity. So the smart programer will do most of the work in BASIC, Pascal or other languages and then create routines for sorting operations in assembly language. Although it requires a long time to write these sort routines, the execution speed is very fast.

If you like to program in BASIC, Pascal or other higher languages, you'll enjoy working with the bits and bytes of assembly language. Programming in assembly language is similar to working at ground level. As you can see, there are several good reasons for programming in assembly language but it can also be fun.

# 2. Number Systems

If you purchased this book hoping it would spare you from learning about hexadecimal calculations and miraculously lead you into the world of the 80x86, we're going to disappoint you. Binary or hexadecimal numbering systems aren't used just to make programming in assembly language more difficult. Without them programming would be impossible.

While it's possible to learn assembly language without working with hexadecimal numbers, it would actually be more difficult. You'll soon discover that you'll have to work twice as hard without hexadecimal numbers than if you had learned it from the beginning.

## 2.1    Twelve is 12 But Also 1100

Numbers are specific characters that, when combined, provide a very precise numeric definition. For example, combining a "1" with "2" gives us a new number of 12. Although we can represent the figure with dots:

```
. . . . . . . . . . . .
```

or just as many Xs:

```
X X X X X X X X X X X X
```

it's still a very exact figure. However, neither the dots nor the Xs by themselves contain the concept of "twelve". For example, suppose that a group of people have agreed that from now on "*" represents 12 and "#" represents 17. They believe that:

```
* = X X X X X X X X X X X X
```

and

```
# = X X X X X X X X X X X X X X X X X
```

However, using this system for performing mathematical calculations would be quite difficult. For example, how can you calculate * divided by #? Normal notation won't work when we require a system with decimal numbers. Therefore, we'd have to memorize all the possible combinations for multiplication and division involving * and #.

This example isn't as improbable as you might think. Remember the Roman Empire. Their numbering system was as primitive as our * and # example:

```
LXXIX / XIV
```

The best way to solve this problem today is to convert these two numbers into "normal" ones and then perform the division. Then you would have to convert the result back to Roman numerals.

Unfortunately, "normal" numerals didn't exist in this time period. It wasn't until around 500 A.D. that an Arab astrologer devised a new system of Arabic numerals which were easier to use in representing large numbers and easier to perform mathematical operations.

Let's see why this system of notation works so well. The numbers defined in this system can be systematically split into parts of the original number. The value of the digits depends on their position in the number. In any given number, the number N is always ten times greater than the same number N placed at its right and ten times less than the same number N placed at its left. This is illustrated in the following table:

| Thousands Digit | Hundreds Digit | Tens Digit | One Digit |
|---|---|---|---|
| $10^3$ | $10^2$ | $10^1$ | $10^0$ |
| 1000 | 100 | 10 | 1 |

In mathematics, a number raised to the power of zero is always 1. In the decimal system the numbers can be represented as a sum of individual products of base-ten. Each number is assigned a specific power of ten. For example, you can break down 3,479 as:

| Thousands Digit | Hundreds Digit | Tens Digit | One Digit |
|---|---|---|---|
| $10^3$ | $10^2$ | $10^1$ | $10^0$ |
| 1000*3 | 100*4 | 10*7 | 1*9 |
| 3000 | 400 | 70 | 9 |

This system is called the *decimal system*. The term is from the Latin "demem" (or "ten"), since ten is the base of the value of each number. A number can be converted into a number in any number system.

However, no matter how ten is represented, it isn't more important than any other number. So why select ten as the base value in our system of numerical notation? The reason we use base-ten deals more with tradition. The decimal system (and not an octal system) remains unchanged for nearly 1500 years.

Unfortunately for computer programming, especially programming in assembly language, using the decimal system is as inefficient as using Roman numerals. The very nature of processors limits them to a vocabulary composed of only two symbols: "1" and "0".

Why only two symbols? Why not use computers capable of calculating in base-ten. Although this type of computer is possible, it would actually further complicate work. The problem is in representing discrete (digital) values in a world composed of continuous (analog) values.

The solution might be to have computers using light pulses for storing data as is now being researched by several manufacturers. Such a machine would use variations of light in a decimal base to represent the numbers 0 to 9.

It's possible to create bulbs of defined luminosity and light detectors calibrated on a scale of ten distinct levels. As you can see with the following illustration, the appearance of the pulse light for 0 is quite different from the appearance of the pulse light for 9:

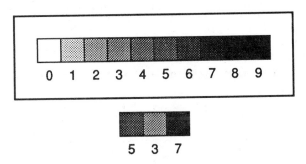

However, the difference between 3 and 4 or 8 and 9 is very slight. Therefore, it's simpler, more economical and more reliable to have a system using base-two: light on, light off.

A computer uses semiconductors which can represent two states: 1 for on and 0 for off. Instead of transmitting differences of light intensity, they receive and transmit voltage. Strong voltage means 1 and no voltage means 0.

The base-two type of notation which computers use is called a *binary system*. Each task your PC carries out, whether you're using Lotus 1-2-3, a BASIC program or Pacman, is the result of intensive manipulations of 0 and 1 or on and off.

Just as our decimal system doesn't need any more than ten digits to represent values above 0, so the binary system doesn't need special symbols to represent values from 2 to 9 because these values can be formed by combinations of 1 and 0.

The binary system is based on the same principle of individual powers as the decimal system. The difference is that the base is two and not ten. The places of the individual digits, as in the decimal system, correspond to individual powers (powers of two). The following table shows the first four values of the binary system:

| Fourth Digit | Third Digit | Second Digit | First Digit |
|:---:|:---:|:---:|:---:|
| $2^3$ | $2^2$ | $2^1$ | $2^0$ |
| 8 | 4 | 2 | 1 |

For example, you can break down the following numbers as:

| Hexadecimal number is 1010 | 1*8 + | 0*4 + | 1*2 + | 0*1 | = 10 in decimal |
|---|---|---|---|---|---|
| Hexadecimal number 1110 | 1*8 + | 1*4 + | 1*2 + | 0*1 | = 14 in decimal |

Binary system requires the use of zeros even when they're not necessary. Therefore 101 must be written as 00000101.

In 80x86 programming, you'll often encounter binary numerals of 8 and 16 characters called *bits*. This term is derived from binary digit. They're numbered from left to right (see below). Bit 0 is called the least significant bit and bit 7 is the most significant bit.

| Bits: | 7 | 6 | 5 | 4 | 3 | 2 | 1 | 0 |
|---|---|---|---|---|---|---|---|---|

Adding and subtracting binary numbers is very similar to adding and subtracting decimal numbers:

```
0 + 0 = 0

0 + 1 = 1

1 + 0 = 1

1 + 1 = 0, carry 1 (10)
```

Carrying is common in binary addition and subtraction.

```
              1                 1 1      <-- carry

    1 0 1 0       1 0 1 0       1 0 0 1

  + 0 1 0 0     + 0 0 1 0     + 0 0 1 1

    1 1 1 0       1 1 0 0       1 1 0 0

                      1             1 1      <-- carry

    1 0 1 0       1 0 1 0       1 0 0 1

  - 0 1 0 0     - 0 0 1 0     - 0 0 1 1

    0 1 1 0       1 0 0 0       0 1 1 0
```

Whole numbers in binary are all powers of two: 1, 2, 4, 8, 16, 32, 64 and so forth. This is very important. This notion constantly appears in assembly language programming.

The number of possible combinations of bits for making a binary numeral is a geometric progression or a series of multiplications by 2. Each time you add a digit you double the number of possible combinations.

You can, in fact, organize the bits in two new ways: one more series when the new bit is activated and one more series with the new bit is deactivated. So, with 3 bits, you have eight possible combinations of bits. With 4 bits, you have eight possible combinations when bit 4 is activated and eight when it is deactivated, for a total of 16 combinations.

Although this progression starts slowly, you don't need to proceed too far before becoming overwhelmed:

| Number of bits | Possible combinations |
|----------------|-----------------------|
| 4              | 16                    |
| 20             | 1,048,576             |
| 24             | 16,777,216            |

A good example of this progression is the story of a king so enchanted by the game of chess that he offered a bag of gold as a reward to its inventor. The inventor refused it. Perplexed, the king asked him how he wanted to be rewarded. After thinking for a moment, the inventor asked the king to place a grain of rice on the first square of the chessboard, two grains on the next square, then four, then eight and so on until all the squares would be filled. The king quickly granted what he considered as a modest request. Obviously his calculation skills were limited. The inventor got away with the deal of the century: more than 18 quadrillion grains of rice (about a trillion tons of rice).

The formula for calculating the largest number of X combinations of n numbers with a base B is:

```
X = B^n + 1
```

The greatest decimal value that can be represented with 3 digits is .999 (or $10^3$-1). A three digit number with a base of 7 can go up to ($7^3$-1). With 3 digits, the binary system can only go to 7 (or $2^3$-1). Consequently, in binary system, even numbers of modest size can take useless space.

The following table shows decimal numbers and their binary equivalents:

| Decimal | Binary equivalent |
|:---:|:---:|
| 0 | 0000 |
| 1 | 0001 |
| 2 | 0010 |
| 3 | 0011 |
| 4 | 0100 |
| 5 | 0101 |
| 6 | 0110 |
| 7 | 0111 |
| 8 | 1000 |
| 9 | 1001 |
| 10 | 1010 |

Although these digits certainly confuse things, they help break the bits down into equal groups. So four bits form a *nibble* (also called *nybble*) and eight bits form a *byte*. In the context of 80x86 programming, 16 bits make up a *word*. The decimal number 531 is 0010

0001 0011 in nibbles. Although slightly better than 1000010011, it still doesn't say much.

Of course, it isn't because computers need to work in binary that people have to program numbers with "1"s and "0"s. You can still continue to use decimal numbers in the "advanced" languages such as BASIC, Pascal or C. However, since you intend to program in assembly language, you'll often have to use the binary system.

To avoid this problem, you can work in decimal notation and convert values in both directions. The idea is a good one but, like mathematicians say, this type of conversion isn't "trivial". It's easier to convert from binary to decimal so we'll start with that method.

Select a binary number. Beginning with the number on the extreme left (the most significant), add up all the decimal values corresponding to the activated bits (1):

| Position | 5 | 4 | 3 | 2 | 1 | 0 | |
|---|---|---|---|---|---|---|---|
| Dec. equival. | 32 | 16 | 8 | 4 | 2 | 1 | |
| 0000 1001 = | | | 8 + | | | 1 | = 9 |
| 0001 1010 = | | 16 + | 8 + | | 2 | | = 26 |
| 0010 0101 = | 32 + | | | 4 + | 1 | | = 37 |

If you can remember the powers of 2 and if you're able to add the numbers, conversion from binary to decimal will be very easy for you.

Converting decimal to binary is slightly more complicated. For example, to convert the decimal number 167 to its binary equivalent:

1.      Determine the highest power of 2 but which is less than 167:
        $2^7 = 128$

2.      Subtract this value from the number to be converted:
        167-128=39

3.      Then repeat steps 1 and 2 for every remainder:
        $2^5 = 32$

4.     Once you have determined all the powers of 2 in the number, write a 1 under the powers of 2 which are in the number. A zero is written below the other powers of 2:

| $2^7$ | $2^6$ | $2^5$ | $2^4$ | $2^3$ | $2^2$ | $2^1$ | $2^0$ |
|-------|-------|-------|-------|-------|-------|-------|-------|
| 1 | 0 | 1 | 0 | 0 | 1 | 1 | 1 |

Then note the columns where a 1 appears in the bottom row. Add these columns together (128+32+4+2+1) and you should receive 163 as the answer.

## 2.1.1     Telephones with two buttons

Suppose that an upstart telephone company releases a new telephone system using only two buttons: "0" and "1".

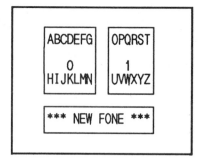

Each subscriber receives a telephone number converted into binary system. Therefore, the phone number for Abacus, which was 698-0330 in decimal, now becomes:

```
0110 1010 1000 0010 1110 1010
```

However, many subscribers have experienced problems. It's almost impossible to make calls correctly and most customers cannot remember even frequently called numbers such as (0010 1100 1001) 0101 0000 1000 1001 0011 1000.

The phone company proposes a compromise:

"Here's what we propose to do in North America. We'll reedit the phone books with subscribers' numbers listed under the old decimal form. You'll easily remember the numbers just like before. To call someone, simply convert the number into its binary equivalent before making your call.

"This conversion is very simple. First try to divide the number by 8,388,608. If that works, the first digit will be 1. If not, it will be 0. Then divide what remains by 4,194,304. If that works, the second digit is 1. If not, it's 0. And so on..."

However, the subscribers don't appreciate spending ten minutes using a pocket calculator in order to make a call. The telephone company devises a new plan.

The solution is a new type of phone book where the new numbering is in its original form, easy to remember and easily converted into binary system. The trick is called *hexadecimal*, a numerical notation system that is more "human" than binary notation. Although this system isn't as convenient as the decimal system, it's still better than the binary system. And it lets you make conversions rapidly and simply.

While the decimal system is based on 10 and binary on 2, the hexadecimal system is based on the number 16. Therefore you have 16 (including zero) different "digits". But that poses a problem since we don't have 16 digits in our system. So what should we do about the values 10 to 15?

To distinguish between the digits which represent values larger than 9, we'll use the letters A-F (first six letters of the alphabet). The following table compares the sequence of decimal numbers (top row) with their equivalent in hexadecimal notation (bottom row):

| Decimal | 0 | 1 | 2 | 3 | 4 | 5 | 6 | 7 | 8 | 9 | 10 | 11 | 12 | 13 | 14 | 15 | 16 | 17 | ... |
|---|---|---|---|---|---|---|---|---|---|---|---|---|---|---|---|---|---|---|---|
| Hexadecimal | 0 | 1 | 2 | 3 | 4 | 5 | 6 | 7 | 8 | 9 | A | B | C | D | E | F | 10 | 11 | ... |

Now that you know that letters sometimes represent numbers, here's a new hexadecimal positions table:

| Fourth Digit | Third Digit | Second Digit | First Digit |
|---|---|---|---|
| $16^3$ | $16^2$ | $16^1$ | $16^0$ |
| 4096 | 256 | 16 | 1 |

From these two tables you should be able to quickly determine the equivalents of the following decimal numbers:

For A3F:

| Hexadecimal | Decimal | Equivalent |
|:-----------:|:-------:|:----------:|
| A | 10 * 256 | 2560+ |
| 3 | 3 * 16 | 48+ |
| F | 15 * 1 | 15 |

Therefore the hexadecimal number A3F becomes 2623 in decimal. Next we'll convert D006 into hexadecimal:

| Hexadecimal | Decimal | Equivalent |
|:-----------:|:-------:|:----------:|
| D | 13 * 4096 | 53,248+ |
| 0 | 0 * 256 | 0+ |
| 0 | 0 * 16 | 0+ |
| 6 | 6*1 | 6 |

The hexadecimal number D006 becomes 53,254 in decimal.

What makes using the hexadecimal system convenient isn't the ease with which you can convert into decimal and vice versa, but the simplicity of conversion into binary. It furnishes numbers of a manageable size while making it easier to convert numbers into binary. The value "A03" may appear strange to you at the beginning but you'll get used to it and it will be easier to work with than "1010 0000 0011".

Each hexadecimal numeral represents a nibble in binary. Once you remember the hexadecimal equivalent of each of the 16 possible nibble formats, converting from hexadecimal into binary is very simple.

The following table shows the equivalents for decimal, binary and hexadecimal numbers:

| Dec | Binary | Hex | Dec | Binary | Hex |
|-----|--------|-----|-----|--------|-----|
| 0 | 0000 0000 | 00 | 16 | 0001 0000 | 10 |
| 1 | 0000 0001 | 01 | 17 | 0001 0001 | 11 |
| 2 | 0000 0010 | 02 | 18 | 0001 0010 | 12 |
| 3 | 0000 0011 | 03 | 19 | 0001 0011 | 13 |
| 4 | 0000 0100 | 04 | 20 | 0001 0100 | 14 |
| 5 | 0000 0101 | 05 | 21 | 0001 0101 | 15 |
| 6 | 0000 0110 | 06 | 22 | 0001 0110 | 16 |
| 7 | 0000 0111 | 07 | 23 | 0001 0111 | 17 |
| 8 | 0000 1000 | 08 | 24 | 0001 1000 | 18 |
| 9 | 0000 1001 | 09 | 25 | 0001 1001 | 19 |
| 10 | 0000 1010 | 0A | 26 | 0001 1010 | 1A |
| 11 | 0000 1011 | 0B | 27 | 0001 1011 | 1B |
| 12 | 0000 1100 | 0C | 28 | 0001 1100 | 1C |
| 13 | 0000 1101 | 0D | 29 | 0001 1101 | 1D |
| 14 | 0000 1110 | 0E | 30 | 0001 1110 | 1E |
| 15 | 0000 1111 | 0F | 31 | 0001 1111 | 1F |

From this table you should easily be able to convert a hexadecimal number such as 456CA0:

| Hexadecimal | 4 | 5 | 6 | C | A | 0 |
|-------------|------|------|------|------|------|------|
| Binary | 0100 | 0101 | 0110 | 1100 | 1010 | 0000 |

Notice that when the binary equivalent is placed on a single line:

```
0100 0101 0110 1100 1010 0000
```

**17**

that a string of eight bits (one byte) is divided into two halves. Since each half is converted into one hexadecimal digit, it's just as simple to convert from binary into hexadecimal. All you need to do is to convert each nibble into hexadecimal:

| Binary | 0011 | 0111 | 0001 | 1000 | 1100 | 0010 |
|---|---|---|---|---|---|---|
| Hexadecimal | 3 | 7 | 1 | 8 | C | 2 |

You can add hexadecimal numbers in the conventional way but it requires some practice.

```
              1        1 1     <-- carry

  3 C      7 A      2 F      F F

+ 2 1    + 3 2    + 1 3    + 1 6

  5 D      A C      4 2      1 1 5
```

Even though you now understand converting decimal numbers and hexadecimal numbers, you might wonder how to determine whether a number is decimal or hexadecimal and how to pronounce a hexadecimal number.

1. How to determine whether a number like "345" is decimal or hexadecimal.

> Most programmers add an "h" to hexadecimal numbers. Therefore, "345" is a decimal number but "345h" is a hexadecimal number representing 837 in decimal. Therefore we'll also designate hexadecimal numbers by adding "h" to the number. Most programmers add an "h" because Intel (the company that designed the 80x86 processor) uses it and this makes it the best choice for programming in 80x86 assembly language.

> Although "h" is the designation we'll use in this book, there are other possibilities for hexadecimal notation. You may see these in other books and manuals:

> - Place a $ before the number such as $C34 or $F123

> - BASIC uses the &H prefix

> - C language uses 0x prefix

2. How to pronounce a hexadecimal number like F3C0.

> There is no standard way of pronouncing hexadecimal numbers. Even the designer of hexadecimal numbers remain uncertain on the pronunciation. However, as a

general rule, we recommend reading the characters exactly as they appear. For example, you would pronounce 0C13h as "Zero-c-one-three."

There are, however, a few exceptions to this rule. For numbers such as F000h, we recommend pronouncing it as "f-thousand" and for numbers such as C00h we recommend pronouncing it as"see-hundred" or "see zero zero".

Whenever you encounter hex numbers in this book remember that computers only use binary. The hexadecimal system is used to simplify calculations.

## 2.1.2    Logical operators

Comparisons and bit manipulations are possible by using *logical operators*. These are encountered in almost every program. Binary numbers can be used with logic operators. These operators are also called *Boolean operators* (named after George Boole, an English mathematician). There are four of these operators.

A database application provides an excellent analogy for using logical operators. In this example we'll use a database containing information about your customers. We'll use logical operators to search for specific information:

OR

> You can use OR to increase the number of data records retrieved. Therefore our example becomes "a list of customers on the east coast OR the west coast".

AND

> You can use AND to limit the number of records retrieved. Our example, therefore, changes to "a list of your customers on the west coast AND who placed orders after June 15".

NOT

> This is similar to AND because it restricts the number of records retrieved. A search might be "a list of customers but NOT those on the east coast".

XOR

> This is a combination of the other three operators. It represents exclusive OR. For example, you can drive a car or ride a bike to go to the store but you cannot do both. You either ride the bike and not drive the car or drive the car and not ride the bike. The result of an XOR function is true if only one of the two statements is true–if the two statements have different truth values.

These operators are comparable to the four common mathematical signs (+, -, *, /). However, the operators are concerned with bits. The logical operators also have a priority.

NOT has the highest priority, AND the second highest. The lowest priority is OR. A negation is performed first before AND and OR.

A computer can distinguish only between two of the states of ON and OFF or TRUE and FALSE. Replace 1 and 0. Here are some examples:

```
1 AND 1 = 1

0 OR 1 = 1

True AND False = False
```

You've probably already used these logic operators in BASIC programs and maybe weren't even aware of it. The IFs in BASIC are based on logic operators:

```
IF (it's true) THEN (do this)

IF A > B THEN GOTO 1000
```

To process this instruction, BASIC begins by resolving the assertive part (A > B) into a simple logic value of "true or false". When A is less than or equal to B, FALSE is produced. When A is greater than B, we have TRUE. From this, a FALSE value will ignore the THEN while TRUE makes the THEN execute what it should.

```
IF A OR B THEN GOTO 1000
```

This command branches to line 1000 when either one variable or the other (A or B) is different from zero. (In BASIC everything that is different from zero has TRUE for a value.)

You can regroup logic operators to express complex relations:

```
IF NOT (A>B) OR ((FLAG>15) AND (G<14)) THEN GOTO 1000
```

This syntax seems easy because we use it in every day conversation.

"If I find it and if you give me the money, I'll buy it."

```
IF  F       AND     M       THEN    B
```

"If it doesn't rain or if you leave me the car, I'll go."

```
IF NOT   R     OR      C       THEN  G
```

## 2.2    Chapter Exercises

1)    Calculate the following additions on binary numbers:

```
100001 + 11110
111111 + 111111
00000001 + 10000000
11 + 00100101
10101010 + 01010101
00010000 + 0010010
```

2)    Calculate the decimal equivalent of the following numbers:

```
10001001
11111101
11111
111111
00000100
00001000
00000011
10000011
```

3)    Calculate the binary equivalent of the following decimal numbers:

```
256
512
13
347
1023
752
12
21
```

4)    Convert the following hexadecimal numbers to decimal numbers:

```
FF
FE
F3E
```

A2B

221

34E

8000

44F

5)     Convert the following hexadecimal numbers to binary numbers:

11

BA

CF3B

4E43

1234

FF

F34E

6)     Add the following hexadecimal numbers:

FFE + FEF

FA + A2

A3B4 + F654

8987 + A567

1 + 12

23 + A4E

7)     Calculate the following operations:

11011 OR 111001

11101 AND 111001

11101 AND 11101 OR 11011

111011 XOR 11011

11011 AND (11011 OR 110110)

111011 AND ((NOT(1111001)) OR 111100)

NOT (111001 XOR (11101 AND 101001))

# 3. Understanding Integrated Circuits

An important key to understanding and learning assembly language is knowing how your computer works. If you don't have a clear idea about how the computer works, you can't really understand the best ways to use assembly language.

## 3.1    What Is An IC?

Computers and related equipment (such as video recorders, calculators and digital watches) are based on the principle of physically processing the boolean concepts TRUE and FALSE (or 1 and 0). The key components used for this processing are integrated circuits (ICs). This is a semiconductor circuit containing at least one transistor and related electronic components.

In the late 1940s vacuum tubes (referred to as valves in Britain) were used as switching devices. However, they burned out quickly and required huge amounts of electricity. In the late 1950s vacuum tubes were replaced by transistors and semiconductors. The engineers realized that semiconductors such as silicon could transform alternating current into direct current.

They also discovered that adding other materials to the silicon chip (a process called *doping*) resulted in the chip behaving like a vacuum tube. They also considered adding transistors onto the chip, now called an *integrated circuit*. By the 1960s the amount of transistors possible on a chip doubled every year. Also as important was the cost of the integrated circuits declined to the point where ICs became popular in products ranging from stereos to nuclear missiles.

Now because of the semiconductor and the IC, there is an enormous advantage in terms of speed, size and price compared to using vacuum tubes, relays and cathode tubes. Unfortunately it's harder to understand how they work.

So you'll have a better idea how your computer functions, we'll construct a primitive, although working, RBL (*Relay Battery Logic*) model. It will consist of relays, wires and a 6-volt battery.

## 3.2    Relays

A relay is just a switch that is tripped electronically instead of being turned on or off with a finger. If you turn on the switch, the current passes. If you turn it off, the current no longer goes through.

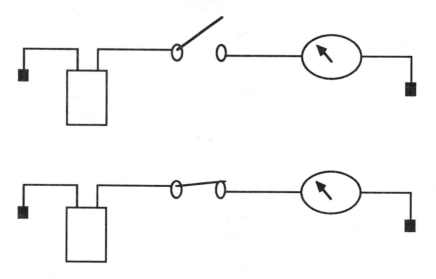

When you turn off the manual switch, the first relay closes. This breaks the connection of the second relay and forces it to open.

In this example, when the switch is open the first relay stays open, letting current pass to the second relay and keeping it shut. With more and more complex interrelationships like this you can get some really interesting results.

# 3.3    Logic Gates

As we discussed in Chapter 2, computers (i.e., digital systems) are designed around three elements: OR, AND and NOT *logic gates*. These logic gates carry out boolean operations by using binary numbers. They're the basic building block in digital systems. Because they use binary numbers the gates are known as *binary logic gates*.

Each logic gate must have clearly different 0 and 1 states as a base. In our RBL system, the logic levels are defined by:

0 = 0V

> This open relay breaks the battery/dial connection.

1 = 6V

> This closes a relay which then makes a connection between the battery and the dial.

### 3.3.1     OR gates: "any or all"

These gates usually have two inputs. Sometimes there are more inputs which are referred to as a 3-input OR gate or 4-input OR gate, etc.

The typical OR gate must follow this rule:

*If one or more inputs are equal to 1, the output is 1. If not, the output is 0.*

The following illustration shows a typical OR gate.

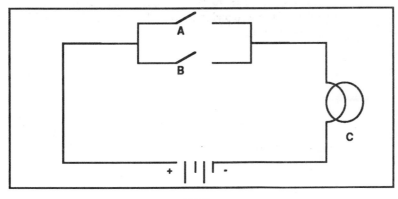

*OR Gate*

As you can see from the following *truth table*, one (or more) relays close if one or both inputs have a value of 1. This establishes a connection with the battery. The output will only be at 0 if the two inputs are also zero.

| Input<br>If B is: and A is: | | Output<br>Then C is: |
|---|---|---|
| 0 | 0 | 0 |
| 0 | 1 | 1 |
| 1 | 0 | 1 |
| 1 | 1 | 1 |

## 3.3.2    AND gates: "all or nothing"

The output of the AND gate will be 6V if and only if, the two inputs are 6V.

The following illustration shows a typical AND gate.

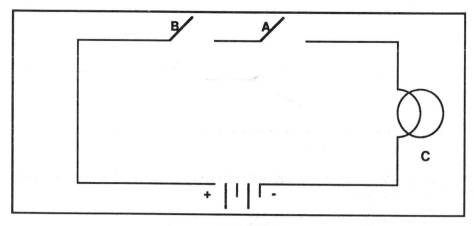

*AND Gate*

As you can see from the following truth table, the output (C) is enabled only when both inputs (A and B) are closed:

| Input | | Output |
|---|---|---|
| If B is: | and A is: | Then C is: |
| open | open | closed |
| open | closed | closed |
| closed | open | closed |
| closed | closed | open |

### 3.3.3    NOT gate

The NOT gates, also called *inverters*, has only one input and only one output. NOT gates follow a simple rule:

*The output is always the opposite of the input.*

If the input to the NOT gate is 1 then the circuit will complement it to give a 0. Because the NOT gate complements the input, it's also known as complementing or negating.

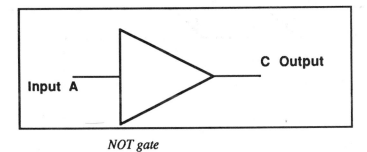

*NOT gate*

As you can see from the following truth table, the output (C) is enabled only when both inputs (A and B) are closed:

| Input | Output |
|---|---|
| If A is: | Then C is: |
| 0 | 1 |
| 1 | 0 |

27

# 3.4   How To Determine Quality

Besides any price consideration, the two most important factors which determine the quality of the logic unit are speed and reliability. We'll discuss both in this section.

## 3.4.1   Speed

How much time does a gate need to move from state 1 to state 0 or vice versa after the input is changed? Ideally, an AND gate should have no time delay at all.

Internal switching delays are important due to the high operating speeds of most digital circuits. The delay time in the waveform of the input and output is called the *propagation delay*. The propagation delay ranges, depending on the logic element used, from a picosecond (0.0000000001 seconds) to almost a full second. The propagation delay is the factor which determines the working speed of a particular computer when using given logic units.

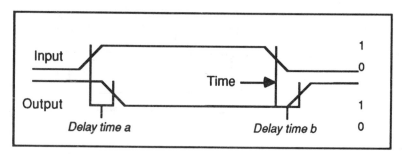

*Waveforms displaying propagation delays*

Relays, because of their mechanics, may require up to a second to change. The RBL we are building has a propagation delay of 0.2 seconds. If we connect an entire series of relays similar to this, it would take some time before the last gate changes its state.

## 3.4.2   Reliability

You may be wondering how reliable a logic unit can switch between states 1 and 0.

We'll often encounter reliability problems with Relay Battery Logic. The contacts wear down, springs weaken and batteries deteriorate. A computer constructed with RBL consists of thousands of relays. It takes only one spring to deteriorate to the point it no longer breaks contact. Then, within a few minutes the whole system breaks down.

There are several *families* of digital ICs (integrated circuits) You can use these families to build a digital system because the ICs in a family are compatible. Manufacturers use *bipolar technology* in one group. These ICs consists of discrete bipolar transistors, diodes and resistors.

An alternative to our RBL model is the bipolar TTL (Transistor-Transistor Logic) family. With a TTL the gates are microscopic structures implemented on thin slices of silicon called *microchips*. This not only makes them reliable but also extremely fast. Instead of using relays, we use transistors as switches. When everything is protected by a plastic or ceramic envelope, it's an integrated circuit, or a *chip*.

Texas Instruments introduced the 7400 series of TTL logic circuits in 1964. Today there are several subfamilies of TTL logic circuits each improving on the original. Although most computers, including PCs, use the TTL family, some chips may require a slightly different technology. This depends on their function. For example, the 80x86 uses NMOS (N channel Metal Oxide Semiconductor) internal logic and TTL compatible outputs to communicate with other circuits. NMOS is especially popular in microprocessors and memories.

Tandy uses 7408 integrated circuits made up of four TTL "AND" gates. Here is the diagram of the 7408 from Tandy:

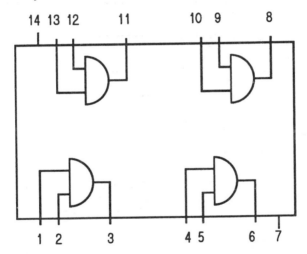

It's easy today to include four AND gates that designers are to the point of placing some 80,000 preprogrammed gates in chips.

Future advances may include a multiprocessor emerging from logic circuits made of carbon molecules. Amino-acids and polypeptides will act in a liquid to give us multi-input AND and OR gates.

## 3.5    Chapter Exercises

1)      What does the OR gate do?

2)      What does the AND gate do?

3)      What does the NOT gate do?

4)      The TTL logic family was developed in what year?

5)      What are the two most important factors that determine the quality of the logic family?

6)      What does TTL stand for?

# 4. Your PC Hardware

The first computer available in North America was the ENIAC. It was so large it required the floor space of a 3-bedroom apartment and weighed an incredible 60,000 pounds. Another early computer, the Cyber 6600 computer from Control Data Corporation was so large that it fit inside a small house.

Fortunately, as the power of computers increased, the cost decreased and the size decreased. Your PC performs much faster at a lower cost with much less space than the huge computers of the 1950s and 1960s.

However, regardless of size, power, speed and cost, all computers have much in common. For example, as the following illustration shows, each requires memory, a central processing unit, operator (user) to input data and a mass storage device such as a disk drive or hard drive.

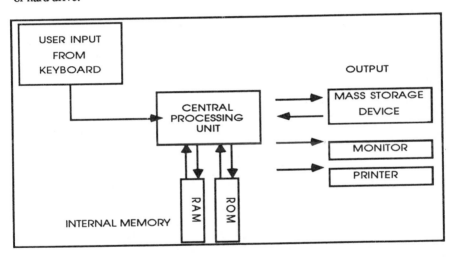

In this illustration, the keyboard is the primary input device. Other input devices include a mouse, lightpen and trackball. The different output devices include monitor and printer. The central processing unit (CPU) controls the system. The internal memory of the CPU includes RAM and ROM. We'll discuss these components in this chapter.

# 4.1    CPU and Processors

The actual "brain" of your computer is its *CPU* or *Central Processing Unit*. The main component of the CPU is the *processor* or *microprocessor*. It controls all of the functions of the computer system and data processing.

The CPU makes all the decisions and manages the other parts of the computer. Even though there are almost as many different types of CPUs as machines, they all execute the same tasks of control, decision and calculating.

You can easily recognize the CPU inside a PC computer. It's usually right next to the slots for expansion boards. On XT compatible computers you can recognize this chip by the copyright printed on its top. The name of the chip, "P8088", "P8088-1" or "P8088-2" is also printed on the chip. The "P" represents processor. These processors are usually manufactured by Intel Corporation.

The essential components of the CPU include the following:

Arithmetic/Logic Unit (ALU)
> Controls the execution of fundamental math and logical data operations.

Control unit
> Deciphers and executes program instructions.

Primary storage
> The main memory of the computer which is directly accessed by the CPU. Primary storage consists of random access memory and read-only memory. Do not confuse primary storage with the mass storage devices such as the hard drive.

Although the CPU and processor combination is the key part of the computer, it has no memory to store programs and other information. We'll discuss memory more in the next section.

## 4.1.1    IBM/PC is a microcomputer

There are many different classes of computers. Programmers and manufacturers have divided these classes into minicomputer and microcomputer and others. Your PC is called a microcomputer because it has an AALU and control unit on one integrated circuit (microprocessor).

## 4.2 Memory

The memory is the most valuable part of a computer. The amount of memory varies with the type of computer but a typical computer is composed of two types of memory. These two types of memory are random access memory (RAM) and read-only memory (ROM).

### 4.2.1 RAM

RAM refers to the memory area where information is first stored (written) and later accessed (read). This information can then be erased and the memory can be used again for other application programs.

RAM is the working memory or main memory of the computer. This memory is volatile or short term because data is stored only as long as the computer is switched on. Therefore, the data sent to this memory is only temporarily stored. You must permanently save the data to a diskette or hard drive or the data is lost after the computer is switched off.

The RAM in your computer is stored in many different chips. These chips have different memory capacity, sizes and operating speeds. One type of RAM chip is the static RAM chip (SRAM). These chips are high speed and do not require refreshing (a process of writing to a chip after reading from it) to retain their contents.

A second type of RAM chips are dynamic RAM (DRAM). Because they're more common than SRAM chips, they're usually what users refer to as their PC's RAM. Although slower than SRAM, the DRAM chips are less expensive and widely available.

The computer operating system reserves a portion of RAM for loading applications or programs into the main memory every time you switch on the computer. These could include programs which you need to write with the computer or for certain applications.

The CPU looks in the memory for "sequences of digits" which let it manage all this memory. These "sequence of digits" are actually programs in assembly language. The basic process carried out by the CPU is simply reading and writing numbers in memory. If they didn't have to communicate with humans, the CPU and memory could operate without any other elements.

You can look at the memory as a series of boxes. In each box is a piece of paper with a number from 0 to 255 written on it. Perhaps more precisely, we should say that each box has eight pieces of paper that each have a 0 or 1 written on it.

To read in the memory, begin by specifying the box you've chosen, then look for the value written there. Writing in the memory amounts to picking the right box and then writing a new value there.

You can directly access a specific memory location in RAM. Therefore, it requires the same amount of time to reach location #00003 as location #52319. Compare this to a magnetic tape on a cassette drive. Here the data are saved and read sequentially. So to reach byte #52319, you have to read the 52,318 bytes before it.

## 4.2.2 ROM

The second type of memory is ROM. All microcomputers must store certain permanent *system information*. ROM chips store program routines that the processor requires when it starts the computer. Unlike RAM, the information in ROM is not lost after you switch off the computer. The system requires the information stored in ROM to run the computer.

You can only read data from ROM memory. Because it's impossible to write to ROM, it's called read-only memory. However, because ROM is nonvolatile, it is not lost when the power is switched off. Many manufacturers have written programs into ROM. Some older IBM-PCs included the BASIC programming language in ROM. Other manufacturers have complete application programs, such as Lotus 1-2-3, saved in the ROM. The advantage of having software in ROM is that it's immediately available after booting the system.

ROM components can also have different capacities. Most XTs include 64K of ROM but ATs require 256K of ROM.

ROM, depending on the computer, consists of one or more medium sized chips with 28 pins each. You can usually find these chips inside your PC between the expansion slots and the memory chips. If you have difficulty locating the ROM chips, look for chips with the manufacturer's name of your PC BIOS printed on top. These manufacturers include IBM, Compaq, PHOENIX, Award, AMI or DTK.

## 4.2.3 Mass storage devices

As we discussed, RAM stores information only for as long as the computer is switched on. You'll need to store this information in order to have a permanent record. There are several types of mass storage devices. These include diskettes, hard drives and tape drives. Furthermore, this mass storage costs less per byte than RAM or ROM.

The CPU can access and use mass memory thanks to its operating system. The operating system of your PC is called MS-DOS or PC-DOS. In fact, most of what DOS does is manipulating binary numbers between the internal memory of the machine and the mass storage. An analogy for DOS is to compare DOS to an airplane pilot. The pilot controls the aircraft similar to DOS controlling everything that goes on in your computer.

The most common mass storage devices are disk drives. They vary in size, portability, data security, durability, as well as in memory and access capacities. Although there are many different types and styles of disk drives, they all have the same basic functions. Their task is to read data from the diskette and send it to the CPU. A disk drive also performs the reverse; it copies data sent to it by the CPU.

The disk drives are connected to a controller card. This card is a board where expansion slots are inserted. The controller represents the connection between the data bus of the computer and the disk drive.

Floppy disk drives and hard drives are two types of disk drives which your PC can use. PCs have always used floppy disk drives. The first PCs had disk drives which would read/write on only one side of the diskette. The storage capacity of one of these disks was 180K. Although too small for most of today's applications, when you consider that the working memory of the first IBM PC was only 64K, a storage capacity of 180K was remarkably high.

Shortly thereafter, double sided disk drives were developed which were capable of reading from and writing to both sides of diskettes. Therefore these disk drives had a storage capacity of 360K (180K on each side). These disk drives became the standard XT disk drive. They process 5 1/4-inch double sided diskettes.

The ATs feature a high capacity disk drive. This disk drive formats 5 1/4-inch diskettes with a storage capacity of 1.2 megabytes. One megabyte (abbreviated Mb) is equal to 1,048,576 bytes. This figure is usually rounded off to equal to one million bytes. However, you have to use special high density diskettes. This disk drive can also read and format diskettes for MS/PC-DOS with standard 360K diskettes.

Since 1987 the 3 1/2-inch diskette has emerged as a popular diskette format. Although smaller, since it comes in a plastic case, the 3 1/2-inch diskette is more durable and sturdier than a 5 1/4-inch diskette.

Obviously a new disk format requires a new type of disk drive. This is the the 3 1/2-inch disk drive. These disk drives format normal 3 1/2-inch diskettes at a capacity of 720K and are used mainly in XT compatible computers. The high capacity disk drives can format from 10Mb to 140Mb. You must, however, use special high density disks (HDs). In addition to the IBM-PS/2 Series and laptop computers, you'll find this disk drive as a second disk drive with high capacity on ATs and 386s.

Hard drives are the mass storage device of choice for most PC users. A hard drive consists of several rotating nonflexible disks. A read/write head can write on both sides of each disk. Each disk is continuously rotated by the hard drive actuator (motor). While floppy disks rotate at a speed of 360 revolutions per minute, the hard drive motor rotates the disks ten times faster (3600 revolutions per minute). Therefore, far more data can be saved on a hard disk. Typical storage capacities range from 10 to 140Mb.

## 4.2.4　　Input/Output Devices (I/O)

You must be able to communicate with a computer before you can use it. The way to communicate with the computer is by using input/output devices. These devices move between the digital world of the computer and your analog world.

Your monitor is the most important output device on your computer. A monitor must be connected to your computer system so that you can communicate with it and the computer can communicate with you.

A printer is the second most important output device in your computer system. This allows you to obtain a "hardcopy" or printout of your data or information. Almost anything which can produce a character on paper from a dot matrix printer to an old typewriter can be connected to a PC.

The keyboard is the central input device which allows you to communicate with the computer system. Since computers were used, the keyboard has been the central input device.

Since an increasing amount of software is designed with the mouse as a primary input device, the supply of computer mice on the PC market has also grown. The development of powerful video standards such as EGA and VGA have also increased the popularity of the mouse.

A recent type of input device is the trackball. As the you spin the ball, the cursor moves at the same speed and in the same direction as the trackball.

# 4.3   History of The 8088

In 1969, Intel released the 4009. This 4-bit microprocessor, designed to work in a calculator, was the first microprocessor. A year later, Intel released the 8008, which was an 8-bit microprocessor. It was designed to work with a monitor and included 16K of addressable memory.

It wasn't until 1973 that the most significant microprocessor was released. This was the Intel 8080 microprocessor. The 8080 is regarded as a gigantic technical improvement because it was the first complete central unit incorporated in a chip which was powerful enough to manage a computer by itself. The 8080 could address up to 64K of memory and possessed an adaptable set of 8 and 16 bit instructions.

The 8080 became the standard microprocessor of the time. Early software applications such as CP/M, Microsoft BASIC, WordStar and dBASE II were written specifically for the 8080 processor.

In 1978, Intel released a newer version of the 8080 processor called the 8086 microprocessor. It included a full 16-bit data bus structure. However, the first IBM-PCs did not use the 8086 because of the high costs involved. Therefore, although the costs are much lower today, few computers use the 8086 microprocessor.

Instead IBM selected the 8088, which was released by Intel shortly after the 8086 microprocessor. The 8088 is similar to the 8086 with one important exception. The 8088 can process 16-bits internally and 8-bits (byte-by-byte) with the rest of the computer. Therefore, the 8088 is more easily integrated into systems using complementary chips of 8-bit technology.

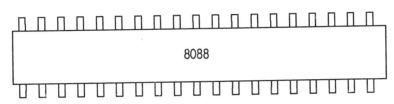

The 8088 reserves 20 of its 40 pins for memory addressing. Since each pin is capable of transmitting the TTL equivalent of 0 and 1, you can address the equivalent of the greatest binary number into an area of memory which can be obtained with 20 bits (1,048,576 or $2^{20}$ ). The pins are connected to the address bus of the PC which links several devices to each other.

The 8088 consists of 29,000 NMOS transistors (about 9000 gates). It's arranged on a silver silicon chip about 1/10 square inch in size. Intel estimates that 90% of the 8088s will still be working after running continuously for 500 years. The 8088 uses so little energy that the power used by a 60-watt bulb is sufficient to run 40 of them at the same time.

# 4.4    A Look Inside Your PC

In this section we'll describe the different components inside your PC. If you own a PC compatible, most of what we're discussing will also apply to your computer. You may want to remove the cover and follow what we're describing.

If you do want to remove the cover to your PC, first switch off the power and remove the power cord. Then remove the screws to the case. Make sure to remove the case screws and not the screws to the PC power supply.

You can slide the cover forward by pulling it towards the front of the case. You don't have to remove the cover completely but slide it far enough forward so you can see inside. If you do want to remove it, lift it slowly so that the threading of the middle case screw doesn't catch any cables.

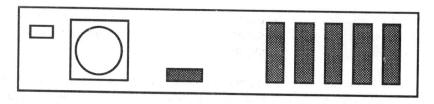

*The Back of the PC*

## 4.4.1    The power supply

If the CPU is the "brain" of your PC, then the power supply is its "heart". It supplies the necessary electricity to all of the components. It's usually found inside the computer case in the back right corner. This location allows easy access to the power switch and power connections. The power supply usually includes a fan and fan intake which prevents the components from overheating.

A watt is an electrical term referring to an amount of work per unit of time. Every component in your PC system requires a certain amount of power to operate. Therefore, your power supply must have a high enough rating to supply power to all of the components. If not, your system will not work to its maximum efficiency and may not work at all.

The first IBM PC included a 65 watt power supply. This was sufficient to power two disk drives. Later, the IBM PC/XT computer included a 135 watt power supply so that it could provide power to two hard drive motors. The computer power supply can also provide power for the monitor or some other peripheral device with the proper jack. Most IBM PC/AT computers today have 200-220 watt power supplies.

Although perhaps sounding formidable, the power supply is nothing more than a transformer which converts high voltages to lower voltages. In the United States, the power supply is set at 115 volts but some countries require the power supply to be set between 220-230 volts.

## 4.4.2    Disk drives

The disk drives are usually located below and in front of the power supply. Some PCs have one floppy disk drive stacked on top of a second floppy disk drive. Other PCs have floppy disk drives side-by-side. To the left of the floppy disk drive is the hard disk.

For more information about the functions of disk drives, refer to Section 4.2.3.

## 4.4.3    The motherboard

The main circuit board of your computer is the *motherboard* or the *system board*. The motherboard, usually located on the bottom left side of the PC, is a thin green rectangular component consisting of a nonconducting material.

The motherboard consists of several layers of printed circuitry. A current flows through several fine conducting lines on each of these layers. These lines are connected to the various chips and other components on the surface of the board. You'll be able to see these lines if you closely examine the motherboard.

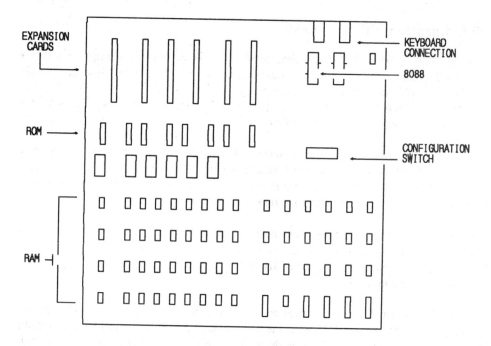

EXPANSION CARDS

KEYBOARD CONNECTION

8088

ROM

CONFIGURATION SWITCH

RAM

## 4.4.4 Expansion slots

Although there are several different manufacturers of motherboards, you should be able to recognize the expansion slots on most boards. This area is located to the rear and left of the motherboard. Although any number are possible, most PCs have between five and eight expansion slots.

An expansion slot is a socket soldered to the board for receiving the connector block of another board. The slot is the interface between the motherboard and an extension board (for example a graphics card).

The expansion slots are connected to a data bus through the socket. The data bus is a system of wires of a board which transmit data to various components of the computer. These components include the CPU (central processing unit), disk drives and all input/output devices. This allows the processor to send data to the cards, for example, to print a file or display the disk directory on the screen. The cards receive power through the slots from the power supply.

The slots are, at least electronically, identical. Therefore you can insert any card in any slot providing it fits. There are always a minimum of two cards on a PC: a disk controller and a video card (either monochrome or color). The other slots are available for serial or parallel interfaces, memory expansion and other system upgrades.

### 4.4.5 Location of the 80x86

You can easily locate the 80x86 processor (or the microprocessor your system uses). As we mentioned earlier in this chapter, it's usually right next to the slots for expansion boards. On XT compatible computers you can recognize this chip by the copyright and "P8088", "P8088-1" or "P8088-2" printed on the chip. On AT computers the chip will be a large square. It will have 80286 or 80386 printed on it.

The 80x86 processor is excellent at basic calculations such as addition, subtraction, multiplication and division. Advanced mathematical calculations, such as cosine or root functions, require more time. Too often the advanced mathematical calculations require so much time that your work and computer time slow down.

Therefore, most computers usually have a socket for the mathematical co-processor located next to the processor. Although the socket is usually empty (the mathematical co-processor is an option), it should have an identifying mark such as a label indicating "math", "co-processor" or a number.

If your PC does have a mathematical co-processor, the chip will have a copyright and specific name. This name differs from the main processor only in the last number and the letter in front of it. For example, it might read "C8087" or "C80287". The "C" represents co-processor.

We'll discuss the 8087 in more detail later.

### 4.4.6   RAM

The motherboard of your machine contains between 64K and 640K of RAM. The first PCs had 64K of RAM (each with 4 rows of 8 chips with 16K). Each 16K chip contains 16,384 bits, which means a row (eight of these chips) provides 16,384 bytes of memory. Recent motherboards accept 64K chips; four rows of 64K provide 256K.

A ninth chip, called the *parity bit*, is added to each row for *parity checking*. This is a technique for detecting memory and data communication errors. If the parity check discovers an error, a corresponding error message is displayed.

Today, many PCs can increase their available memory (or RAM) by using expansion cards. The 8088 makes no distinction between an expansion card and a motherboard.

## 4.4.7    ROM

ROM, depending on the computer, consists of one or more medium sized chips with 28 pins each. You can usually find these chips between the expansion slots and the memory chips.

ROM also includes the *BIOS (Basic Input/Output System)* programs and routines required by your computer. BIOS controls the interplay of the individual hardware components. It customizes the operating system to a specific computer. On XT compatible computers BIOS determines which components are connected by the position of switches on the motherboard. If they're set wrong, BIOS displays an error message. Mastering the PC requires a good knowledge of BIOS routines.

## 4.4.8    POST

After you switch on your PC, one of the first jobs of the 8088 and BIOS is running the Power-On Self Test (POST). This program checks and verifies your PC configuration by counting the number of disk drives, serial and parallel ports and counts and checks available memory.

If POST detects an error, it either displays an error message on the screen or alerts you to the problem by sending a series of beeps.

# 5.  Introducing SIM

This chapter introduces the SIM program. SIM is a simulator which executes assembly language programs one step at a time and displays the various contents of the CPU. Before continuing, you should backup the companion disk to either a floppy diskette or to a directory on the hard drive.

SIM consists of the SIM.EXE main program, several demo files (with a .DEM or .COM extension) and the assembler code source (.ASM) of some of these demos. For information on setting up SIM, refer to Appendix G.

If you're using floppy disk drives rather than a hard drive, we recommend that you copy SIM.EXE to your system diskette (the one that you keep in drive A:) and copy the demos to a second diskette and insert this diskette in drive B:.

# 5.1 The SIM Screen

Start SIM by typing:

C>SIM <Enter>

SIM displays a screen with several different areas:

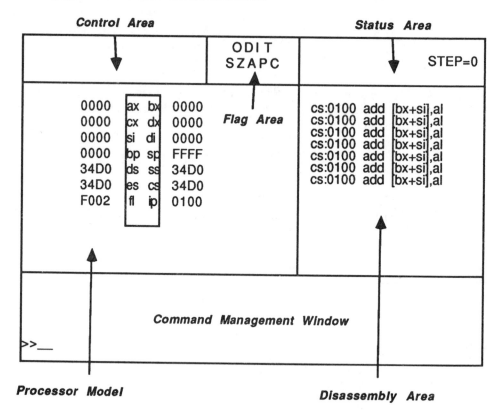

The Status Area is displayed at the top right of the screen. It displays the current filename and the current state of the simulator including any error messages.

The Disassembly Area is located below the Status Area. Here the 80x86 instructions at the specified address are displayed.

The Processor Window is located to the left. This window is subdivided into three parts.

The largest of these is the Processor Model. Here the register contents are displayed (see diagram A).

Above the Processor Model is the Control Area and the Flag Area.

*Registers* are special memory locations of the 80x86 processor. They are high speed "scratch pad" areas that are used to hold numeric and character data, memory addresses and processor control information.

The bottom most window is the Command Management Window. The SIM command prompt ">>" appears at the bottom of the screen. The command appears regardless of the mode or operation and allows you to enter commands and other information. Many of the SIM commands are similar to DOS commands. So, <Ctrl><S>stops movement on the screen, <Ctrl><P> starts printing and so on.

So, the SIM screen consists of a command management area and a simulation area. The command management area controls the memory and simulation. The simulation area executes the programs of the 80x86.

We'll refer to the Command Management Window often in this book. You'll be interacting with the Command Management Window when the cursor appears at the SIM command prompt (the >> at the bottom of the screen).

To exit SIM and return to DOS, press <Q>. Be certain you want to return to DOS because SIM does not ask you to confirm your choice.

## 5.2    Entering Commands

To enter a command, type its name at the >> prompt and press <Enter>. You can type the command in either upper or lowercase. You can type multiple commands but each command must be separated with spaces. If you make a mistake press the <Backspace> key (or the <←> on some keyboards) or cancel the command by typing <Ctrl><C> and reentering the correct command. If SIM doesn't recognize a command, it will display an error message.

Two commands are used quite frequently:

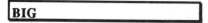

BIG

You may need to change the size of the management window to display more registers (essential to the 80x86 simulator). Type this command:

```
>>BIG <Enter>
```

You can switch the size of the window by typing the BIG command again.

Once the window is the larger size, you will see several more registers listed in the processor window. These include the AB and DB registers located at the bottom of the window. They represent the state of the connections of the 80x86 with the address busses and PC data, and consequently, the entire system. The AB (*Address Bus*) register is a 20-bit link for addressing memory. The DB (*Data Bus*) register is a channel for transmitting the 8-bit data that the processor writes to and reads from memory. We'll discuss AB and DB registers later in this book.

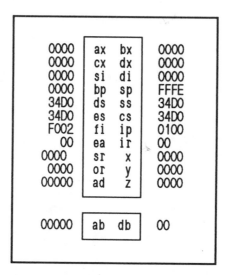

## DIR

Many SIM commands are similar to DOS commands. The DIR command is an example:

```
>>DIR *.* <Enter>
```

Notice that the processor area remains on the screen while the filenames in the directory are displayed below it. You can also display specific extensions. For example, type the following to list the demo files:

```
>>DIR C:*.DEM <Enter>
```

# 5.3   Loading Registers

To load a value in a register, type the name of the register followed by the value in hexadecimal. For example, type the following to put 1234h in register AX:

>>AX 1234 <Enter>

Try loading a few values in the registers on your own.

## BASE

SIM normally accepts hexadecimal numbers. If you specify a non-hexadecimal number, an error message is displayed. Therefore, "1234", which we just loaded in AX, is the same as 4660 in decimal. However, you can change the default so SIM accepts binary values. Switch SIM to accept binary numbers by typing the following command:

>>BASE * BIN <Enter>

or to only convert values into decimal for the AX register:

>>BASE AX DEC <Enter>

Note:     Although the values of the registers are displayed according to the mode specified with "BASE", they're always executed in hexadecimal mode.

After executing this command, the AX register no longer displays 1234h in AX but 4660 in decimal. Modifying a register is only one of the many applications of the BASE command. At this point you may want to experiment using hexadecimal, decimal and binary values.

## ERASE and DSCRN

There will be times when you will want to clear the screen to execute a program. Use the ERASE command to clear the SIM screen. Type the following:

>>ERASE <Enter>

Type the following to redisplay the SIM windows:

>>DSCRN <Enter>

| CALC |
|---|

To use the calculator, type CALC at the SIM command prompt and press <Enter>. The cursor appears in the third line of the Status Area (at the upper right of the screen) and displays the following message:

H:0000

The "H" indicates that you're in hexadecimal mode and only hexadecimal numbers can be entered. Also, all the results are displayed as hexadecimals. You can switch between the different modes by typing:

^B to switch to BINARY base

^D to switch to DECIMAL base

^H to switch to  HEXADECIMAL base

Make certain you're in hexadecimal before continuing and type the following:

2+2 <Enter>

Notice that "2+2" is replaced by "0004". Next experiment with other calculations:

H: 3 + 3 <Enter>

H: 4 * 4 <Enter>

H: 6 / 2 <Enter>

H: 3EA * 2 <Enter>

Remember that the calculations are performed in hexadecimal even though they're displayed in binary.

## 5.3.1    Converting between bases

Using the calculator, it's easy to convert between bases. For example, to convert 65,000 from decimal to hexadecimal, type the following:

^D

65000 <Enter>

^H

Now try converting to binary with ^B then back into decimal with ^D. Next let's try this addition problem (make certain you're in decimal mode):

```
FF + 3
```

You'll receive an N1 error message in the status window. This error is because SIM unable to find a decimal number at the beginning of the operation. When you're in binary base, operations in hex are accepted, but the result is displayed in binary. All mathematical operations must be typed in one of these two formats:

```
N1 operator N2
```

> N1 and N2 represent numbers written in the current base and "operator" is one of the following signs:  +, -, * and /.

```
N1
```

> N1 represents a number written in the current base.

## 5.3.2    Limitations of the calculator

Even though the calculator is handy, it cannot take the place of your desktop or pocket calculator. Keep the following limitations in mind as you use the SIM calculator:

> It only performs operations using whole numbers.

> Floating numbers (numbers with a decimal point) can't be used.

> Only the quotient of any division operation is displayed. The result is not rounded off. For example 6/2=3 but 5/2=2 and 9/11=0.

> You cannot use negative numbers (unless you're in the decimal base). If your operation results in a negative number (15-30) in hexadecimal, the result is the remainder in two (a binary technique for managing negative numbers).

The SIM calculator is used to help you write and debug assembly language programs.

Exit the calculator by pressing the <Esc> key.

---

| CASE |
|------|

Hexadecimal numbers can appear as uppercase letters or lowercase letters. The CASE command lets you select lowercase or uppercase letters for hexadecimal numbers:

```
>>CASE <Enter>
```

# 5.4    Chapter Exercises

1)    What is the SIM command BIG used for?

2)    Load the value 77h in the AX register?

3)    Set the BX register to a binary base.

4)    Make the SIM screen change by using the appropriate command.

5)    Calculate the following in hexadecimal using the calculator:

          345h * FF5h

          234h / 12h

          FF4h + 5FABh

          F6h - 6h

6)    Convert the following decimal values to hexadecimal values using the calculator:

          45, 457, 255, 127, 78

7)    Convert the following hexadecimal values to decreased values using the calculator:

          45h, FF2h, 6Bh, 87h, 8FFh, 8890h

# 6. Registers and Segments

Registers are specialized memory locations within the 80x86 processor. These registers can be accessed much faster than conventional RAM. The CPU uses registers to perform mathematical and logical operations.

All registers are 16 bits in size. The largest number which can be represented within 16 bits is the decimal number 65535 (64 * 1024).

The 8088 is a 16-bit processor. The integrated circuit technology used in this processor provides a useful number of 16-bit registers and a 16-bit *arithmetic/logical unit* (ALU).

One of the basic functions of a processor is to manage addresses. Generally, addresses are loaded and manipulated by registers.

You can also specify memory addresses in a register. When programming you specify the name of the register to determine which address it contains. This lets you use an abbreviated notation.

Since the maximum value of a 16-bit register is 65535, it appears that this is the limit to memory that can be addressed. By using *segmentation* the designers of the 80x86 were able to increase the memory capacity or *address space* of the microprocessor by a factor of 16 to one megabyte.

# 6.1    80x86 Registers

The number of memory locations which a processor can access depends on the width of the *address register*. Since every memory location is accessed by specifying a unique number or *address*, the maximum value contained in the address register determines the address space.

The address register must be a minimum of 20-bits wide to address one megabyte of memory. It was not possible to use a 20-bit address register when the 80x86 was originally developed. Instead, the designers used an alternate method to achieve the 20-bit width: two 16-bit numbers are added together to create a 20-bit number.

One of these numbers is contained in a segment register. The 80x86 has four segment registers. The second number is contained in either another register or in a memory location.

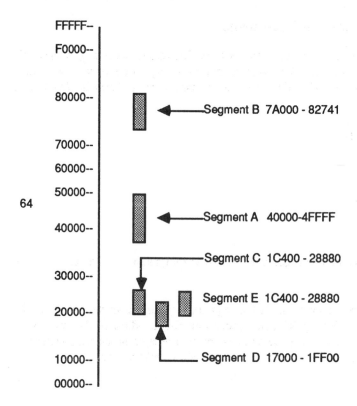

When we mention the "segment at 40000h" we are referring to the segment starting at address 40000h. This segment has a minimum size of one byte and a maximum size of 64K. Segments don't have to start at an address with a multiple of 64. Therefore, they can overlap or begin at the same address like segments C, D and E in the diagram above.

**Note:** Each segment address has to be a multiple of 16 which translates into hexadecimal by a segment beginning address ending in 0. These addresses (divisible by 16) are called "paragraph boundaries."

A segment could, therefore, begin in 43210h or 40010h but not in 4321h or 40008h. Let's move over to binary for a moment. You could theoretically write the beginning address of a segment on 20-bits but we have just seen that the 4 low-bits are zeros (or multiples of 16). So 16-bits are enough to provide a segment beginning address. This is the exact length of the 80x86 registers.

## 6.1.1    Four important segments

The 80x86 has four segment registers. Each has a specific role in executing an assembly language program. The values contained in these four registers provide the starting address of each of the four segments. Each of these segments has a name and specific function in 80x86 assembly language:

• DS for Data Segment

• SS for Stack Segment

• CS for Code Segment

• ES for Extra Segment

At any given time, the 80x86 can execute read/write operations in only one of these 64K areas.

To form a 20-bit number the contents of the segment register are shifted left four bits (thereby multiplying the value by 16) and a second number is added to the first. These addresses are called the *segment address* and *offset address*. The segment address is created by a segment register and indicates the start of a segment (64K chunk) of memory.

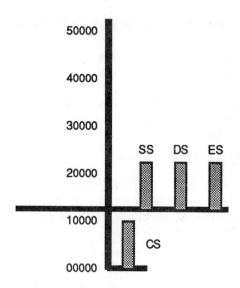

In this diagram, the data segment begins at 13C00h and ends at 29BFFh. The CPU can neither read nor write in memory location 30002h without first loading a new value in the segment register to access memory at that address.

## 6.1.2  Offset Address

The *offset address* indicates the number of memory locations from the beginning of the segment defined by the segment address. The maximum value of an offset is FFFFh or 65,535.

The offset address is a 16-bit value which tells us of the memory location within the segment. For example:

```
2100:0003
```

This formula explains that we have to go 3 locations past 2100h to find the desired location. In the same way, you can add these two numbers to determine the 20-bit effective address:

```
    21000     segment address

 +    0003     offset address

    21003     effective address
```

2100:F090 is an address which points to F090h locations beyond the beginning of segment 21000h. This provides (expressed as 20-bits):

```
   21000      segment address

+   F090      offset address

   30090      effective address
```

The 80x86 addresses using 20-bits are expressed by the following format:

   segment:offset

Both the segment and offset are values on 16-bits. To the segment value, you add a zero. Then you add the offset value to produce a 20-bit effective address.

Now try to find the effective address in the examples below:

```
   2000:1000    = _____

   2001:F000    = _____

   2F00:F000    = _____

   2111:C034    = _____
```

Change these addresses into segment:offset address couples:

```
   10332   = _____ : _____

   2C307   = _____ : _____

   F0001   = _____ : _____

   00155   = _____ : _____
```

## 6.1.3    Segment:offset notation

Next we'll move to the peculiarities of *segment:offset* notation. You may have already noticed that in reality you use 32-bits (2 x 16) where 20 would be enough to express the address. This still leaves several valid possibilities for writing the same address. The segment:offset pairs which follow all points to the same effective address of 89620h.

   8000:9620

   8900:0620

   8962:0000

These are not quite as obvious but still point to the same address:

85F2:3700

82F9:6690

In your PC there is only one address segment called 89620h. However, because of segment:offset notation, there are different ways of writing 89620h. You can use whichever one you wish.

You may never understand the hexadecimal system as well as the decimal system but it will eventually seem more familiar. Use the SIM calculator if necessary.

Don't panic if you still don't completely understand segment:offset notation, You rarely have to worry about the segment being used. The 64K of accessible memory inside a segment are sufficient for your programming needs described in this book.

The majority of cases, 64K of memory is a lot. For example, a database listing of 1000 names and addresses might require 64K.

Programs in assembly language use offsets more than segments. Generally, at the moment of initialization, a program chooses a segment then it no longer needs to change the segment registers.

# 6.2    Chapter Exercises

1)    What is a segment?

2)    What is offset?

3)    Calculate the effective address of the following:

        1200:2300

        3F54:F000

        2200:5F60

# 7. SIM and Memory

In the last chapter we discussed how the 80x86 uses an address bus of 20-bits and that it can therefore address 1,048,576 memory locations. What can you find at these addresses? This is something that every 80x86 programmer needs to know.

The following is a diagram of the memory map of a typical PC:

| | |
|---|---|
| ROMS | FFFF:000FH |
| Memory for Applications (user area) | A000:0000H |
| SIM | 3DC0:0000H |
| Resident programs | 2B3B:0000H |
| DOS operating system | 0000:0600H |
| DOS tables | 0000:0500H |
| BIOS tables | 0000:0400H |
| Interrupt Vectors | 0000:0000H |

These locations will vary depending on your system. (applies to 3DC0:0000H, 2B3B:0000H, 0000:0600H)

In most PCs, the ROM is placed at the top (high address) of the CPU's address range and the RAM at the bottom (low address) of the range. The amount of addressable RAM varies from 64K to 640K.

As you can see in this diagram, RAM is divided into several distinct areas.

## 7.1    RAM Allocation

At the bottom of memory, there are 400h addresses containing 256 interrupt vectors. An interrupt is a signal from a peripheral device or a request from a program to perform a specific function. When an interrupt occurs, the computer branches to the program which begins at the address contained in the respective interrupt vector. Each interrupt vector consists of four bytes (or two words). Interrupt vector 0 extends from addresses 0 to 3, interrupt 1 from addresses 4 to 7, interrupt 2 from addresses 8 to 11, and so on through interrupt 255 (3FCh to 3FFh). We'll discuss interrupts in more detail later.

Next we'll discuss the relationship between the contents of the interrupt vectors and segment:offset notation. Although it's possible to manipulate a few interrupt vector addresses, you must do so very carefully. The system can become completely disorganized if you randomly change a vector address.

Next come the two RAM "note pad" areas of 256 bytes. One begins at 400h (0040:0000) for BIOS, the other at 500h (0050:0000) for DOS. These two areas, just like the interrupt vectors, are reserved exclusively for special DOS and BIOS functions so be careful if you try to change the values here.

However, unlike the interrupt vectors, they are not specific to the 80x86. These areas are reserved for the exclusive use of the operating system.

The DOS operating system is located above these two "note pad" areas. It starts at address 600h and is loaded when the PC is "booted". In fact, initializing the computer consists of loading and starting DOS in memory.

# 7.2 Memory Above DOS

Because DOS versions are different for each computer, it's impossible to say where it ends. Factors such as the version and size of DOS, whether you're using memory resident programs or print spoolers also determine the ending point of DOS. Since these different programs and applications are loaded above DOS, you may get the impression that DOS is larger than it really is.

Above the area reserved for DOS are the resident programs. You can identify these programs because they have ".COM" and ".EXE" or other extensions. DOS assumes that each filename with an EXE extension is an assembly language program. Therefore, you can find the programs that perform the DISKCOPY, FORMAT, CHKDSK and SIM commands, for example, in this area. As one program ends, the next program begins.

## DSTAT

If you have not started SIM, do so now. One of the first tasks which SIM executes when it boots is calculating these three key boundaries: top of RAM, top of SIM and top of DOS. The DSTAT (Display STATus) command allows you to display these three boundaries. At the SIM command prompt type:

```
DSTAT <Enter>
```

You can then modify the memory map according to the information you receive:

```
>>DSTAT

Top of DOS = 2B3B0

User Area   = 3DCD0 - 9FFFF

User Interrupt = 00
```

The memory layout should be similar to the following:

| | |
|---|---|
| ROMS | FFFF:000FH |
| Memory for Applications (user area) | A000:0000H |
| SIM | 3DC0:0000H |
| Resident programs | 2B3B:0000H |
| DOS operating system | 0000:0600H |
| DOS tables | 0000:0500H |
| BIOS tables | 0000:0400H |
| Interrupt Vectors | 0000:0000H |

These locations will vary depending on your system.

The area between the end of SIM and the top of RAM is available for application programs without affecting the interrupt vectors, DOS or SIM.

The programs listed in the book and contained on the companion diskette are written to occupy this area. You can also write your own programs to occupy this area if they don't exceed the memory limits of your PC. Also, observe that SIM only executes on computers with more than 4K of reserved memory.

When you first start SIM, the segment address of the user area is placed in the 4 segment registers. In this book, this number is represented by ssss. Each time you encounter ssss, simply substitute the segment address of the user area of your computer.

## 7.2.1 Normal and Confirmed Mode

You can use SIM on two different levels: normal and confirmed. We'll discuss the confirmed mode in later chapters.

The normal mode was designed for beginners. You can only write in memory locations of the user area because SIM prevents you from writing in "delicate locations" where you could shut the computer down. In the normal mode, messages help you by appearing as soon as you try to do something you don't really want to do (like writing to ROM or in locations that are neither in ROM nor in RAM).

## 7.2.2 Using the SIM Screen

If you're familiar with the DEBUG program in DOS, you'll realize that most SIM commands are very similar to DEBUG commands. If you're not familiar with DEBUG, learning to use SIM is the same as learning DEBUG. Although not as impressive as SIM, DEBUG is a useful and indispensable tool for debugging programs.

The SIM screen has two functions. It displays and controls the 80x86 simulator and also displays and controls information concerning memory. Keep the following formula in mind:

```
Memory + processor = assembly language
```

The command window lets you manage both of them.

## 7.3    Examining and Modifying Memory

One of the fundamental tasks of the command window is to let you read and modify memory.

| E            Enter  command |

The E command (for Enter) lets you do this. The syntax of the command is simple:

    E address

with "address" representing [segment:]offset.

The notation "[ ]" indicates that the element inside the brackets is optional. If you don't specify the segment in the command line, "E" defaults to the address of the segment contained in the DS (Data Segment) register of SIM. The offset is then added to the data segment.

| NEW          New  command |

Type the following command at the SIM command prompt:

    NEW

This command reinitializes the registers. As you already know, the number (ssss) in DS is the segment address of the first location of the user area. If you specify only an offset in the E command, the value contained in DS is used to determine the segment. You do not want SIM to guess the segment by not specifying one.

Since the four segment registers contain the same value or address, all you need to consider is offsets.

Type:

    >>E 211 <Enter>

SIM responds with:

    ssss:0211: 00

The two numbers to the left of the cursor represent the current value at offset 0211. It may not be 00 on your PC because some data or information from the preceding program may still remain or the result of switching on your PC.

You can modify the value located at offset 211h. Enter any hexadecimal number (without the "h"). Hexadecimal is the default base for the command window and SIM expects hex numbers unless you change the base.

Press <Enter> to confirm your choice. Then SIM writes the new value to location ssss:211 and increments the location by one. Now you should see this on the screen:

```
ssss:0212: 00
```

Next, press <Enter> instead of entering a value. This increments the address counter without modifying the contents of location 212h.

```
ssss:0213: 00
```

After you make several changes, you probably want to see if these changes have indeed taken place. Press the "-" (minus sign key) to decrement the address counter. You will see the new values. Leave the edit mode by pressing <Ctrl><C>.

## 7.3.1    Modifying Memory Values

```
E                    Edit command
```

There are situations when changing individual memory values requires too much time. You can edit faster using a slightly different E command. Simply indicate the address followed by the values to store into the memory:

```
E address list
```

where the list consists of one or several bytes in hexadecimal. For example:

```
>>E 211 CC 33 11 FF <Enter>
```

This command stores CCh in ssss:211, 33h in ssss:212, 11h in ssss:213 and FFh in ssss:214.

Practice this by storing 11h, 22h, 33h, 44h and 55h in the memory from offset 500h (DS). Activate the interactive mode beginning from ssss:500h like this:

```
>>E 500 <Enter>
```

## 7.4    Segment Limits

A word (16-bits) in the memory of the 80x86 consists of two sequential bytes. The 8 least significant bits are located at the lower address. For example, here are four memory locations:

```
ssss:0203 65

ssss:0202 10

ssss:0201 BD

ssss:0200 AA
```

In each case, you (or rather the 80x86) can say that address 200h contains the value BDAAh and that address 202h contains the value 1065h.

At this point you may be wondering what happens when you move past the offset FFFFh locations in the memory or when you move backwards beyond offset 0000h.

The answer is to wrap around. Although the offset begins again at zero, you remain in the same segment. For example, if we write something at address 3000:FFFF, the new address located after you confirm what you just wrote is 3000:0000. Wrapping around within a segment is something that you'll need to remember in 80x86 assembly language programming.

As we've mentioned, one of the major differences between SIM and DEBUG is that SIM won't let you write to most reserved locations. That means it's impossible for you to accidentally change the contents of a RAM address which would destroy DOS, SIM or any other program. If you attempt to write to these addresses (for example, 0000:0020 in the area of the interruption vectors), SIM displays a warning.

Don't panic if you see one of these warnings. The worse that can happen is that you may have to perform a warm boot (press <Ctrl><Alt><Del> key combination) or switch off the computer. You can do nothing from the keyboard which would physically damage the computer. The only exception we know is trying to reformat the hard disk. But that's not something you have to worry about now.

Let's try writing to one of these locations. Type the following at the SIM command prompt:

```
>>E 0:0020 FF <Enter>
```

The "bad list" error message is displayed. If SIM had executed this command, the system would have locked up or crashed and you would have to perform a warm boot.

SIM also protects you from other errors. For example, if you write to an address which doesn't exist in RAM, the message "No RAM" is displayed. An attempt to write between F000:6000 and F000:FFFF results in a "Write to ROM" error message in the status window.

A good safety rule to remember is that SIM leaves you a user area at least three times larger than that which other computers offer (and in some cases, it can be up to 300 times larger).

So the Edit command ("E") is a useful tool for examining and modifying memory. Even though it lets us read and modify the contents of memory, SIM has a more effective method of displaying this information.

## D        Dump command

The Dump command from DEBUG displays everything in memory. It allows you to simultaneously read and display a series of consecutive memory locations. You can dump any area of memory.

Dump displays up to 128 bytes at a time. Type the following to dump a group of 128 bytes:

```
>>D 200 <Enter>
```

This command displays 128 bytes starting at offset 200 (ssss:0200 to ssss:0270). Each one of the eight lines appear in three parts:

- a segmented address of 32-bits

- 16 bytes of hex code

- these same 16 bytes coded in ASCII

To form a number above 255, you can group several bytes together (a pair of bytes is a *word*). A byte can also be a part of a program. These are small sequences of bytes with a specific meaning for the 80x86 but are meaningless for any other processor. In some cases, the byte might be a dot on the screen or an element in a diagram.

An 8-bit number represents a specific alphabetical character. However, we cannot store the pattern for the letter "A" in only a single byte. On the other hand, we could easily store a code representing this letter. And if we always use the same code and succeed in convincing other programmers to use the same code, we always know that the letter "A" corresponds to this code. By placing these codes of letters one after another, we can store the equivalent of a document.

In 1968, manufacturers created the American Standard Code for Information Interchange (ASCII). It defined 96 standard and 32 nonstandard characters. The standard characters include alphanumeric characters (0 to 9 and lower/uppercase letters) and the most common punctuation signs. Nonstandard characters include control characters for skipping lines, carriage return, end of a file and others. We've included an ASCII table in Appendix C.

The main purpose of ASCII was provide more efficient data communication and more compatible information exchange between computers and different peripherals. This allows one computer from one manufacturer to work with a printer from another manufacturer. The ASCII system has since become so universal that even IBM has adapted a version of it for the PC.

So does it mean that every time that we see 41h in a memory location of the PC, we should read "A"? It depends on how and where it's used. For example, if the bytes surrounding this code also resemble ASCII characters, then 41h is most likely an "A".

In fact, even though 41h is the ASCII code for "A", it's also the instruction in assembly language which increments the CX register and it's the second byte of the sequence of four bytes that represents the value of pi ($\pi$ or 3.14159).

Therefore, don't be surprised if Dump doesn't always know the exact meaning to give to the bytes that it displays. Nonetheless, since the "bytes in ASCII" conversion is undoubtedly the most useful one available, Dump displays the equivalent in ASCII (codes 0-31, control characters and the dot). If the display appears as nonsense similar to the following examples:

```
1000:0040 8B 76 06 C6 04 00 00 C6-46 FA 00 A1 2A E9 89 46
.v.G...FFz.!*i.F

1000:0050 FC B8 EC FE 50 8B 5E 04-FF 77 04 E8 74 FC B8 EE |81
P.^..w.ht|8n

1000:0060 FE 50 8B 5E 04 FF 77 04-E8 67 FC D1 E8 72 03 E9
~P.^..w.hg|Qhr.i

1000:0070 A7 00 8B 1E 2C E9 32 FF-EB 30 8B 76 0A 80 3C 00
"...,i2.kO.v..<.
```

Then you're working with 80x86 symbolic code. However, a display similar to the following is what you should see:

```
1600:0030 1A 20 0F 7A 65 72 6F 20-72 65 67 69 73 74 65 72 . .zero
register

1600:0040 3A 20 1D 10 23 10 1D 10-1B 10 1A 10 1D 10 1B 11 :
..#..........

1600:0050 1A 11 1D 11 0E 49 2F 4F-20 77 72 69 74 65 20 62 ....I/O write
b

1600:0060 79 74 65 00 0A 77 72 69-74 65 20 62 79 74 65 00 yte..write
byte.
```

Dump automatically retains the last address of the preceding dump. Therefore, to see the next 128 bytes type:

```
>>D <Enter>
```

Now Dump displays the next 128 bytes (ssss:0280 up to ssss:02FF). Any value not having an ASCII equivalent that can be displayed is represented by a dot in the ASCII part of the screen. In this area of the screen, the most significant bit of each byte is ignored. For example, 41h (or 0100 0001) and C1h (1100 0001) are displayed as "A."

Practice displaying various memory locations. As with the "E" command, to display a location outside the current data segment you have to specify the segment in the address:

```
>>D 40:0 <Enter>
```

The numbers from 0400:0000 to 0400:0079 seem to be nonsensical, but without them, available programs from BIOS couldn't work. And then the PC couldn't read the keys pressed on the keyboard nor display a text on the screen.

Rather than displaying memory as groups of 128 bytes, you can display it in groups of 1 to 64K bytes. The command for doing this is:

```
D beginaddress endaddress
```

The `endaddress` should include only the offset. It cannot include a segment. These ROM programs are at the beginning of memory. Try to experiment and display the BIOS contents (F000:E000 to FFFF).

To display 2000h of BIOS bytes type:

```
>>D F000:E000 FFFF <Enter>
```

Because Dump must display hundreds of lines (many more than the 25 lines on our screen), press <Ctrl><S> to stop the display. Then press any key to continue or <Ctrl><C> to quit.

There are two ways to specify the extent of an area to display with Dump. The method just discussed consists of specifying the beginning and ending addresses. Then the command displays everything that is between these two addresses. The other method consists of selecting the beginning address followed by a "L" (length) and the number of bytes to display.

So to display 231h bytes beginning from offset 100h, type the following:

```
>>D 100 L 231 <Enter>
```

This command displays everything between ssss:0100 and ssss:0330. You can use either uppercase or lowercase letters.

# 7.5   Displaying Memory

| DMEM |
|---|

You can open a memory window using the DMEM command (Display MEMory). The DMEM display is different from Dump because it does not scroll but remains fixed in the location.

The DMEM command immediately displays any writing in the memory. You can display the first 16 bytes in the memory by typing:

>>DMEM 0 <Enter>

Now write to this memory by typing:

>>E 6 FF <Enter>

Type the DMEM command again. SIM displays another series of 16 bytes in memory.

If you prefer to work using words instead of bytes SIM lets you do this. Open a second window at the same address but display the memory as words:

>>DMEM 0 W <Enter>

The "W" parameter displays the memory as words.

Type the following to close the DMEM window:

>>DMEM OFF <Enter>

# 7.6   Review

The E command (Edit command) modifies memory contents. It consists of two modes:

- The interactive mode which displays the contents of an address. The command then waits for you to modify it:

    ```
    E address
    ```

- The immediate mode which writes a "list" of values without displaying the contents beforehand:

    ```
    E address list
    ```

The D command (Dump command) displays the contents of memory. It has two formats:

- By 128 bytes (with or without address specification).

- Displaying a certain number of bytes (from 1 to 64K) while specifying the beginning and ending address as well as the number of bytes to display separated by an "L".

    ```
    D

    D address

    D offset address

    D L value address
    ```

When we discuss the commands, we'll indicate the two methods of describing the memory area where work (offset address and L value address) by the expression "Area".

# 7.7    Chapter Exercises

1)      Display and modify the contents of the following memory locations:

     `ssss:212`   `write in it:`  21h

     `ssss:215`   `write in it:`  30h

     `ssss:217`   `write in it:`  4Fh

2)      Display each contents of memory locations ssss:217 to ssss:212 backwards.

3)      Put the following values in memory locations ssss:212 to ssss:217:

     `15h, 13h, 1Fh, FAh, 11h, 2Ah`

4)      Display the contents of memory locations ssss:212 to ssss:217.

5)      Display the contents of the 128 bytes that follow.

6)      Display the contents of memory locations 0020:012B to 0020:02A0.

7)      Display 300h bytes from memory location 00A1:02F0.

8)      Display 16 bytes on the screen statically beginning with address ssss:0212h.

9)      Display 8 words on the screen statically beginning with address ssss:0216h.

10)     Modify byte ssss:0218h by inscribing the value 4Bh. Observe the result on the screen.

# 8. Additional SIM Commands

There are over 30 commands which SIM provides to examine and to modify memory. The two primary commands are Edit ("E") and DUMP ("D") which we discussed in the last chapter.

In this chapter we'll present four new commands.

COMPARE ("C") moves through two areas looking for possible differences. FILL ("F") fills a specific area with bytes. SEARCH ("S") looks for characters or sequences of characters and displays the result. Finally, MOVE ("M") allows you to copy the bytes in one area and paste them into another area.

## C    COMPARE command

Executes a comparison, byte by byte between two memory areas. It's used to locate and identify bytes which do not match in two different memory areas. COMPARE is non-destructive; it does not write to memory.

The syntax is:

```
C area address
```

The "area" can take two distinct forms of "beginning address" and "ending address" or the more usual format where you specify a departure address, a length ("L") and the number of bytes to compare.

For example, to compare the first 20h addresses of your user area with the 20h addresses beginning at 800h, type:

```
>>C 0 L 20 800 <Enter>
```

COMPARE displays the address of each different byte. Since you've only started using SIM, it's quite possible that no byte of your computer is alike in the two areas. So COMPARE might take a long time to execute. Here is an example of what COMPARE can do when it has found FFh in the first area and 31 in the second:

```
ssss:0000: ff-31 :ssss:0800
```

---

| **F** | **FILL command** |
|---|---|

FILL loads a specific memory area with bytes or a series of bytes. The syntax for FILL ("F") is:

```
F area list
```

For example, to fill 800h bytes from your user area with the value CCh, type:

```
>>F 200 L 800 CC <Enter>
```

If you're experienced with DEBUG, you may find the FILL command executes somewhat slower. This is because DEBUG was written in assembly language while SIM is written in Pascal and SIM must make a security check for each of the 2000 bytes.

Try using the command we wrote above to see how FILL works. Use DUMP from 200h to A00h to verify that CCh does in fact fill the entire area.

Of course, the memory can be filled with a sequence of different bytes rather than only one byte. Therefore, to load a series of "01 02 03 04" in the area between the ssss:8000 area at ssss:FFF, type:

```
>>F 800 L 800 1 2 3 4 <Enter>
```

You will most often use FILL to clears a part of RAM by loading zeros or other known and useless value in it. If the area to be filled includes an address located outside the user area, a warning message "Unsafe Address" appears in the status window.

For example, type the following at the SIM command prompt:

```
F 0:100 L 500 1 2 3 4 5 <Enter>
```

| **S** | **SEARCH command** |
|---|---|

SEARCH is a more intelligent form of DUMP. You have two methods of knowing if the sequence of values 66h, 32h and 12h are in a determined area of 30K. You can either do a DUMP of the entire area and examine every line or you can let SIM do the work.

The syntax for the S command is:

```
S area list
```

For example, determine if the sequence 66h, 32h, 12h is actually in the first 1000 bytes of your user area:

```
>>S 0 L 1000 66 32 12 <Enter>
```

SIM is probably unable to locate this particular sequence in your user area. A message is displayed if SEARCH finds the 66 32 12 sequence. It continues searching and a sequence may repeat itself several times. No message is displayed if SEARCH is unable to match the search criteria.

Type the following two lines at the SIM command prompt.

```
>>E 209c 9 8 7 6 5 <Enter>
```

```
>>S 0 L 3000 9 8 7 6 5 <Enter>
```

SIM displays 20D5:209C in the SIM command prompt.

## M        MOVE command

This command allows you to copy and paste bytes from one area into another area.

Its syntax is:

```
M area address
```

For example, to move 345h bytes beginning at ssss:200 to ssss:800, type:

```
>>M 200 L 345 800 <Enter>
```

In this case, area 200-544h is copied in 800-B44h. You can verify this by using COMPARE:

```
>>C 200 L 345 800 <Enter>
```

If MOVE did its work well, COMPARE lets you know that there is no difference between the bytes of the two areas.

## 8.1     Chapter Exercises

1)      In the user zone, enter the value FF FE in an area of 3000 bytes.

2)      Use "D" to verify that FF FE is in fact in a part of this new area.

3)      Load some useful data somewhere in the user area.

4)      Pretend that you've forgotten where you loaded the data in Step #3 above and use S
        to find the data.

5)      MOVE 400h bytes from one region to another. Then use "C" to compare the two
        areas and to verify by this comparison that everything went like you wanted it to.

# 9.  Registers

Now let's clear the Simulator by using the NEW command. The registers are given values by default. Use the BIG command to see the display of the entire processor.

```
        0000  ax bx  0000
        0000  cx dx  0000
        0000  si di  0000
        0000  bp sp  FFFE
        34D0  ds ss  34D0
        34D0  es cs  34D0
        F002  fi ip  0100
          00  ea ir  00
        0000  sr x   0000
        0000  or y   0000
       00000  ad z   0000


       00000  ab db  00  ilnit
```

**Real and simulated processors**

Although your IBM PC or compatible uses an 80x86 processor, it is possible to simulate another processor. All that's required is appropriate *simulator* software. A simulator not only simulates instructions on the screen and controls the speed of execution but also prevents errors from instructions that are capable of stopping or crashing the system.

As we mentioned in Chapter 4, learning 80x86 assembly language requires studying the microprocessor. In this chapter we'll discuss the names, operations and functions of registers. As you learn how to read and write in memory, programming 80x86 assembly language will become much easier for you.

# 9.1 80x86 Registers Closeup

The 80x86 has 22 registers. Remember that a register is only an area for storing binary numbers inside the processor.

The registers are the most important elements for the programmer in a microprocessor. Programmers frequently use registers and you'll use them in the .DEM programs on the companion diskette.

In this section we'll discuss the five groups of registers.

## 9.1.1 Data registers

Data registers, also called *scratch-pad registers*, maintain frequently used operands inside the 80x86. There are four common 16-bit registers which are used for calculating and storing:

- AX

- BX

- CX

- DX

The contents of these registers instruct the computer as to which tasks it must perform and what data to use to execute the tasks. These four registers are affected mainly by mathematical and input/output instructions. They're assigned a specific position within the registers of the 80x86 because they can be separated into two 8-bit (1 byte) registers. Therefore, you have the option of using each of them as two 8-bit registers.

The registers are designated as H (high) and L (low). Therefore when you subdivide the AX register into two 8-bit registers, they become two registers:

- AH (AX High)

- AL (AX Low)

The AL register contains the 0-7 bits (lower 8 bits) of the AX register and the AH register contains bits 8-15 (higher 8 bits).

The same is true for each of the other data registers. Assembly language programs move numbers from memory into these registers to execute operations there and then store the results in memory. Very few programs work differently from this basic outline. As for the other registers, they are often intended for moving numbers between memory and these four registers.

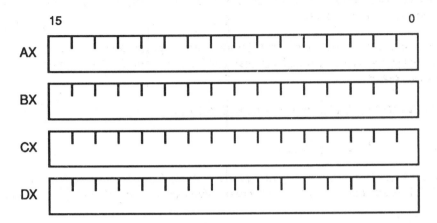

You can use these 16 bit registers as 2 registers of 8 bits each. The 8-bit registers corresponding to AX, BX, CX and DX are called AL, AH, BL, BH, CL, CH, DL and DH (the L always represents the lower 8 bits and H represents the higher 8 bits). Therefore, you can assign any value the 8 bits in the BL register without affecting the contents of register BH.

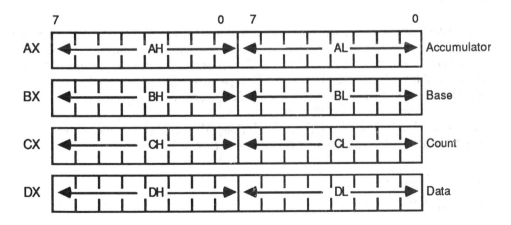

Registers are generally interchangeable and are widely used despite their functions. However, you often use AX for simple jobs with instructions which implicitly address this register. AX is named the "Accumulator."

You can sometimes use BX, the "Base" register, as an indexing register (see below). CX is the "Count" register. You should be aware of the fact that the processor directly carries out numerous counting operations with CX. As for DX, it's the "Data" register. In 32-bit operations, the higher 16 bits are load in CX and the lower ones in DX.

## 9.1.2    Offset registers

There are five offset registers which are used with the segment registers to contain segmented addresses.

The BP and SP registers, known as the *stack registers*, provide offsets into the stack segment. The BP (base pointer) register is the base register of the stack. It points to the address at the base of the stack. We'll discuss this in more detail soon. The SP register, or stack pointer, points to the top of the stack.

The SI and DI registers are *index registers*. SI (source index) and DI (destination index) are used in basic addressing of data in indexing operations. These index registers "point" to a memory location. So, if SI contains F000h, it points to offset F000h.

DI and SI index registers and the "stack pointers" are specific tools in assembly language.

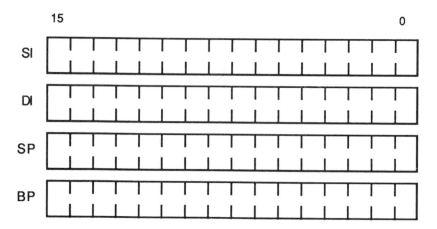

These index registers are 16-bit registers which, unlike data registers, can only function on 16 bits. They let you do certain mathematical operations and are generally used for storing data.

The IP register is the *instruction pointer*. It's also called the *program counter* or *PC register*. It's responsible for guiding the 80x86 instruction by instruction while the assembly language program is executing.

The IP is constantly modified after executing each instruction so it points to the next instruction. The 80x86 depends entirely on the IP to know what the next instruction is. That's why it always keeps the offset in the code segment.

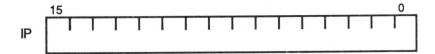

## 9.1.3    Segment registers

Traditionally, processors have always used the 16-bit word to indicate addresses in the memory. And since each address consists of 16 bits, the number of single individual addresses is 65,536 or 64K.

The memory requirements of processors has increased at the same time their performance has become greater. The 80x86 still uses the 16-bit address word. However, the total memory capacity has been increased to a megabyte (1,024K) due to segmenting memory addressing.

By using 20 bit words we should be able to represent any number from 0 to 1,048,575 to generate addresses that a memory of one megabyte finds necessary. The 80x86 uses 20-bit words to address real memory. The complete set of 1,048,576 different addresses is called the "addressable space of one megabyte". However, we'll refer to memory addressed in blocks as segments.

Each segment can be 64K. This lets us use the standard 16-bit addressing word. Each segment can begin at any limit of 16 bytes (a paragraph) inside the memory space of one megabyte. Notice that the address for the beginning of a segment can take 64,536 possible locations and that for each of the segments, the last four bits are at zero.

Also remember that the maximum size of a segment is 64K; it can contain any amount up to that point. Also, segments can overlap. This means that we can reach a given byte from more than one segment.

Every time that the 80x86 accesses memory, it chooses one of the four segment registers (CS, DS, SS or ES) to calculate the beginning address of the segment. This value is shifted four bits, then added to the offset to form the 20-bit physical address. This is the complete address used to access the memory.

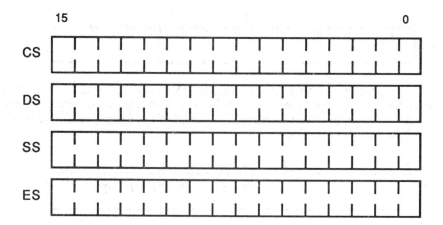

Each time that the processor reads or writes in the memory, one of these registers supplies the segment part of the memory address (depending on the situation):

CS register (code segment) indicates the locations of the programs in memory. The code segment register contains the addresses of the instructions of a program.

The SS register (stack segment) determines the load where operations are performed on the stack.

DS register (data segment) controls most of the memory locations intended for reading and writing data in memory. When an instruction reads or writes a number in a memory location, most of the time that location will be inscribed in the data segment.

As its name indicates, the ES register (extra segment) register is an extra data segment. It's used by some assembly language instructions to address more than 64K of data or to transfer data between two different segments of memory.

When SIM starts working, the four segments contain only ssss (the user segment). In that case, the address segment of the processor puts it in a situation like that of a processor without a segment register which can only address 64K.

These are the first 12 registers which are easy to classify. Four of them have various uses (AX, BX, CX and DX), four others help with indexing (SI, DI, BP and SP) and the four segment registers (CS, DS, SS and ES).

## 9.1.4    Flag registers

The Flag is a specific signal bit. For example, the 0 bit of FL is the "Carry Flag" bit. Programs often test this bit to determine the resulting condition of a mathematical operation.

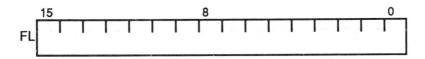

This register appears in two places on the screen in SIM: as an "FL" register on 16 bits and as an indicator in the Command Management Window. This is due to the particular interest that we attach to the 9 bits of the FL register. You might think that any modification of FL will modify the display of the flags.

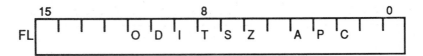

If you glance at the flag display area on your screen (the area that's highlighted), you'll see that the heavy bytes contain flags O, D, I and T. The second line (still on the screen) displays the light weight bytes and contains S, Z, A, P and C. The 7 other bits aren't displayed. Their value has no interest to us.

Let's modify the value of FL in binary:

```
>>BASE FL BIN <Enter>
```

Now it's easy to compare the contents of FL with the flag display. Let's examine the effect that modifying the contents of FL has on the other bits. By default, the value of "FL" is F002h.

```
xxxxODIT    SZxAxPxC

11110000    00000010 FL (F002h)
```

You see that 9 flags are highlighted. Use the L command to load F003h in FL:

```
>>FL F003 <Enter>
```

The "C" in the Flag Area becomes highlighted because bit 0 has been activated. Similarly, if you load FFFFh in FL, all the indicators in the Flag Area become highlighted.

```
xxxxODIT    SZxAxPxC

11110000    00000011 FL (F0003h)
```

So the program lets you selectively modify the contents of the flags without converting hexadecimal to binary conversions.

---

### SET and CLEAR

Activate or deactivate a bit by using the SET and CLEAR commands:

```
>>SET I <Enter>

>>CLEAR I <Enter>
```

SIM may be influenced by the value of certain flags. These must be cleared before you can proceed. To do this, type several CLEAR commands or execute this command:

```
>>FL 0 <Enter>
```

We'll discuss these flag bits in more detail later.

## 9.1.5    Simulator registers

The instruction register (IR) is a one-byte register where instructions (8-bit numbers read in memory) are decoded in order to determine the command that they contain and how to carry them out. In many instructions, you have to use the effective address (EA) register as an extension to the IR. The X and Y registers play a minor role in the 80x86. Some instructions call them for temporary storage.

*Read/write registers*

The offset register (OR), segment register (SR), address latch (AL) and data latch (Z) registers control loading and extracting numbers in the processor. SR usually contains the same value (one of the four segment registers). If this isn't the case now, it will be changed when the first instruction is executed.

During read/write operations, OR and SR are added to produce a value on 20 bits stored in AD. This way you can always be sure that the processor of your PC has enough bits to address position #1,048,576 of the memory diagram.

No digit enters or leaves the processor without first passing through the Z register, also known as the "data latch". Like all data registers, you can use this one as two 8-bit registers called ZL and ZH. Values on a byte always pass through ZL, but values on a word pass through the entire Z register.

*Memory registers*

Communication between the 80x86 and the PC memory is performed through AB (Address Bus) and DB (Data Bus) registers. During read/write operations, AB specifies the address while DB contains the value currently there (or will eventually be loaded there).

# 9.2    Control Pins

You'll often see the letters i l n i t appearing to the right of certain memory registers. These are "control pins" of the 80x86 and represent the following:

| E/S | processor output |
|------|------------------|
| LOCK | processor output |
| NMI | processor input |
| INTR | processor input |
| TEST | processor input |

By implied agreement, AX, BX, CX, DX, SI, DI, BP, SP, SS, DS, ES, FL and IP are the names of standard registers accepted by 80x86 programmers. Registers that aren't displayed as soon as you begin to use SIM (such as SR, OR, AD, EA, IR, X, Y and Z) have less standard names.

These registers play a necessary role in keeping programs executing well on the 80x86. But since they execute intermediate jobs, you don't need to use them when you create a program.

## 9.2.1    First program

The first program you'll write will add numbers. This mathematical operation is so much a part of assembly languages that the creators of the 80x86 anticipated a specific set of instructions for a very particular form of addition known as adding one to a given number or *incrementing* by one.

Incrementing a register containing 3011h produces 3012h. If you increment AX while it contains FFFFh, you get 0000h or just plain zero. This is just like an escalator that keeps going back to its starting point once it has reached the end of its course.

If you increment the CH register (remember you can split the data registers into two 8-bit registers) while it contains 3Fh, you get 40h. Increment DL while it contains the value FFh and you get 0 (without it changing the DH register).

The value 41h is the instruction code (or opcode) which instructs the microprocessor to increment the CX register. For this simple program, you only need to tell the 80x86 to execute instruction 41h.

PROG1 is the first program you'll write in assembly but since it's only one byte long you will not find it on the companion diskette. You will be using the E command in SIM.

    41h (01000001 in binary or 65 in decimal)

In order for the simulator to increment its CX register, you must put 41H in a very special location - the address that the CS:IP of the simulator points to at the present time.

By definition, CS:IP (*Code Segment:Instruction Pointer*) is the memory location (the Segment:Offset address) where the 80x86 finds the instruction to execute as soon as it moves into action.

You'll need to determine the default values for these two registers. Use the NEW command to clear the registers. CS contains ssss, which is the segment address of the user area similar to all the other segment registers. IP has a default value of 100h.

CS:IP currently points to ssss:0100. That's the address where PROG1 should be. In fact, if we load these bytes elsewhere in the user area (for example, ssss:1033) the simulator will execute what is at address ssss:0100 instead of executing the increment instruction of CX.

Try loading this byte at ssss:0100:

    >>E 100 41 <Enter>

Although it contains only one instruction, you've now written a program in memory. And not just anywhere in memory but at the CS:IP address, exactly where you wanted it.

The highlight bar in the Disassembly Area always indicates the instruction which the CS:IP points to. If you enter 41h at the CS:IP address, the bar displays:

    CS:0100 INC CX

This window also displays instructions in memory load after the operation INC CX in address ssss:0100.

Before starting the simulator to see how it uses the value 41h as an instruction to increment register CX, load the value 7CFh into register CX:

    >>CX 7CF <Enter>

Use the STEP command to instruct SIM to move one step at a time:.

>>STEP 4 <Enter>

| SIM |
|-----|

Then type:

>>SIM <Enter>

This command activates the simulator. Be very careful here. When the simulator is active, you can't use keyboard commands because there is no cursor or prompt. SIM is now in control and executes the programs.

Look at the Control Area. Despite their special uses, the, DATA registers are usually interchangeable.

| fetch opcode |
|--------------|
| read byte |

The first line contains the name of the instruction in its standard form. This line is currently empty since neither SIM nor the 80x86 currently know the instruction to execute. However, we know which instruction comes next because the program window displays it.

The other lines progressively display the stages of how 80x86 functions. The second and third lines display respectively the "macrostep" and the "microstep" that will be executed. Therefore, we've divided each instruction into macrosteps which are in turn composed of microsteps.

If you look at the macrosteps you'll get a very good idea of the way the instructions are executed. We've added microsteps for more detail in order to break down a complex operation into several stages. However, quite often, macrosteps represent the most fascinating level of execution and microstep sequences aren't quite as interesting.

Because it's easier to demonstrate this in smaller steps or parts, we'll first work in mode 4 (STEP=4). The simulator will pause each time it executes a microstep. Then, when you know assembly language and the simulator, you can work with other modes while stopping after each macrostep and finally after each instruction. Although this may sound confusing to you right now, you'll soon find it very easy.

Let's return to increment CX. In our example the Macrostep line displays, "Fetch opcode". In fact, the first phase in executing an 80x86 instruction is to read the *operation code* (or OPCODE) in memory. As long as you haven't performed this step, the 80x86 doesn't know which instruction to execute nor how to execute it. Remember that the operation code is the value representing a given instruction in memory.

"Fetch opcode" consists of a series of microsteps intended to inscribe a byte located at memory address CS:IP in ZL (input port of the 80x86) and then move it into the instruction register.

Press <Spacebar> to view the first microstep of "Fetch opcode" executed. The Microstep line displays:

```
TRANSFER: OR <--- IP
```

This means "Transfer the contents of the instruction pointer in the offset register". The affected registers are highlighted on the display. These transfers are the most frequently used operation when you execute an instruction.

The transfer takes place as soon as you press <Spacebar> to continue the program execution. You may want to slow down the simulator so you can better observe reading in memory. Press <5> to slow down the simulator. You can also use the <C> key.

Notice that the transfer operation hasn't modified the IP register. The next opcode microstep is:

```
INCREMENT IP
```

This operation does not contribute to executing the 41h instruction but will be used later for executing the next instruction. When the simulator is in the analysis mode, IP always points to the next instruction.

Remember that the 80x86 cannot wait for you because it must execute thousands of instructions per second. Furthermore, it must make certain that the IP points to the first byte of the next instruction.

CS is now transferred into SR (Segment Register). The table is now in place to read memory. We have a segment and an offset. That's all that is required to move anywhere within 1,048,576 memory locations.

The next microstep consists of reading the byte. The only distinction between the different modes of execution of the simulator resides in the fact that STEP=4 divides reading and writing instructions into stages of "mini" microsteps.

The following is a list of these stages. They will not be displayed on the screen:

1. SR and OR are combined to give a standard segment:offset address. The result is displayed in the address window (or Address Latch).

2. Next, this is transmitted to the address bus.

3 The memory location is read and its contents loaded to the data bus.

4 The value of the data bus is transmitted to ZL.

So ZL should now contain 41h. If this isn't the case, there are two possible explanations. Either you didn't previously load it at address SSSS:0100 or CS:IP is not at address SSSS:0100.

The last microstep of the opcode selection is a third transfer:

```
TRANSFER:  IR <--- ZL
```

Here the 80x86 looked for an instruction and load it in IR.

## Decoding

During the "Decode" macrostep, the 80x86 analyses the instruction to find out what you expect it to do. Decode isn't divided into microsteps. Press the <Spacebar> for the 80x86 to decode.

Now "INC CX", the mnemonic name for the 41h opcode, displays in the control window. Up to this point this window was empty since the processor hadn't yet determined the nature of the instruction.

Next the processor executes the actions set off by INC CX. First it increments. Up until now, everything done has only been to prepare the ground for this process.

```
INCREMENT : CX
```

Next, we move to the flag test stage. Bit 4 of FL is known as the "assistant carry flag". Right now, indicator "A" is highlighted. If either another flag or if no flag is activated, then you did not load 7 CFH in CX. We'll study flags in the second part of this series.

We're almost finished; only a little housework remains. It's the same for each instruction. The macrostep called "end of instruction" does this "housework."

The first chore consists of controlling possible interrupts which amounts to verifying "Control Pins" N and I and flags IF and TF. Press the space bar to skim through the flags. Don't worry at this stage if it doesn't go smoothly. Also, accept the "clear prefixes" stage without trying to understand it.

After this bit of housework the execution of opcode 41h, also known as INC CX, is completely finished. The simulator returns the controls to you and places you in the Analysis Mode.

Congratulations, you've just watched your first program execute. If you followed these steps completely, you already know 90% of assembly language.

It's not so important to remember the exact sequence of the macrosteps and microsteps. What is important is to make 80x86 look in memory and then execute opcode 41 to increment the CX register.

For the time being, let's put aside everything we learned concerning setting up flags. There are two consequences as a result of execution of this opcode. First, CX is incremented. In fact, if you have followed this closely, IP now points to ssss:0101. Second, if we had to now execute a new simulation, we would no longer send the instruction 41H (INC CX) but rather what is in CS:0101.

Let's go through this one more time.

To start INC CX again, you have to position the instruction pointer on 100H:

```
>>IP 100 <Enter>
```

Then we have to again select the SIM command, but this time, INC CX will end with the value 7D1H in CX.

# 9.3 Incrementing Other Registers

Each of the data registers can be incremented. You use opcode 40h for AX, 43h for BX, 42h for DX, 44h for SP, 45h for BP, 46h for SI and finally 47h to increment DI. The following table is a list of these opcodes:

| Operations | Opcode binary | Opcode hex |
|---|---|---|
| INC AX | 0100 0000 | 40h |
| INC CX | 0100 0001 | 41h |
| INC DX | 0100 0010 | 42h |
| INC BX | 0100 0011 | 43h |
| INC SP | 0100 0100 | 44h |
| INC BP | 0100 0101 | 45h |
| INC SI | 0100 0110 | 46h |
| INC DI | 0100 0111 | 47h |

You've notice that, when the first five bits of the opcode are 01000, the processor recognizes that it's an instruction for incrementing a register. The last three bits are used to specify the register.

The following is a table for decoding 16 bit registers:

| | |
|---|---|
| AX | 000 |
| CX | 001 |
| DX | 010 |
| BX | 011 |
| SP | 100 |
| BP | 101 |
| SI | 110 |
| DI | 111 |

Here is a more formal description of the INC instruction:

| 0 1 0 0 0 reg | Increment Register

REG represents any index or data register.

The "INC reg" instruction follows an outline common to all 80x86 coding instructions. The first part describes the operation to be executed and the second part describes what the operation is done on.

This division of opcodes into verbs and direct objects doesn't usually lend itself to working with nibbles. Sometimes it even spills over on to neighboring bytes. An opcode can do more than just work with two bytes.

Now that you know this, we can consider constructing an increment instruction of the index source register by combining the first five bits that mean "increment the register" (INC) with the last three bits specifying SI. Don't touch the first four bits. If you attempt to change them at this stage in the game, you might change the INC instruction into who knows what.

```
01000 110       (0100 0110 = 46h)

(INC) (SI)
```

Test your work by starting the simulator with opcode 46h. Inscribe this opcode in memory at address ssss:0100, put the IP at 100 and type SIM to start the simulator.

# 9.4    Decrementing

It's possible for the 80x86 to go "backwards" and to decrement a register instead. The decrement instruction is also one byte long. The first five bits are used to define the operation and the last three to identify the corresponding register.

| 0 1 0 0 1 reg | Decrement Register |
|---|---|

So 01001 000 (or 48h) "decrements" AX, while 01001 001 (49h) decrements CX and so forth.

Now we're ready to execute programs with two instructions. First we'll increment and then decrement a register.

Load this program at CS:100:

```
>>E 100 45 4D <Enter>
```

and then start the program. Be certain that IP is at 100H. If it isn't at this address, type:

```
IP 100 <Enter>
```

You'll return to the execution mode after executing the first instruction (45h or INC BP) unless you expressly specify to the simulator that you want it to execute two instructions:

```
>>SIM 2 <Enter>
```

Now SIM will execute two instructions one right after another.

Until now we've only seen two different instructions from more than a hundred possible ones:

```
01000 + reg (INC reg, incrementing a 16-bit register)

01010 + reg (DEC reg, decrementing a 16-bit register)
```

Because the 80x86 doesn't understand INC when you want it to increment the CX register, you must specify opcode 41h. Every 80x86 instruction has a corresponding mnemonic device made up of from two to six letters. Some of them are more informative than others but each one is easy to remember.

Mnemonic devices are generally associated with an operand so you have a symbolic representation of the instruction. In the case of opcode 41h, "INC" is the mnemonic and "CX" the operand:.

```
Mnemonic     operand

Do this      with this thing
```

# 9.5  Assemble and Disassemble

We've seen how the "U" window (the Disassemble window on the right) and the first line of the control window display the official mnemonic of the instruction being carried out. The relation between the "bytes in memory" of an instruction and its shortened description leads us into a discussion about assemblers and disassemblers.

Disassemble means transforming bytes in memory into mnemonics and operands. In the SIM program you "disassemble" something by using the Disassemble (or "U") command. Basically, however, the two terms mean the same thing and we will use them interchangeably.

Assemble is the opposite. It means translating mnemonics and operands furnished by humans into bytes. When a person works with an assembly program, you say that he or she is working in assembly language. If you want to be particular from a technical point of view, programmers work in assembly language and the result of their work is actually assembly language in the form of binary numbers in memory or in a file.

| Assembled | Disassembled |
|-----------|--------------|
| 01000011  | INC BX       |

The SIM command Disassemble disassembles large areas of memory areas or an area which isn't in CS:IP. This command is very similar to DUMP from DOS.

To see your previous work, type:

```
>>U 100 <Enter>
```

You may notice that although the result is similar to what is in the Disassembly Area, there is one important difference. The segment code value is clearly displayed with the values of the bytes making up the instruction given as a bonus. This wasn't possible in the border of the Disassembly Area because of the limited space. Already, a few instructions go beyond the border of this area.

Now let's take a quick look in BIOS ROM to see how the screen management was written. You can do this by instructing the U command to disassemble up to the BIOS ROM level. Don't worry if you still don't understand mnemonics and operands.

```
>>U F000:F065 <Enter>
```

Your computer displays garbage when you attempt to disassemble memory which doesn't contain assembly language. In the same way, we've seen that a DUMP of bytes that aren't a text produces ASCII translations without meaning. So you may find data for BIOS routines at address 0040:0.

```
>>U 40:0 <Enter>
```

Since almost every 8-bit value corresponds to an authentic 80x86 instruction, it might prove to be difficult to determine if a given area contains assembly language or not. One tip is that areas without assembly language present useless repetitions.

For example, an area filled with 0 produces a series of "ADD [BX+SI]". In the same way, if one of the opcodes and there are about 20 of them, appears without having been defined beforehand, the assembler displays "???". This is a sure indication that a code is absent.

The trouble is that, if you don't start at the right place, you may get a wrong disassembly of an area really containing assembly language. The vast majority of instructions in assembly language make up more than a byte. So if you begin disassembling on the second or third byte of a 3 byte instruction, the reading might be shifted forward or backward.

## A     Assembler

SIM includes an assembler. The assembler can simplify programming by avoiding bits and bytes in the set of instructions of the 80x86. They just have to know INC CX and the assembler takes care of the rest and loads 41h in memory by itself.

Start the assembler using the Assembler command ("A") followed by the address where you want it to start.

```
>>A 100 <Enter>
```

We'll start with the two mnemonic instructions we've already discussed:

| When the display shows: | Then type: |
|---|---|
| ssss:0100 | INC CX <Enter> |
| ssss:0101 | INC AX <Enter> |
| ssss:0102 | DEC BP <Enter> |

SIM decodes your lines after you press <Enter>. If they contain correct 80x86 assembly, SIM loads the appropriate byte in memory. The effect of each choice should be visible immediately in the Disassemble ("U") window. To exit the assembler, press <Ctrl><C>.

You can compare assembly and disassembly commands to DUMP and Enter respectively. When information that you want to load in memory is a program in assembly language, the assembler acts like a turbo version of the Enter command ("E"). In the same way, when you want to read a computer program, Disassemble is a better performing DUMP command.

```
1709:0100 41                            INC CX
1709:0101 40                            INC AX
1709:0102 4D                            DEC BP
1709: 0100 41 40 4D 00 00 00 00 00   00 00 00 00 00 00 00 00 ...
1709: 0100 00 00 00 00 00 00 00 00   00 00 00 00 00 00 00 00 ...
1709: 0100 00 00 00 00 00 00 00 00   00 00 00 00 00 00 00 00 ...
```

Of these two displays, which provides the most information addresses 0100 and 0101?

## 9.6    Try Experimenting

Use the simulator to simulate INC and DEC instructions until you've had all you can take. Mastering the basic mechanisms of the 80x86, such as the increment instruction pointer, the fetch/decode procedure and addressing memory by segment:offset, is now within your reach.

While you're experimenting with the INC and DEC instructions, experiment with the STEP command:

- The difference from STEP=3 and STEP=4 is that STEP=3 doesn't pause between reading and writing.

- STEP=2 only pauses at macrosteps. Displaying microsteps in this mode is done so quickly that it is impossible to see it. That's why STEP=2 only displays the significant stages in the execution of an instruction and leaves out redundant transfers and increments the instruction pointer.

- STEP=1 only pauses between instructions. STEP=0 doesn't pause at all, unless you press the <Spacebar>.

Change the execution speed by pressing the following keys:

- Press <1> for maximum speed.

- Press <9> for minimum speed.

Other keys you'll use include:

- Press <Spacebar> to stop and press it again to restart execution.

- Press <Ctrl><C> or execute a BRK command to stop SIM and return to the Command Management Window.

- Press <Ctrl><P> to activate the printer; press it again to stop the printer. When using a printer, you have to leave SIM and switch to DOS. A description of the current state of the processor is printed after each instruction is executed.

Try to experiment and simulate an instruction with all the registers in binary mode (>>BASE * BIN). What you see on the screen is a real representation of the contents of the 80x86. After this hexadecimal notation will seem as easy as 1, 2, 3.

# 9.7    Chapter Exercises

1)    What are data registers used for? Which ones are they?

2)    What are index registers? What are they generally used for?

3)    What is a segment? What are segment registers used for? Which ones are they?

4)    What is the instruction pointer used for? Is it really a register?

5)    What is the flag register used for? What is it called?

6)    What is the Z register used for? What are ZL and ZH?

7)    What does "I L N I T" mean?

8)    What do we mean by "CS:IP"?

9)    What does the SIM expression "Fetch Opcode" mean?

10)    What is the mnemonic device that lets you increment AX? And the one that lets you increment DX?

11)    What is the mnemonic device that lets you decrement the BX register?

12)    What does the term "disassemble" mean?

13)    What is the SIM command for disassembling a memory area?

14)    What is the SIM command for assembling a series of instructions?

15)    Make a little program that increments AX once and then decrements it.

16)    Put all the registers in binary mode and execute the program in STEP=4 mode.

# 10. The MOV Instruction

Single byte instructions, like INC and DEC, are rare. Most instructions cannot be contained in a single byte. This is especially the case of the MOVE instruction (MOV).

The MOV instruction of the 80x86 is used to transfer values from one register to another register or from a register to memory. Incrementing a register is useful, but it's not very useful if you can't easily load values into that register.

The MOV mnemonic lets you execute several distinct instructions corresponding to several ways of transferring. These methods include from memory to a data register, from memory to a segment register and others. All these instructions require two operands but they can take two different formats:

```
MOV destination, source

MOV destination_register, immediate_value
```

We'll discuss the "MOV destination_register, immediate_value" first. The term "immediate_value" means that the second operator is the value that you're loading into the destination register. It's the equivalent of the BASIC command LET X = 14.

The following three byte machine code:

```
B8h C6h F0h
```

translates to the following mnemonic form of the instruction:

```
MOV AX,F0C6
```

The result of this operation is to load the AX register with the value F0C6h. This explains the meaning of the arrow that SIM displays in the Microstep mode. This corresponds to the agreement adopted by Intel that in assembly language the operation is indicated as moving from the right operation to the left operand.

Let's do a detailed analysis of these three bytes. "B8h" is an opcode byte and means, "Load in the AX register the word that follows this code." The next two bytes (C6h and F0h) actually are stored in reverse order. Remember that the least significant part of the word is in the lowest memory location.

# 10.1   Using MOV

Before loading MOV1.DEM from the companion diskette, make sure that SIM is in memory and type the command NEW:

```
>> NEW <Enter>
```

Then type:

```
>>LOAD MOV1.DEM <Enter>
```

**Note:**    If you're not using a hard drive, type:
>>LOAD B:DEM1.DEM
(Switch this to the A: drive if the companion diskette is in that drive).

The SIM command loads the selected file into memory at the address CS:100. The Status Area will display MOV1.DEM. You can load any files with .COM, .EXE or other extensions in memory providing the size doesn't exceed the memory limits of your computer.

The length of the file is entered in BX (containing the high 8-bits) and CX. Since the size of MOV1.DEM is 80h bytes (3 program bytes and 125 padding bytes), BX-CX contains 00000080h. The program has been loaded successfully when MOV AX,F0C6 is displayed in CS:0100 (Disassembly Area).

SIM automatically changes the size of the SIM screen even if you did not previously use the BIG command. After the command is executed, the screen returns to its former size.

Type the STEP command to switch to mode 4:

```
>>Step 4 <Enter>
```

Then perform a simulation of this instruction. As always, the processor begins with a "fetch opcode". As soon as B8H is in the instruction register, the 80x86 recognizes the instruction "MOV AX, immediate value" and executes the macro fetch word. After this, Z contains "F0C6h".

To understand these explanations, we recommend following the instructions on the SIM screen. You can easily tell the difference between each stage because you'll see one or more parameters change on the screen.

Now the processor reads offset 0101 in the code segment and loads the 8-bit value that's there (C6h, the low 8-bits in F0C6h) in ZL. Then it reads offset 0102 where the high 8-bits are located. Finally the entire word is read and transferred to AX.

After this end of instruction "housework," here we are back in the command mode. The IP instruction pointer (0103) points to the instruction BRK.

## BRK

The BREAK has an opcode of CCH at address ssss:0103.

BRK is the end of program signal used by SIM. It's loaded in memory by the MOV1.DEM file and allows the simulator to return control to you by automatically coming back to the command mode. This is very useful for executing multiple instructions in the STEP=1 mode.

Now you can modify the 16-bit number at address 101h and start the simulator again. Be careful that you do not use the opcode value (100h) or we would need a different command than MOV to execute it.

Now execute the BRK command at 103h. You see that after the simulator executes BRK, it immediately turns the controls back to you. The IP still points to 103h, which proves that BRK has in fact been executed.

Look at the opcode bytes, the eight codes of "MOV register, immediate_value" and especially the last three bits:

| | | |
|---|---|---|
| MOV AX,value | B8 | 1011 1000 |
| MOV CX,value | B9 | 1011 1001 |
| MOV DX,value | BA | 1011 1010 |
| MOV BX,value | BB | 1011 1011 |
| MOV SP,value | BC | 1011 1100 |
| MOV BP,value | BD | 1011 1101 |
| MOV SI,value | BE | 1011 1110 |
| MOV DI,value | BF | 1011 1111 |

As you've already seen with INC and DEC, the three least significant 3 bits specify the register:

```
MOV register, immediate value

 1 0 1 1 W  reg    data    data    if W=1
```

Remember that data registers can be subdivided into two 8-bit registers. The MOV instruction can also take advantage of the "separable" registers. "MOV reg, value" has a format that can exploit this alternative. To load FFh into AL (remember that AL is an 8-bit register of AX) type:

```
MOV AL,FF

 1 0 1 1 0 0 0 0    1 1 1 1 1 1 1 1
```

COMPARE the above instruction with the MOV AX,FFFF code:

```
MOV AX,FFFF

 1 0 1 1 1 0 0 0    1 1 1 1 1 1 1 1 1 1 1 1 1 1 1 1
```

It appears that the first four bits actually contain the opcode for "MOV reg, value". Bit 4 of the opcode (W) is the Word/byte flag. During the instruction decoding phase, the 80x86 reads this bit to determine whether it's an 8-bit or 16-bit operation. If it finds that W is set (1), it loads the next word following the opcode into the appropriate register.

But if W is clear (0), it loads the next byte following the opcode into the appropriate register.

How does the MOV instruction know which register? In fact, the processor decides on the register according to the table below:

| 8-bit register | Decoding table |
|:---:|:---:|
| 000 | AL |
| 001 | CL |
| 010 | DL |
| 011 | BL |
| 100 | AH |
| 101 | CH |
| 110 | DH |
| 111 | BH |

The three bits identifying the register let you code eight different registers. If "W" is set, it's one of the eight 16-bit registers that will be used. If "W" is clear, it's one of the eight 8-bit registers.

By analogy, you might think that the INC and DEC instructions benefit from a word flag permitting manipulation of 8-bit registers. Although sounding logical, it's nevertheless wrong. No flag like this exists for these instructions. So there is no way to use these instructions to increment or decrement 8-bit registers.

Practice assembling these instructions:

```
MOV AH,FF    =

MOV AX,134C  =

MOV AX,14    =

MOV CX,0     =

DEC CX       =
```

Load the bytes that you have selected in memory so you can verify your work. SIM doesn't have to be used. The results you get after disassembly (the U window) will be instructive.

The ability of the assembler to translate mnemonics and operands into assembly language saves us the trouble of memorizing operation codes and register tables. It shouldn't prevent us from understanding the internal mechanisms of instructions in assembly language. That's our objective in the following chapters.

## 10.2 Chapter Exercises

1) What is the SIM command that lets you put everything back at the initial state?

2) What is the mnemonic MOV used for?

3) What is the mnemonic device used to load the value 6787h in the AX register?

4) What is the mnemonic device used to load the value 76h in the SI register?

5) Use the instruction MOV to modify the value of CX. For example, load F004 in it. Note what happens when you start the instruction.

6) Write a small program which has to first load the value 64 in AL then decrement AL. Start SIM to see the procedure.

7) Write a small program which manipulates AL by loading F5 in it and then AH by loading 55h in it.

# 11. The EA Byte

In the preceding chapter, we introduced the 80x86 MOV instructions.

The "MOV register immediate_value" version of this instruction reflects only one of the many possible ways to move data in assembly language. First of all, this instruction cannot read the value at a given memory location. It's limited to writing. Next, it can only load "immediate" data (or defined value) into a register.

So how can we move data from one register to another (for example, BX into BP)? The assembler takes care of that:

```
ssss:0100  MOV  BP,BX
```

At the level of mnemonics and operands (or assembly language), this is only slightly different from MOV BP,F000. At the level of assembly language, the necessary instruction for copying one register to another is completely different.

At times the similarities between 80x86 assembly language and 80x86 machine language aren't as obvious as you would wish. For example, the MOV instruction used in assembly language can take on a number of forms when written in machine language. The form used depends on the move and the location.

The 80x86 assembly language is simpler since you have to use only one and not several MOV mnemonics. However, it's also more complex because you can quickly confuse MOV AX,F000 (which is possible) and MOV ES,F000 (not possible). The difference isn't obvious when you examine only mnemonics.

A MOV from register to register is similar to the BASIC command "LET A = B". You must use a format of MOV which is more general and capable of transferring one register to another. We'll later discuss the possibilities of doing even more.

```
MOV    reg/mem      to/from reg

| 1 0 0 0 1 0 D W | MOD  REG  R/M |
      byte 1            byte 2
```

The "MOV" mnemonic is almost the only thing that this instruction has in common with "MOV register immediate_value". In reality this a totally different instruction for the processor:

Let's take the instruction MOV BX,BP as an example:

```
MOV   BX, BP

1 0 0 0 0 1 0 1   1 1   0 1 1   1 0 1

            D W     MOD   REG   R/M

                    (BX)
```

Let's look at the effects the MOV instruction has on registers. Notice that below the opcode are the names of several fields (such as MOD, REG, R/M, D or W) which corresponds to a single or a group of bits that make up the instruction.

# 11.1 MOD, REG and R/M

What do the fields MOD (md), REG and R/M represent?

## 11.1.1 MOD

MOD (mode) is a two-bit field which can take on four different values ($2^2$). The case we'll discuss is when MOD = 11h (3 in decimal). When MOD is not equal to 11, the processor executes an unexpected operation which we'll discuss later.

## 11.1.2 REG and R/M fields

REG and R/M are each 3-bit fields able to take on eight different values ($2^3$). REG (or Register) represents one of two registers concerned by a MOV instruction and R/M (Register or Memory) indicates the second.

The "R/M" name is somewhat misleading. In fact, especially for MOD values not equal to 11, it so happens that R/M doesn't really process registers but rather a number of memory locations.

We already know that the two registers referenced by a MOV instruction are entered in the REG and R/M fields. To know which of the registers is the source and which is the destination, we have to look at a new indicator of the opcode byte.

We have:

```
1 0 0 0 1 0 D W MOD  REG   R/M
```

When Destination (D) is set, then the register contained in the REG field is the target register. If Destination is clear, the register contained in the R/M is the target register.

For example:

```
1 0 0 0 1 0 1 1 1 0 1 1 1 0 1   = MOV  BX,BP

            D       BX    BP

1 0 0 0 1 0 0 1 1 1 0 1 1 1 0 1   = MOV  BP,BX

            D       BX    BP
```

There is also a word indicator in the opcode byte. When W is set, the processor knows that it must "decode" (or read) REG and R/M with the help of the 16 register table. When W is clear, it means that the two fields, REG and R/M, are 8-bit data registers.

```
1 0 0 0 1 0 1 1 1 1 0 1 1 1 0 1   = MOV  BX,BP

                W     BX    BP

1 0 0 0 1 0 1 0 1 1 0 1 1 1 0 1   = MOV  BL,CH

                W     BL    CH
```

## 11.1.3    Quick review

Let's take a moment to review this chapter and especially this section.

There are many variants of the "MOV reg_destination/reg_source" although it is a unique instruction. The first six bits of the opcode inform the 80x86 about what we have to do with this variant of the MOV instruction. Next come the D and W indicators and finally a byte of information divided into REG and R/M fields.

Let's see how the 80x86 works with these instructions. Load MOV2.DEM in memory in mode 3. The MOV instructions will be more interesting if you put values other than 0 (zero) in the concerned registers.

Here are some details that you should carefully observe. After the macro decodes, the SIM command line displays:

```
MOVE  W REG,R/M
```

That's what the 80x86 decoded. So according to the operation code, it observes that it's indeed dealing with a MOV instruction.

It sees that the W bit is set. The operation is performed on a word. The destination register is 16-bits in any case.

It also sees that MOV is performed on a register (REG) into which memory (M) or register (R) data will be transferred. This should not surprise you because it's the only case possible.

This is all that the 80x86 knows concerning the MOV instruction after reading the opcode byte. It still must determine the name of this register and the name of the register or memory box where the data to transfer is coming from. To do this, it must read the EA (Effective Address) byte; and to this, it must read the byte containing REG, MOD and R/M so it knows what it actually contains.

**114**

After that, the EA byte is decoded in two steps:

- The processor translates the REG field (the three central bits) into "BX". It then knows the destination register.

- It decodes the MOD and R/M fields. These two combined fields represent the BP register. Observe the contents of the SIM command line during this decoding. It indicates the progress of the processor in decoding the instruction.

This produces the final result of the simple transfer of one register to another. The description of the following instruction would be similar to the difference of the W that is reloaded by a D meaning an opposite MOV operation (from BX to BP). That seems very complicated because we're explaining in detail what happens in the processor. Remember that MOV transfers values between the memory and a register or from register to register.

Now it's your turn to assemble the following instructions. (Use the assembler if you can't do it yourself).

```
MOV    AX,BX    = ____ ____

MOV    SI,CX    = ____ ____

MOV    CX,SI    = ____ ____

MOV    BL,CL    = ____ ____

MOV    DL,DH    = ____ ____
```

You're now familiar with the two most important instructions of the mnemonic MOV. The others are only minor variations on these two. An example being a special format for moving to a segment register.

After you've worked for a time with the many variations of the MOV instruction, you'll welcome the ease of using XCHG.

## 11.2   XCHG  (XCHG.DEM)  Instruction

The XCHG (or Exchange) instruction exchanges values between two registers or between a register and a memory location. It's a type of bidirectional MOV. It has two formats: a general format (the EA format) and another format less complete but more efficient (the distinctive format of the accumulator).

```
XCHG register, register/memory

1 0 0 0 0 1 1 W MOD  REG  R/M
```

XCHG exchanges values (byte or word) contained in REG and MOD or R/M fields. There's no need for a destination indicator since REG and R/M are both source and target registers.

Let's use the assembler to generate an XCHG DX,BP instruction.

```
ssss:0100 XCHG DX,BP
```

This assembly generates the coding of two bytes that we have just seen. This is the general format. Now let's assemble the following instruction:

```
ssss:0102 XCHG AX,BP
```

This results in an instruction only one byte long. XCHG has a specific format for the accumulator to execute exchanges between AX and one of the index registers or 16-bit data registers. Although you can obviously generate a 2-byte code, it's better to generate a more efficient one.

```
XCHG accum,register

1 0 0 1 0  REG
```

## 11.3  Chapter Exercises

1)      What does the EA byte represent?

2)      What is the meaning of the R/M field?

3)      What happens when the D field is active?

4)      What is the W indicator used for?

5)      What is the mnemonic that lets you transfer the contents of BL into AL?

6)      What is the mnemonic that lets you exchange values contained in the SI and CX registers?

7)      MOVE the AX register into the BX register.

8)      Then exchange the AX and CX registers.

9)      Next decrement the CX register.

# 12. Flags

In this chapter we'll discuss the flags which have been mentioned previously. Flags are really just indicators. In the FL register are bits with individual meaning rather than an overall value. In other words, if FL and AX both contain 111101100 01011110, we generally agree that AX contains the value F45Eh while FL contains a certain number of 1s and 0s.

Therefore, we've provided a name and special location on the SIM screen for the nine bits of the FL register.

| Position | Indicator | Function | Abbreviation |
|----------|-----------|----------|--------------|
| 0 | Carry Flag | (state) | CF |
| 2 | Parity | (state) | PF |
| 4 | Auxiliary | (state) | AF |
| 6 | Zero | (state) | ZF |
| 7 | Sign | (state) | SF |
| 8 | Trap | (control) | TF |
| 9 | Interrupt | (control) | IF |
| 10 | Direction | (control) | DF |
| 11 | Overflow | (state) | OF |

These flags are logically divided into two groups: state and control flags. Several flags supply key information on instructions - Carry, Auxiliary, Overflow, Zero, Sign and Parity flags. Programs can check the state of these flags to determine the result of the preceding instruction.

The Direction, Interruption and Trap flags are control flags. They determine the way the processor responds in given situations. Programs may change these flags to control execution of certain instructions.

Flags are generally called by their abbreviation. For example, "DF" (or just "D") is the Direction flag.

The first thing that you should know about flags is that the set of 80x86 instructions for changing flags is very incomplete:

| Mnemonic | Opcode | Operation |
|----------|--------|-----------|
| CLD | FC | Clear Direction Flag |
| STD | FD | Set Direction Flag |
| CLI | FA | Clear Interrupt Flag |
| STI | FB | Set Interrupt Flag |
| CLC | F8 | Clear Carry Flag |
| CMC | F5 | Complement Carry Flag |
| STC | F9 | Set Carry Flag |

There are only 7 instead of 18 possible instructions that you might expect for setting and clearing flags. Of the six state flags, only the carry flag (CF) can easily be changed. The reason is simple: Since these state flags are used to signal the status of a previous instruction, there's no reason to have to change them beforehand.

As for the control flags, you can set and clear DF and IF but you can't change the TF (the trap flag). That's an understandable shortcoming because unless you write a program with DEBUG, SIM or other simulator, it's best to assume that this flag doesn't exist. Otherwise, using the TF flag is one of the best ways to crash or lockup the computer.

# 12.1   The Zero Flag (ZF)

The Zero flag (ZF) is a state flag which shows the arithmetic result of an instruction. The 80x86 sets or clears the ZF based on the execution of the previous instruction.

The state of ZF follows this rule:

*When an operation produces a zero as a result, ZF is set. If the operation does not produce a zero as a result, ZF is clear.*

For example, with the instruction INC AX:

```
IF AX=FFFF then Z is set
```

or, with the instruction DEC AX:

```
IF AX=0001 then Z is set

IF AX=178C then Z is clear
```

This seems to work backwards from what you might imagine. When a mathematical operation has 0 for a result, the ZF flag is set and it remains set until another mathematical operation produces a result different from zero. Afterwards, the flag remains cleared at zero until the next operation which produces a zero.

## 12.2   The Sign Flag (SF)

The sign flag (SF) follows a completely different rule. SF is only set if an operation produces a result where the most significant bit is set. If not, it remains clear.

For example, with the instruction INC AX:

```
IF AX=0026h then SF is clear

IF AX=FC23h then SF is set

IF AX=7FFFh then SF is set
```

When the operation affects only eight bits (such as INC AL), then the setting of bit 7 that determines the state of the SF flag.

For example, with the instruction INC BH:

```
IF BH=87h then S is set
```

But with the instruction INC CL:

```
IF CL=14h then S is clear
```

The name of this flag comes from the fact that the most significant bit of a number indicates its sign (either positive or negative). Unfortunately you can't use the + and - signs in binary.

We'll discuss signed numbers in more detail later but an important rule to remember now is:

> *When a program in assembly language uses negative numbers, the highest bit of a number determines the sign (either positive (0) or negative (1)) of this number.*

In most cases you won't use "signed" numbers, so the state of the SF flag usually is not important.

# 12.3   The Parity Flag (PF)

You may have written many 80x86 assembly routines without ever feeling like a parity flag was required (especially since PF follows a rather uncommon rule):

*When the result of an operation has an even number of set bits, then PF is set.*

Let's take the instruction INC AX as an example:

PF is clear if AX starts out with zero. In that case, the result (0001h or 00000000 00000001) contains an uneven number of 1s. If you execute the same instruction again (INC AX), the result is 00000000 00000010 and PF is still clear. But if you execute the same instruction a third time, the result is then 00000000 00000011, which sets PF with an even number of "1"s.

The INC and DEC instructions affect these three flag indicators simultaneously.

Load the FLAGCOND.DEM program and execute a simulation and choose a simulation in Mode 2.

Now carefully watch the "allocation flag" macro (condition flags). Try to anticipate the values that SF, PF and ZF will take after each instruction. (OF and AF will also be modified but we aren't interested in them for the moment.)

## 12.3.1   Why use flags?

The automatic updating of the state of a flag lets you test the results of an operation and modify the sequence of subsequent instructions to control execution of the program. This procedure exists in every program language. For example,

| | The BASIC equivalent is: |
|---|---|
| DEC AX | 100 A = A - 1 |
| [if AX <> 0, repeat] | 110 IF A <> 0 THEN GOTO 100 |

In Chapter 13 we'll discuss the assembly equivalent of the BASIC IF GOTO commands.

## 12.4 Chapter Exercises

1)      How is the overflow flag demoted on the SIM screen?

2)      How is the sign flag denoted?

3)      How can you clear the carry flag? What is that used for?

4)      What is the zero flag used for?

5)      Write a program that clears the zero flag, places the value 01h in AX and then decrements AX.

6)      Write a short program to execute the following operations:

>      a) Enter the value FFFC in AX.

>      b) Increment AX four times in a row.

Then start the program and note what happened.

7)      Write and then start a program that loads the value 88h in CL and then decrements CL. Note the settings of the flags after running it.

# 13. Conditional Jumps

It's sometimes necessary to break the sequential execution of 80x86 instructions and execute another sequence of instructions.

Without this possibility, every program would only be a succession of sequential instructions processed in only one direction, from the top to the bottom, and on only one pass. It would be incapable of performing loops, repetitions and tests that are the very essence of programming.

Your first program in BASIC was probably very simple such as the following:

```
100 INPUT "WHAT IS YOUR NAME ?";A$

110 PRINT "HELLO, ";A$

120 END
```

Although this is an executable program, it isn't very interesting. As you gained experience working with loops, more difficult programs and routines became possible:

```
100 N = 0

110 PRINT N, N * N

120 N = N + 1

130 IF N <= 10 THEN 110

140 END
```

Programming isn't just loops and repeating or automatic decision making. This is just as true for an assembly language as for Pascal or BASIC. Since loops are fundamental operations, the 80x86 offers a series of instructions for this purpose.

## 13.1   Looping Principles

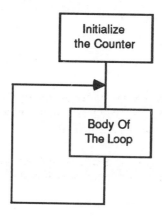

Recall that the instruction pointer (IP) is the register used for executing instructions. You might conclude that a conditional jump changes the value in the IP. This is exactly what happens. If a conditional instruction proves true, a new value is placed into the program counter.

However, if the conditional instruction proves not true, then the IP is not altered and execution continues normally with the next instruction. For example, this happens when the ZF is set and the conditional instruction JNZ (Jump if Not Zero) is encountered.

If a conditional instruction is executed and proves true, the byte following the conditional instruction is added to the IP. For example, if IP contains 102h and if the ZF is clear, a JNZ 10 instruction sets the new value of the IP to 102h + 10h = 112h. So the next instruction to be executed is found at 112h.

This does not mean that conditional jumps can only take place in forward direction. Backward ("negative") jumps are not only possible but occur more frequently than forward ("positive") jumps.

During a conditional branch, when the displacement byte is greater than or equal to 80h, the 80x86 "knows" to subtract rather than add the value to the IP.

FFh=-1

FEh=-2

FDh=-3

... 80h=-128

We'll examine this in more detail when we discuss binary arithmetic. Conditional jumps are executed in both forward and backward directions, depending upon the value of the displacement byte (byte following the instruction).

Using only one displacement byte to determine whether the jump is forward (positive) or backward (negative) implies that these jumps are within a range of 127 bytes forward or 128 bytes backward.

The LOOP1.DEM program shows how to use the JNZ instruction to perform a loop. Type the following to load this demonstration:

```
>>LOAD LOOP1.DEM <Enter>
```

In the Disassembly Window you'll see the following:

| | |
|---|---|
| 0100 MOV | DX,04 |
| 0103 STC | |
| 0104 CLC | |
| 0105 DEC | DX |
| 0106 JNZ | 0103 |
| 0108 BRK | |
| 0109 BRK | |

**Note:**     This screen appears when the BIG command is not set.

Remember that STC sets the carry flag and that CLC clears it (refer to Chapter 12). Although it might seem meaningless now to do one right after the other, it's sufficient for the demonstration.

The program begins by loading 4 into register DX. The goal is to execute a series of flag settings/clearings within the loop.

Next is "DEC DX". Without DEC, which affects the zero flag, the loop in the routine would not be possible.

The JNZ instruction consists of an opcode byte (75h) and an offset byte (FBh). The branch is negative since bit 7 of FBh is set. So IP is decremented by 5 if the condition is true (zero flag is not set).

Now the disassembler helps you determine where the jump will end after the testing condition is true. JNZ 0103 is preferable to JNZ FB to describe a jump. Let's start the routine.

DX takes 03h as its value the first time that DEC DX is encountered. Since this is different from zero, the ZF is clear and therefore the condition of JNZ is true and execution proceeds by looping.

The "IP form" macro defines a new value for the instruction pointer. With the sign, the displacement byte becomes a word in ZL (we'll discuss this operation in more detail later).

Next, because of the Boolean signed numbers, the resulting word (FFFBh) is added to the IP and decremented to 103h. Finally, after four loops, the DEC DX zero flag is eventually set. The JNZ test is false and the loop is interrupted.

The following is a list of the 17 possible conditional jumps:

| Instruction | Opcode | Operation |
|---|---|---|
| JO | 70 | Jump if O=1 (Jump if Overflow) |
| JNO | 71 | Jump if O=0 (Jump if No Overflow) |
| JC | 72 | Jump if C=1 (Jump if Carry) |
| JNC | 73 | Jump if C=0 (Jump if No Carry) |
| JZ | 74 | Jump if Z=1 (Jump if Zero) |
| JNZ | 75 | Jump if Z=0 (Jump if No Zero) |
| JS | 78 | Jump if S=1 (Jump if Sign) |
| JNS | 79 | Jump if S=0 (Jump if Not Signed) |
| JP | 7A | Jump if P=1 (Jump if Parity) |
| JNP | 7B | Jump if P=0 (Jump if No Parity) |
| JBE | 76 | Jump if(C=1) OR (Z=1) (Jump if Below or Equal) |
| JA | 77 | Jump if(C=0) AND (Z=0) (Jump if Above) |
| JL | 7C | Jump if S <> 0 (Jump if Less than) |
| JGE | 7D | Jump if S = 0 (Jump if Greater or Equal) |
| JLE | 7E | Jump if((S XOR 0) OR Z)= 1 (Jump if Less than or Equal) |
| JG | 7F | Jump if((S XOR 0) OR Z)= 0 (Jump if Greater) |
| JCXZ | E3 | Jump if CX=0 (Jump if CX is Zero) |

Some of the above instructions are used with the CMP instruction (Compare). The CMP instruction is capable of performing more complex comparisons of two values. For example, you can use CMP to determine if one number is less than or equal to another. Finally, JCXZ isn't an indicator test at all, but rather a method to check the CX register.

You should know that some conditional jumps have several "equivalent" mnemonics. For example, you can express the JNZ command as "JNE" (Jump if Not Equal) in some cases. If you take a pen and notepad and list the mnemonics and operands during an assembly program coding, JNE is sometimes more judicious for describing the operation executed by opcode 75h. This is particularly true when you carry out tests after a CMP command (a comparison command that we will look at later). In other cases, your first priority is the state of the zero indicator and it's preferable to use "JNZ".

The 80x86 assemblers, just like SIM, use multiple mnemonics for the following instructions:

| Instruction | Opcode | Operation |
|---|---|---|
| JO | 70 | Jump if O=1 (if overflow) |
| JNO | 71 | Jump if O=0 (if no overflow) |
| JC | 72 | Jump if C=1 (if carry) |
| JNC | 73 | Jump if C=0 (if no carry) |
| JZ | 74 | Jump if Z=1 (if zero) |
| JNZ | 75 | Jump if Z=0 (if different from zero) |
| JS | 78 | Jump if S=1 (if sign) |
| JNS | 79 | Jump if S=0 (if not signed) |
| JP | 7A | Jump if P=1 (if parity) |
| JNP | 7B | Jump if P=0 (if no parity) |
| JBE | 76 | Jump if(C=1) OR (Z=1) |
| JA | 77 | Jump if(C=0) AND (Z=0) |
| JL | 7C | Jump if S <> 0 |
| JGE | 7D | Jump if S = 0 |
| JLE | 7E | Jump if((S XOR 0) OR Z)= 1 |
| JG | 7F | Jump if((S XOR 0) OR Z)= 0 |
| JCXZ | E3 | Jump if CX=0 |

As you can see, there are several mnemonics at your disposal. But how does a disassembler handle an opcode for which there are several mnemonics? The SIM assembler accepts either JNE or JNZ, but the disassembler uses JNZ.

# 13.2 Chapter Exercises

1) What's the mnemonic that lets you test if the result of an operation is equal to zero and perform a branch?

2) What is the mnemonic that lets you test whether the result of an operation is not zero and performs a branch?

3) What is the mnemonic used to test whether the sign indicator is set and performs a branch?

4) What is the conditional branch mnemonic if the CX register is equal to zero?

5) Write the following program to:

   a) Transfer the AX register into the BX register.

   b) Decrement the AX register.

   c) If the AX register is not zero, decrement AX again and continue.

6) Write the following program to:

   a) Enter the value 80h in the AX register.

   b) Increment AX.

   c) Test the parity flag and branch to step #2 if it's clear.

7) Write the following program to:

   a) Enter the value 00h in the AX register.

   b) Transfer the AX register into the DX register.

   c) Increment AX.

   d) If AX is not zero, jump to step #2.

   e) If not, transfer the DX register into the AX register.

# 14. More Loops

Because loops are so important, the 80x86 offers several ways to structure them. One simple, although little known method, is simply the LOOP instruction. This is a "super" conditional jump. In fact, a single LOOP instruction replaces the two instructions of the preceding demo routine.

| LOOP                     instruction |

LOOP automatically decrements the CX register. If CX is not 0, the jump is executed and the loop continues. Using LOOP requires that the CX register be the counter.

This is the first in a series of cases where CX is used as a counter. What is important to remember now is that cases where registers are used for a specific purpose are a key part to mastering assembly language.

Type the following to load the LOOP2.DEM file:

```
>>LOAD LOOP2.DEM <Enter>
```

## 14.1  Unconditional Jump (JMP)

Even if you don't explicitly change it yourself, modifying the instruction pointer is sometimes very interesting. JMP lets you change the value of the IP register in 80x86 assembly.

The JMP mnemonic lets you execute four types of different jumps which vary in function with the length of the branch desired and the direction of the jump.

The first is an unconditional 2-byte branch with one byte for the command and only one byte containing the size of the jump. The latter is signed with the sign placed in the IP. The new instruction pointer can therefore take values equivalent to an address situated from 128 bytes to 127 bytes preceding this instruction.

JMP follow displacement

131

We obviously need other ways to perform jumps. After all, the 80x86 is capable of processing programs in assembly language that are thousands of bytes long. Fortunately, there are JMPs capable of reaching all the nooks and crannies of the memory.

JMP (opcode E8h) is a 3-byte instruction: one byte of opcode and two bytes containing the length of the displacement. The value of these two bytes is added to that of the IP. This lets you reach any address of the same segment. Like in its abbreviated format (the first JMP we described), it's a relative JMP. The new value of the IP is formed by adding the two bytes.

| 1 1 1 0 1 0 0 0 | displacement LSB | displacement MSB |
|:---:|:---:|:---:|
| byte 1 | byte 2 | byte 3 |

Why use the 2-byte form of JMP when the 3-byte form can be used instead? When you use the 2-byte form (which is probably 90% of the time), it saves one byte and executes the instruction a little quicker. Since it's used so often, it is more efficient.

Programs in assembly language use jumps a lot and any time and space that can be gained is significant, no matter how small it might be. The assembler automatically chooses the shortened form of JMP when the destination is within the range (-127 to +128 bytes) so you won't have to count the displacement yourself.

You can use the 3-byte JMP instruction to extend the distance of the conditional jump. Since it doesn't have a long format, JNZ can't go beyond 128 bytes in one direction or the other. However, if you reverse the condition (JZ instead of JNZ) and add a JMP instruction, you can move anywhere in the code segment.

Instead of:

```
0100    JNZ    7F00    (impossible to reach!)
```

Use:

```
0100    JZ     0105

0102    JMP    7F00
```

Jumps inside the same segment, whatever the number of displacement bytes, are called "intrasegments" or "near" jumps.

# 14.2 Long Jumps

To move to another code segment, there is a 5-byte JMP format called an "intersegment" or "far format". This format includes an opcode byte and two words of data: one designating the address inside the segment for the command pointer and the other showing the desired code segment.

This format follows a structure which has already been discussed. Note that the least significant part of the address (the IP value) is placed in the lower address.

```
far JMP
```

| 1 1 1 0 1 0 1 0 | IP  LSB | IP  MSB | CS  LSB | CS  MSB |
|:---:|:---:|:---:|:---:|:---:|
| byte 1 | byte 2 | byte 3 | byte 4 | byte 5 |

The "intersegment" JMP doesn't use the relative addressing characteristic of the other two formats. You have to accurately enter the new values of CS and IP into the four reserved bytes. The length of the jump isn't calculated by addition like in the preceding formats. For example, type the following command to return control of the program back to address F000:F065:

```
>>s:0100  EA65F000F0    JMP   F000:F065
```

We'll later see that the far JMP and the near JMP can be indirectly obtained in a second method.

In summary, JMP modifies the instruction pointer and lets you continue executing at another place in the program. The CS register is also modified as well with a far JMP.

To simulate various jumps, load the JMP.DEM program. Type the following:

```
>>LOAD JMP.DEM
```

The more you play with JMP.DEM, the more likely that a far JMP will place you sooner or later in a "wild" BIOS routine at the top of the memory (F000:F065). Unless you're a super intelligent computer whiz, leave JMP.DEM when you get to that stage.

## 14.3   Chapter Exercises

1)   What is the instruction to decrement and test of the CX register? What does this instruction do?

2)   What is the mnemonic for jumping to memory box 150h if the result of an operation is not 0?

3)   What is the unconditional jump mnemonic to 130h?

4)   Write the following program:

       a) Enter the value 04h in AX

       b) Enter the value FFh in CX

       c) Decrement CX

       d) If CX is not 0, jump to step #3

       e) If CX = 0, increment AX

       f) Transfer AX to DX

       g) Verify whether DX = 00

       h) If DX is not 00h, jump to step #3

# 15. Addition and Subtraction

In the previous chapters we've discussed incrementing, decrementing, moving numbers and have executed forward and backward jumps. In this chapter we'll discuss mathematical operations such as ADD (addition), ADC (addition with carrying), SUB (subtraction) and SBB (subtraction with borrowing).

Each of these instructions has a format with two operands like the MOV instruction. For example, the ADD command either adds two different registers or a register and a memory location of 8 or 16 bits:

```
ADD  register/memory with register
```

```
| 0 0 0 0 0 0 D W | MOD   REG    R/M |
       byte 1             byte 2
```

The instruction "ADD AX,BX" adds the contents of register BX to the contents of register AX. The result remains in AX (which overwrites the previous contents of AX). In other words:

```
ADD AX,BX    new AX = old AX + BX
```

There is also another form of the ADD instruction that lets you add a specific number (F104h in this case) to the contents of a register:

```
ADD BX,F104
```

This, of course, places the result in BX.

The mechanics of the ADD instruction, which gives the sum of two 8-bit or one 16-bit numbers, is as simple as adding two decimal numbers. The only thing that might confuse you is the way 80x86 handles "carries". The word "carry" is the same as in decimal operations.

The 80x86 uses the carry flag so the program knows if a mathematical operation has resulted in a value greater than can be contained in the target register. In fact, we encounter a problem when we do ADD AX,BX with the values AX=C321h and BX=7DF0h.

```
   C321      (11000011 00100001)

+  7DF0      (01111101 11110000)

  14111   (1 01000001 00010001)
```

The value 14111h cannot be represented in register AX. Since the size or the capacity of a register cannot change, the carry flag is used when a 17th bit is necessary to complete the operation. Are 17 bits enough to contain the largest result obtained by adding two 16-bit numbers?

```
   11111111   11111111    (FFFFh)

+  11111111   11111111    (FFFFh)

 1 11111111   11111110   (1FFFEh)
```

The answer is "yes". The ADD instruction assigns the carry flag according to the following rule:

If the result of an addition operation is above FFFFh (or FFh in the case of operations on one byte), the carry flag is set at 1 (active). If the result is less than FFFFh or FFh, the carry flag remains set at 0 (inactive).

The ADD instruction also sets the Z, P and S flags (Zero, Parity and Sign flags) according to the usual rules you've seen before. Following an ADD operation, if the target register contains 0, the ZF flag is set. The SF flag is set when the result sets the least significant bit in the target register. If the result of an ADD produces an even number of set bits, then the PF flag is also set.

Next, load the ADD.DEM file and watch as the numbers are added:

```
>>LOAD ADD.DEM <Enter>
```

# 15.1  Double Precision Math

Although the 80x86 ALU is 16-bit, it's possible to perform mathematical operations beyond this limit using *double-precision mathematics*. Here three or more bytes are used to store these values. What is the maximum value of a binary number of three bytes?

- 2 to the 24th power $(2^{24})$ - 1 = 16,777,215

Of four bytes:

- 2 to the 32nd power $(2^{32})$ - 1 = 4,294,967,295

Of eight bytes:

- 2 to the 64th power $(2^{64})$ - 1 = 18,446,744,073,709,551,615

| ADC            instruction |

As you can see, binary exponential progressions rapidly reach impressive numbers. The ADC instruction (Add with Carry) is essential for adding numbers occupying more than 16 bits. ADC is completely like ADD except that it uses the carry flag in the addition.

For example, let BL = 44h and CH = 32h, then:

```
ADC BL,CH
```

places 76h in BL if the carry flag is clear, but it places 77h in BL if this flag is set. Just like ADD, ADC assigns the carry flag after an addition. After execution of "ADC BL,CH" the carry flag is clear.

The ADD2.DEM program illustrates the use of the carry flag during double-precision additions. The 32-bit value in DX-AX is added to BX-CX then it's placed in BX-CX.

Before starting the operation, you should load values in these registers.

```
    32C47111  DX-AX

+   2000C212  BX-CX

    ????????
```

This is the type of problem to set up to see if ADD2.DEM routine produces the correct solutions. The answer for this problem is 52C53323. Simulate the routine several times with higher numbers. What happens when adding has a result that's too large to load in 32 bits? Is it enough for the carry flag to intervene?

## SUB and SBB instructions

The SUB (Subtract) and SBB (Subtract with Borrow) instructions work similar to ADD and ADC. However, these instructions use the carry flag instead of using a borrow flag specifically for subtraction operations.

If the carry flag is set following a subtraction, you know that borrowing has been done. Of course, borrowing is done each time the result of the subtraction is negative (in other words when you subtract a number from another that is smaller than it):

```
  11

    00101101

 -   01001000

    11100101    (with borrowing)
```

SBB adds the carry flag to the result during the operation. If BL = 33h and CL = 30h, then the operation "SBB BL,CL" results in BL = 02h if the carry flag was previously set or BL = 03 if the carry flag was clear. But the operation "SUB BL,CL" results in BL = 03 regardless of the previous setting of the carry flag.

Let's execute a simulation with SUB.DEM. Pay close attention to the relationships between SUB and the borrow flag, especially in subtraction with 32-bits: CX-BX minus AX-DX.

## 15.2 Compare

In Chapter 8 we introduced the CMP instruction as a tool for structuring loops. The CMP instruction works similar to subtraction except that only the flags are modified, not the target register.

| CMP | instruction |
| --- | --- |

Let's suppose that we control the commands of a wordprocessor and that we need to identify the command keys used. We can quickly review all the possibilities using a series of multiple comparisons and conditional jumps.

```
CMP     AL,41          (is it the "A" key?)

JE      FNCTA          (jump if yes)

CMP     AL,44          (is it the "D" key?)

JE      FNCTD          (jump if yes)

CMP     AL,1B          (Escape?)

JE      FNCTESC

JMP     ERROR
```

If we had used SUB instruction instead of CMP, the value of AL would have been changed immediately in the first test.

After a comparison, you can simply insert the conditional jumps.

```
CMP     AL,50

JA      SKP      (jump if AL greater than 50)

JE      SKP1     (jump if AL equal to 50)

JNE     SKP2     (jump if AL not equal to 50)

JBE     SKP3     (jump if AL equal or less than 50)
```

Now load and simulate CMP.DEM.

## 15.3 Chapter Exercises

1) What is the instruction to add AX and BX?

2) What is the double-precision addition mnemonic? How does it handle results greater than 16-bits?

3) What is the instruction for testing whether BL equals 23h?

4) Create the following program to:

   a) Place 77h in AH

   b) Place 76h in BX

   c) Add both and put the result in AX

5) Create the following program:

   a) Place 55h in AL

   b) Place 55h in BL

   c) Add both and put the result in CX

   What is the state of carry?

6) Create the following program:

   a) Place 77h in AX

   b) Decrement AX

   c) Test whether AX equals 50h

   d) If not, jump to step #2

   e) If yes, place 96h in CX

   f) Add AX and BX and store the result in register pair BX-CX.

# 16. Memory Operands

In this chapter we'll return to the EA byte (Effective Address) which is used in so many instructions. Up to now the examples have been cases where MOD has been equal to 11. Therefore, R/M had to correspond to a register.

If for an instruction the value of MOD is 00,01 or 10, then R/M is used to specify other memory locations.

There is a maximum of 32 combinations of MOD and R/M (5 bits are equal to/greater than $2^5$ or 32). If you deduct the eight possible combinations in which MOD = 11, there are 24 remaining combinations (or 24 possible operands).

Now we'll discuss a particular state among these 24 operands. This is MOD=00 with R/M=110. When the EA byte contains these values, the processor knows that the byte considered (the byte we want to move, add, subtract or exchange) is at the address indicated by the following two bytes.

The following is a two byte instruction:

```
ssss:0100 8BDD    MOV BX,BP
```

```
|1 0 0 0 1 0 1 1|1 1|0 1 1|1 0 1|
         DW      MOD  REG  R/M

                      BX

                      BP
```

Since MOD=11, the processor automatically decodes the R/M register as the 16-bit BP register.

Now let's take the MOV instruction where the field MOD=00:

```
ssss:0100 8B1E00F0     MOV BX,[00F0]
```

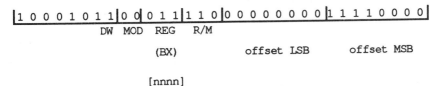

```
|1 0 0 0 1 0 1 1|0 0|0 1 1|1 1 0|0 0 0 0 0 0 0 0|1 1 1 1 0 0 0 0|
         DW      MOD  REG  R/M    offset LSB      offset MSB
                     (BX)

                   [nnnn]
```

This instruction takes four bytes. When MOD=00 and R/M=110, the processor knows that the following word indicates the address of the word to be moved is located. So the instruction "MOV BX,[00F0]" moves the word located at address 00F0 into the BX register. The brackets around 00F0h are used to distinguish this MOV mnemonic from the immediate MOV mnemonic.

We've just seen that the MOV instruction that lets us transfer the contents of a memory location into a register. However, you can structure all of the instructions having an EA byte in the same way:

| | |
|---|---|
| MOV [00F0], BX | Transfer the contents of BX to 00F0h |
| ADD [00F0], BX | Add BX and the value located at address 00F0h and places the result in memory location 00F0h |
| CMP CX, [0080] | Compares the contents of register CX and the word located in offset 80h |
| XCHG AL,[0080] | Exchanges the values contained in register AL and memory address 80h |

With this technique, it's no longer necessary for you to load values in the registers to perform the above operations.

Load the MEMOPS.DEM file and start it in STEP=3 mode. You'll notice that the processor executes two new operations. These operations are designated by the expressions "Form Offset in X" and "Read Byte/Word at effective Address".

"Form Offset in X" indicates that the processor determines the address of the operand according to the bits specified in MOD and R/M. When MOD=00 and R/M=110, the processor knows that the address is specified by the word following the opcode of the instruction.

"Read Byte/Word at effective Address" indicates that the processor reads the byte or the word at the effective address specified by the word following the opcode. Once the byte/word has been read, the processor can begin its processing.

# 16.1   What Is The Segment?

Addresses which are specified by the operand are usually in the data segment (DS) register. So the instruction "MOV BX,[F000]" transfers the word located at address DS:F000 into the BX register.

However, sometimes you might wish to access data at an address which isn't in the current data segment. If this is the case, you must explicitly specify the desired segment. To do this use a segment override prefix which is entered just before the operand like this:

```
MOV CX,ES:[F000]
```

When this instruction is executed, the processor accesses the word at address ES:F000 (address F000 of the Extra Segment). Of course, you can use any of the segment registers.

At the instruction level, the segment override prefix is specified like this:

```
Segment Override Prefix

0 0 1   argument  1 1 0
```

Here is the decoding table for segment registers:

| | |
|---|---|
| 00 | ES |
| 01 | CS |
| 10 | SS |
| 11 | DS |

There are three instruction prefixes for the 80x86 including the *segment override prefix*. A *prefix* modifies execution of an instruction.

A prefix isn't an instruction by itself. In fact, operations normally executed after each instruction (such as verifications of interrupts, etc.) don't occur as a result of a prefix execution.

Prefixes modify certain internal flags of the processor (the simulator displays these as normal flags). Prefix flags are short lived and last for only one instruction and are erased after each execution. That's why they aren't specified in the FL register as bits.

**143**

A prefix is ignored when it appears in front of an instruction for which it has no meaning (for example, a segment override before an INC AX or MOV AX,BX instruction).

Now, we'll simulate our routine SOPREFIX.DEM carefully. In SIM, simply decoding the prefix isn't equivalent to executing an instruction. The screen isn't restored if a real instruction hasn't been executed. Processing prefixes is indicated in the SIM Disassembly Area.

```
>>LOAD SOPREFIX.DEM <Enter>
```

Then use:

```
MOV    CX,ES:[F000]
```

instead of:

```
ES:

MOV    CX,[F000]
```

Instructions which you enter with an illegal prefix are not indicated in the Disassembly Area. The U command (DISASSEMBLE) will nonetheless display the opcode of the illegal prefix in the "bytes" part of the Disassembly Area.

# 16.2   Effective Addresses

The general instruction "MOV register to/from register/memory" that we have used is an instruction with two operands. The effective address (EA) operand is defined by the five bytes of the MOD and R/M fields and the operand register is controlled by the REG field.

Some 80x86 instructions only need to specify one operand. Examples of these include INC and DEC. It isn't necessary to specify the "target" and the "origin" in an increment instruction. Only the operand is required.

Consider the first instruction we discussed in this book. The "INC reg" instruction is one method for modifying a 16-bit register. However, it remains quite limited because it doesn't let you increment a memory location.

Fortunately, the 80x86 features another format of the INC instruction that will handle this case:

```
INC register/memory
```

| 1 1 1 1 1 1 1 W | MOD 0 0 0   R/M |

You usually use the MOD and R/M fields of the EA byte of this instruction to specify the memory location or the register to increment. There are three free bits in an increment instruction since the EA byte doesn't contain a REG field.

Every instruction containing an EA byte and using operands has the REG field as a secondary opcode. This secondary opcode is used to distinguish INC R/M from other mnemonics with the same primary opcode (or first byte). For example, DEC R/M gives:

| 1 1 1 1 1 1 1 W | MOD 0 0 1   R/M |

When 80x86 encounters an opcode of the type 1111111w (whether it's 11111110 or 11111111), it cannot determine by this information alone what type of operation to execute. It does, however, know that the instruction is a part of a group of eight instructions used to process an operand (byte or word).

There are eight operations possible in the case of 1111111w:

| Secondary opcode | Instruction |
|---|---|
| 000 | INC |
| 001 | DEC |
| 010 | CALL near (indirect) |
| 011 | CALL far (indirect) |
| 100 | JMP near (indirect) |
| 101 | JMP far (indirect) |
| 110 | PUSH r/m |
| 111 | ??? (undefined) |

Secondary opcodes are necessary for defining the called instruction. It's obvious that eight bits limit the number of possibilities. And to complicate the situation, some instructions ("INC reg" to name only one) place their operands in the opcode byte.

The 80x86 designers saw that the instructions to an operand, like INC r/m and DEC r/m, didn't require a REG field for their EA byte, therefore they freed these bits so they would be available for describing eight different instructions having the same primary opcode.

When you use your assembler, you must make your intention clear and precise. For example, can you find a problem in the following disassembly of an INC operation?

```
CS:01000: INC   [F000]
```

This example is too ambiguous. Are we incrementing the word or the byte located at DS:F000?

Fortunately, SIM provides information about operands having a special size and specifying "BPTR" (byte pointer) and "WPTR" (word pointer) operators.

```
CS:0100: INC   BPTR [F000]
```

Load INC2.DEM and start the routine. Notice how BPTR and WPTR in the disassembly window are used to indicate the size of the operand. Also, observe how the simulator has to decode the REG field and the EZ byte before knowing the name of the instruction being executed (one of the eight instructions of the second group). In this specific case, REG is in fact only a secondary opcode that has nothing in common with the registers.

## 16.2.1    A quick chapter review

We've learned how the 80x86 determines which register or memory location on which to execute an operation. In the case of instructions with two operands (MOV, for example), one of the operands is always a register indicated in the REG field and EA byte. The second operand is either a register or a memory location, according to the MOD and R/M fields.

In the case of instructions with one operand (such as INC R/M) the combination MOD-R/M specifies the operand on which it has to work, and the REG field serves as secondary opcode which allows more operations than would normally be thinkable.

# 16.3 Chapter Exercises

1) What is the mnemonic that lets you transfer the byte at address 5C8h of the code segment into the BL register?

2) What is the segment prefix used for?

3) What is the mnemonic that lets you decrement memory location 36h of the present segment?

4) Create the following program to:

> a) Enter the value located in address F8h of the data segment in the AX register
>
> b) Decrement data segment memory box F8h
>
> c) Is this memory box equal to zero?
>
> d) If not, jump to step #2
>
> e) If yes, enter the value of AX at address F8h of the data segment
>
> f) Jump immediately at the program beginning

# 17. Multiplication and Division

The 80x86 was one of the first processors to include multiplication and division instructions. Before the 80x86, programmers had to program these functions themselves which resulted in longer and slower programs.

## MUL and DIV    Instruction

The 80x86 quickly resolves the problem by using the MUL and DIV instructions. These instructions take the standard form "EA with an operand":

```
MUL   register/memory
```

| 1 1 1 1 0 1 1 W | MOD 1 0 0 | R/M |

REG

```
DIV   register/memory
```

| 1 1 1 1 0 1 1 W | MOD 1 1 0 | R/M |

REG

As with all instructions using the EA byte, the REG field serves as a secondary operation code. In mnemonic notation we can write code using the multiply instruction as such:

```
MUL   BL
```

```
MUL   WPTR [F000]
```

Have you noticed that to multiply you must have two numbers. Where is the second one?

The second value is still in the *accumulator*. An accumulator is simply a type of temporary memory in which the processor stores intermediate values. Remember that AL is for multiple values of bytes and AX for multiples of words.

So MUL BL multiplies AL by BL and stores the product in AX. Are 16 bits enough to accept the largest product of a multiplication of 8 bits?

```
        FF

*       FF

    FE01
```

## Operands of 16 Bits

"MUL BX" multiplies BX by AX and places the 32-bit product in DX-AX. Are 32 bits enough to contain the product of a multiplication of 16 bits, and so forth?

The answer is yes because "MUL WPTR[F000]" multiplies the word located at address DS:F000 by AX and places the 32-bit product into DX-AX.

"MUL AL" produces the square of a value on a byte in AL. "MUL AX" does the same for 16-bit numbers. By seeing to it that one of the operands is constantly kept in the accumulator, the REG field remains available as a secondary operation code.

Load the multiplication demonstration file called MUL.DEM and you'll see the result.

```
>>LOAD MUL.DEM <Enter>
```

# 17.1   Division

Division with 80x86 is the opposite of the multiplication process. An operation on words divides a 16-bit operand in DX-AX by a quotient in AX and the result is stored in AX with the remainder in DX. If you're dealing with a single byte, for example "DIV BX" divide an 8-bit operand located in AX by the quotient in BX and the result is stored in AL with the remainder in AH.

However, division encounters a special problem. We can't be sure that division of a 32-bit value by a 16-bit value produces a result of 16 bits. For example:

```
FFFFFFFF / 3 = 55555555
```

A value of 55555555h cannot be stored in AX. In the same way, you have the same problem when a division of bytes produces a value greater than FFh. The best way to get this result is to divide any number by zero.

It's the famous "divide overflow" that the 80x86 treats in a very different way than the carry flag often used by ADD and SUB. In this case it generates an interruption. We'll discuss interrupts later. But for now, remember that if you execute a division whose result is too large for the target register there is no warning flag.

The result is that the 80x86 exits the current program and becomes locked up in the "divide overflow" procedure. Unfortunately, if this occurs, your only option may be to perform a warm start (press <Ctrl><Alt><Del> key combination).

Start the DIV.DEM program:

```
>>LOAD DIV.DEM <Enter>
```

Attempt an intentional "divide overflow" error. It shouldn't take you very long to see what happens. After the end of the DIV command, you'll find yourself in a new DOS routine. To return, keep ssss (a value that will always be present in the other segment registers) and enter 1000h in the IP.

### A special note for older IBM-PCs

If you're using an older IBM PC (1982 or before), your computer may have a version of the 8088 that has a difficult time returning from a "divide overflow" interrupt. This causes SIM to lock up on an operand resulting in the "divide overflow" at the same time that the division macro is executed.

To determine whether your computer has an older 8088, simulate the following division instruction:

```
MOV   BL,0

DIV   BL
```

If the system locks up or crashes, your 8088 is an older version.

# 17.2   Chapter Exercises

1)      What is the mnemonic to multiply AX by itself?

2)      How can you divide AX by BX and have the result in BX?

3)      Create the following program to:

        a) Enter the value 04h in BX

        b) Transfer BX into AX

        c) Decrement BX

        d) Multiply BX by AX with the result in AX

        e) Test whether BX=01h

        f) If not, jump to step #3

        What does this program do?

4)      Create a program that calculates the nth power of a number on one byte. Initially load this number in AL. BL contains the value n and the result is entered at the end of the program in AX. Of course, you can use other registers to do your operations.

5)      Write a program to calculate the square upon the hypotenuse of a triangle when you know the length of the two sides opposite the hypotenuse. The length of each side is initially placed in AX and BX. The length of each of the sides can't be greater than a byte (less than 255). Let "a" be the length of the first side, "b" the length of the second side opposite the hypotenuse, and "h" the hypotenuse. The formula is:  h^2=a^2+b^2.

# 18. SHIFT Instruction

The difference between the 80x86 SHIFT instructions and the ADD and SUB instructions is that they process 8-bit and 16-bit values as series of bits rather than as numbers.

Many different operations are possible when numbers in a register are considered in binary form as a chain of 1s and 0s.

## 18.1   SHIFT and ROTATE

**SHL            Instruction**

The 80x86 can move bits from a register or a memory location one position to the left or to the right. For example, let's take the SHL (Shift Left) instruction. SHL shifts each bit one position to the left. Bit 0 is then filled with a value of 0. Bit 15 is shifted into the overflow flag (OF).

The assembler instruction format is "SHL R/M,n". The "n" represents the number of bits to be shifted. For example, let's use "SHL AX,1":

Before SHL, reg,1

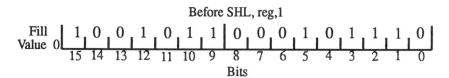

After SHL, reg,1

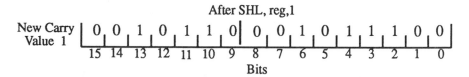

Although this is a useful operation, you may be wondering what comes next. First of all, the effect of shifting one position to the left in a binary number is equivalent to a multiplication by two. Try it yourself:

```
20h (0010 0000) * 2 = 40h (0100 0000)

37h (0011 0111) * 2 = 6Eh (0110 1110)

64h (0110 0100) * 2 = C8h (1100 1000)
```

You aren't limited to multiplications by two. To multiply by four, shift twice in succession to the left. To multiply by eight, you have to shift three times in succession to the left and so forth.

We recommend using the SHL instruction to MUL for multiplications by powers of 2 because they can be up to ten times faster. The reason is simple, since the MUL instruction internally results in a long series of ADDs and SHIFTs.

Additionally, by experimenting we can make SHL execute multiplications other than by powers of 2. Let's multiply AX by 10 (if AX is less than 256):

```
SHL    AX,1        (AX = 2x)

MOV    BX,AX       (temporarily keep 2x in BX)

SHL    AX,1        (AX = 4x)

SHL    AX,1        (AX = 8x)

ADD    AX,BX       (AX = 8x + 2x, or 10x)
```

This five-step program is much faster than:

```
MOV    BL,0A       (move 10 decimals)

MUL    BL
```

## SHR                (Shift Right)

Of course, you can also shift to the right.

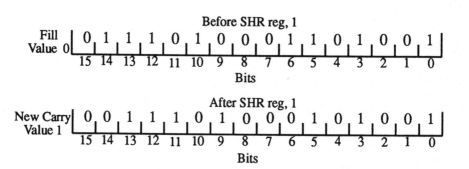

For example, let's use "SHR AX,3" when AX contains 7469h:

```
0 1 1 1 0 1 0 0 0 1 1 0 1 0 0 1

  SHR three positions -->

0 0 0 0 1 1 1 0 1 0 0 0 1 1 0 1   0 0 1

(same as 7469h / 8 = 0E8Dh carrying 1)
```

## 18.2   Rotations

The ROTATE instructions are a variation of the SHIFT instructions. For example, ROL (ROTATE left) operates just like SHL except that instead of a 0 being entered into bit 0 a 1 would be entered. Similarly, ROR (ROTATE right) shifts the previous value of bit 0 into bit 15.

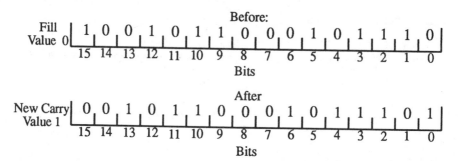

Note that bit 15 is rotated to bit 0.

These rotations are just what we need to reverse the order of bits in a register. In this example, four "ROR AH,1" instructions are enough to exchange the nibbles in AH.

### 18.2.1   Rotation in the carry flag

You can use two types of rotations: Rotation with and rotation without the last bit into the carry flag.

There are two rotations which do not use the carry flag:

*   ROL      (ROTATE Left)

*   ROR      (ROTATE Right)

And there are two rotations which do use the carry flag to  communicate during the rotation:

*   RCL      (ROTATE Left through Carry)

*   RCR      (ROTATE Right through Carry)

For example, with RCL AX,1:

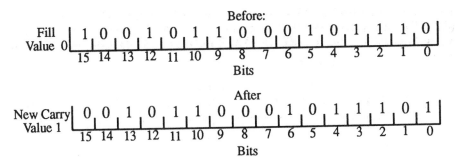

RCL and RCR instructions are useful for executing multiplication and division operations on values that make up more than 16 bits.

For example, to multiply DX-AX by 2:

```
SHL   AX,1    (bit 15 from AX is placed in carry)

RCL   BX      (carry bit rotated to bit 0 of BX)
```

## 18.3   Coding Shifts

SHIFT instructions take the one operand EA format with an opcode byte and an EA byte to indicate the register or the memory location to shift. SHIFTs and ROTATEs share the same primary operation code. This causes the processor to verify the secondary opcode to determine the type of requested shift.

```
SHL   register/memory
```

| 1 1 0 1 0 0 V W | MOD 1 0 0 | R/M |

Variable (V) is an opcode specific to SHIFT instructions. When V is empty, the processor executes a shift of one position on the chosen operand. In the opposite case, 80x86 uses the value in CL (we prefer this counter) to know the length of the shift to execute. For example:

| 1 1 0 1 0 0 0 1 | 1 1 | 1 0 0 | 0 1 0 |

shifts DX once to the left (one position), and:

| 1 1 0 1 0 0 1 1 | 1 1 | 1 0 0 | 0 1 0 |

shifts DX CL times to the left (you can't modify CL).

You may have concluded from this that a form of SHIFT and ROTATE is controllable by the CL register. Unfortunately, this isn't true. Additionally, three consecutive "ROL AX,1" instructions are executed faster than the following:

```
MOV   CL,3

ROL   AX,CL
```

In reality, this "variable" form is anticipated for cases where you cannot predetermine the number of positions to move, that is the number of bits can only be calculated during the program.

Our demonstration file SHIFTS.DEM will let you simulate a whole series of shifts and rotations with or without variables.

```
>>LOAD SHIFTS.DEM
```

# 18.4   Chapter Exercises

1)      Write a program to:

        a) Enter the value 33h in AX

        b) Multiply this value by 2

        (Use only two mnemonics.)

2)      Write a program to:

        a) Enter 44h in BX

        b) Rotate the BX bits to the left with carry

3)      Write a program to:

        a) Enter 44h in BX

        b) ROTATE the BX bits to the right

4)      Write a program to:

        a) Enter 67h in DX

        b) Shift the DX bits three times to the left

        (Use only three instructions for this program.)

# 19. Boolean Instructions

The 80x86 is excellent for Boolean calculations. The AND, OR and XOR (Not OR) instructions are used with two operands to perform logical functions between each bit of the source operand and the corresponding bit of the target operand.

Just like SHIFTs, the value of the individual bits are more important than the value of the entire byte. For example:

```
AND  AL,AH
```

In reality, during this processing, eight logical AND operations are executed simultaneously, one on each bit in the AL and AH registers. The result is then entered in AL. The following are two examples:

```
AL 00110011 (33h)    AL 11000000 (C0h)

AH 01000110 (46h)    AH 01001111 (4Fh)

AL 00000010 (02h)    AL 01000000 (40h)
```

The essential function of the AND instruction is to clear certain bits of a register or a memory location to zero. The following clears bits 6 and 7 of the CL register without changing the state of bits 0 through 5:

```
AND    CL,3F
```

**Note:**     Remember that the least significant bits are numbers 0-7 and not 1-8.

This process is called *masking*. In the example above, we masked bits 6 and 7. The following changes all the AX bits to zero except bit 2 (which will keep its current state of 1 or 0):

```
AND    AX,0004
```

Using the AND instruction to mask bits lets you find the remainder of a division by a power of two (2, 4, 8, etc.). When we discussed SHR (Shift), we mentioned that the zero bit contained in the carry flag after the shift represented the remainder of the division. In fact, if we're only interested in the remainder and no longer in the quotient ("modulo" operations), you only need to mask all the bits except those that would be shifted.

Let's give you an example: To calculate the remainder you get from dividing 7469h by 8, we would mask the 5 most significant bits:

```
        0 1 1 1 0 1 0 0 0 1 1 0 1 0 0 1

AND     0 0 0 0 0 0 0 0 0 0 0 0 0 1 1 1

        0 0 0 0 0 0 0 0 0 0 0 0 0 0 0 1

           carry = 1
```

So to calculate 75h modulo 8 (the remainder of dividing 75h by 8), do this:

```
MOV  AL, 75

AND  AL, 07
```

While AND clears bits, the OR instruction lets you selectively set bits without affecting the other bits. For example, to set bits 4 to 7 in the BH register, do the following:

```
OR  BH, F0
```

As for the XOR instruction, it lets you find the complement of the selected bits. For example, to reverse the state of bit 7 in the BH register without modifying the value of the others:

```
XOR  BH, 80
```

Sometimes XOR is used to quickly set a register to zero. In fact, an XOR operation on two identical numbers always produces zero. So it's interesting to note that a 2-byte sequence like this:

```
XOR   BX, BX
```

is more efficient than the three bytes required by:

```
MOV   BX, 0000
```

By this time you should have noticed that XOR BX,BX produces the same result as SUB BX,BX.

# 19.1   The TEST Instruction

TEST instruction is a combination of AND and CMP. Similar to AND, TEST executes an AND logical operation. And like CMP, only the state flags are modified. Therefore, what TEST does is a logical AND to set the flags but does not store the result. This is very useful for testing the same byte several times.

```
TEST   [F000],08      (Is bit 3 of DS:F000 activated?)

JZ     SKIP           (if not, ignore)

TEST   [F000],04      (Is bit 2?)

JZ     SKIP           (ditto)
```

It's surprising that logical operations are so rarely used to test logic conditions. Let's take the example of the following test taken from a typical accounting program:

```
IF deductions<net AND (day=15 OR day=30) THEN make out check
```

This test is more likely to be executed by a series of conditional jumps than by using ANDs and ORs as in the above example. One of the advantages of using advanced languages in a case like this is their distinction between the course of the program and evaluation of Boolean expressions. This distinction isn't possible in machine language.

Start the BOOLEAN.DEM simulation.

```
>>LOAD BOOLEAN.DEM <Enter>
```

The first two instructions calculate 343Bh modulo 16. All bits, except the least significant ones, are masked immediately. Now we have 0000B, or the remainder of dividing 343B by 16.

Next, the demo presents OR and XOR instructions. These guarantee that bits are put at zero or calculate the complement of certain bits in the AX register.

## 19.2 Chapter Exercises

1) Write a program to:

      a) Enter 37h in AL

      b) Change bits 3 and 5 of AL to 0

2) Write a program to:

      a) Enter 22h in BL

      b) Change bits 2 and 4 of BL to 1

3) Write a program to:

      a) Enter F80Ah in AX

      b) Change the state of bits 9, 10, and 1

4) Write a program to clear the CX register in the most efficient way.

5) Write a program to:

      a) Enter 89h in BX

      b) Test whether bit 2 of BX is at zero

      c) If so, shift all the BX bits to the left with carry

      d) If not, shift all the BX bits to the right

6) Write a program to:

      a) Enter F7h in BX

      b) Increment BX

      c) Test whether bit 3 of BX is zero

      d) If not, jump to step #2

      e) If so, multiply BX by 2 and place the result in AX

# 20. Signed Numbers

We've discussed how 16-bit numbers can represent whole numbers between 0 and 65,535. This scale of values was perfectly sufficient for illustrating the computational capabilities of the 80x86. We learned that F32Dh in AX was the equivalent of 62,253. But there's another way we can look at this because F32Dh can just as easily represent -3,283.

Ask any assembly language programmer to tell you the decimal value of F32Dh. They'll probably ask you in return "Is the number signed?" In fact, the same sequence of bits such as F32Dh, for example, can have two different decimal translations.

Up to now, we've worked only with positive or unsigned numbers because most assembly language programs follow the agreement made for unsigned integers. But let's suppose that we wanted to write a program for managing a bank account. There may be occasional negative balances. How do we represent this negative value?

What will happen when we subtract 6 from 3? Of course, the instruction SUB AX,BX when AX = 0003 and BX = 0006 will put FFFDh in AX. The carry flag will be set but that won't do for reading -3 from FFFDh. There must be a better way.

Consider the most significant bit, called the *sign bit*. What if we use the 15 least significant bits to represent the absolute value of the word and the most significant bit as a sign flag?

```
00001111 11001001 = + 0FC9h   00101011 10000110 = + 2B86h

10001111 11001001 = - 0FC9h   10101011 10000110 = - 2B86h
```

Or again, for a single byte:

```
0011 1111 = + 3Fh     0100 1010 = + 4Ah

1011 1111 = - 3Fh     1100 1010 = - 4Ah
```

This isn't so scary after all. It's very similar to the way we do calculations on paper. When the sign bit is set, it means minus. This makes it simple and efficient.

Using the most significant bit as a +/- sign flag obviously limits the area of the values of 16-bit numbers (from -32,767 to +32,767). This should remind you of when you were programming in BASIC.

This is the size limit of integer variables in BASIC. So we can relate all this to what we've already seen about the SF flag. It's set each time that the processor works on a value where the most significant bit is set.

Although this sounds practical and logical, there's still a catch: It may not work. Are you sure that the answer to $6 + (-3) = 3$?

```
    0000 0110      ( 6)

+      1000 0011       (-3)

    1000 1001      (-9)
```

Unfortunately, no matter how you determine the answer, -9 will never be 3. This is the same reason that $26 + (-14)$ doesn't equal 12:

```
    0001 1010      ( 26)

+      1000 1110       (-14)

    1010 1000      (-40)
```

And what about 00000000 which would correspond to a positive zero and 10000000 which would be a negative zero?

Although the idea was logical, it's not completely accurate, unless we want to revolutionize mathematics. Let's look for another idea instead and find the right way to process negative numbers. In fact, we only have to look for the double complements of numbers.

Here, just like in our first but inaccurate method, the most significant bit indicates the sign but the other bits are processed in a different way. To look for the double complement of a number, reverse each of the bits (single complement) and then add 1 to the number found. In this way, -19h is represented by the double complement of 19h.

```
 19h = 0001 1001

- 19h = 1110 0110 + 1 = 1110 0111 (E7h)
```

This way E7h is at the same time the value 231 using 8 unsigned bits and the value -25 using 8 signed bits.

In the same way:

```
64h = 0110 1000

- 64h = 1001 0111 + 1 = 1001 0000
```

Although this doesn't say as much from a logical point of view as our first attempts, this method has the advantage of finding precise results. It also has only one zero. So when the most significant bit is set, there's no more doubt that the number is negative. Unfortunately, you may not immediately determine its value.

Now let's practice and add 6 to -3. Start by writing -3 while looking for the double complement of 3:

```
- 3     => double complement of 3 => single complement + 1

0000 0011 =>     1111 1100 + 1       =>        1111 1101
```

We know that 1111 1101 is a negative value since bit 8 is set. Let's do the addition:

```
  0000 0110      ( 6)

+ 1111 1101      (-3)

1 0000 0011      ( 3)
```

For the moment we're not concerned with the carry flag. The answer we've obtained is in reality correct. Here's another example:

```
6 + (-8)
```

You have to first express -8 as a double complement of 8:

```
0000 1000 => 1111 0111 + 1 => 1111 1000
```

Now let's add:

```
  0000 0110      ( 6)

+ 1111 1000      (-8)

  1111 1110      (??)
```

Since bit 8 is set, we know that the sum in the result is negative. Now we just have to look for the complement of this result to make it positive and read it:

```
1111 1110 => 0000 0001 + 1 => 0000 0010 => 2
```

In fact, 6 + (-8) is indeed equal to -2.

Determining the 2's complement is the usual way to process negative numbers in binary. However, we're still not completely error-free, especially when manipulating large numbers. For example:

```
  0111 1110      (7Eh)

+ 0110 0110      (66h)

  1110 0100      (E4h)   (-28 in decimal)
```

This example seems to show that when we add two larger positive numbers, we get a negative result. Adding two larger negative numbers would give results that are just as meaningless. Actually, the problem is that the result is either too large or too small for signed representation. In fact, in the 8-bit universe, signed values greater than 127 or less than -128 are nonexistent. When values go beyond these limits, the method comes to a standstill. That's what we call overflow.

The ideal tool for exploring the properties of whole numbers, fractions, the notion of negative and positive infinity and many other mathematic examples is the graduated line. This line went from negative infinity to positive infinity and passing through zero. The following diagrams are small examples of the graduated line.

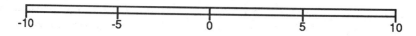

You added positive numbers by marking off the first operand on the line and then moving to the right the number of spaces represented by the value of the second operand. This led you to the result.

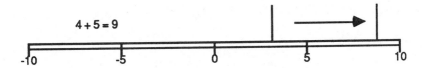

$$4 + 5 = 9$$

To add negative numbers, you just had to move to the left.

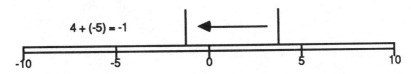

$$4 + (-5) = -1$$

Unfortunately, computers cannot use this graduated line like we do because they cannot express numbers that are infinitely positive or negative. In fact, the area of values on which the computer can work depends on the number of storage bits. You can allocate a 100 storage bytes so you can accomplish a better simulation of infinity but then execution speed would be reduced to that of a turtle.

A good compromise is to store using 16 bits. A 16-bit number is a point on our calculation line between 0 and 65,536. However, when a program needs to manipulate signed numbers, the calculation line is always divided into 65,536 points ranging from -2,768 to +32,767.

A circle is still the best way to illustrate the way a computer manipulates signed numbers. Imagine a graduated line whose positive and negative lines are joined to form the circle. The number of radii or spokes depends on the total bits allocated to the representation of a value. For example, to represent 4-bit numbers, a circle consists of 16 spokes numbered clockwise from 0000 to 1111.

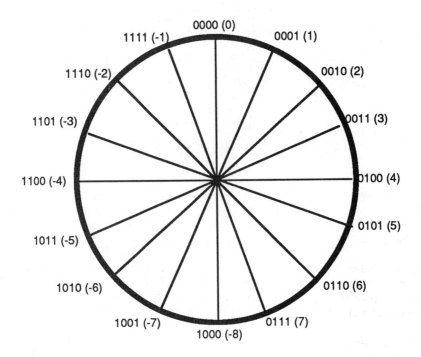

We can add and subtract in the circle by either counting clockwise (addition) or counterclockwise (subtraction).

Therefore, you can add 4 to 3 by advancing three spokes clockwise beginning at spoke #4. The same happens for subtracting 6 from 3. You go counterclockwise 6 spokes beginning at spoke #3, which places you on spoke #-3. And what happens when you want to add 3 to 6?

By advancing three spokes clockwise, you come to spoke #-7 and this places us beyond the boundary of infinity.

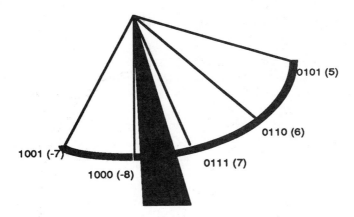

The same result occurs when you move counterclockwise (adding two negative numbers) beyond the boundary. The explanation is simple. Our model of infinity on four bits doesn't move. This is what the 80x86 calls *overflow*.

If our circle represented numbers on eight bits, this overflow would be moved back because the area of possible numbers would increase from -128 to 127. But beyond these limits, your trick is no longer valid. We can never totally avoid an overflow no matter how many bits we assign for storing our numbers or how many radii are present in our circle.

Let's study the ADD AX,BX instruction with AX = 97CAh and BX = 8641h. If you use signed numbers in this case, it comes back to adding real numbers -26,678 and -31,167:

```
  - 26,678

+ - 31,167

  - 57,845
```

Obviously -57,845 doesn't fit into a signed number of 16 bits. Although the 80x86 cannot give you a correct result in this case, it still warns you that it cannot execute your instruction by setting the overflow flag. If you find the overflow flag set after an operation on signed numbers, you can assume the calculation and its result are false.

The processor is indifferent to the fact that the value F000h in AX could be worth either -4096 or +61,440. Whether you do an addition or a subtraction operation on this value, you'll get a correct answer. If you work on unsigned numbers, you'll just have to check the carry flag to know whether the result is reliable or not. And if the operation is on signed numbers, you have to check the overflow flag.

You cannot use MUL and DIV instructions here. To get reliable results on signed numbers you have to resort to their signed equivalents of IMUL (Integer Multiply) and IDIV (Integer Divide).

## 20.1   Sign Extensions

A common activity for the 80x86 is extending signs. If we continue with our comparison to circles, extending signs is the technique which consists of moving from a circle of primitive numbers to a more evolved circle.

Assuming we have a signed number on 4 bits that we want to change to 8-bit for a more refined manipulation. If our number was -3 (1101) we could give it a format on 8 bits by adding a nibble of set bits (1111). If we want to put it in 16-bit format, we have to add 12 set bits:

```
              1101    (- 3 in 4-bit format)

         1111 1101    (- 3 in 8-bit format)

1111 1111 1111 1101    (- 3 in 16-bit format)
```

But if our number was a positive signed value on 4 bits (for example, 6) we'll add nibbles of 0:

```
              0110    (6 in 4 signed bit format)

         0000 0110    (6 in 8 signed bit format)

0000 0000 0000 0110    (6 in 16 signed bit format)
```

The *sign extension* is so named because you shift the initial sign bit according to the new format. You do this through several instructions (for example, conditional jumps), but you can also use the sign extension instructions of CBW (Convert Byte to Word) and CWD (Convert Word To Double Word). These two instructions work exclusively on AX and DX registers.

For example, let's say that AL = O3h. After execution of the CBW instruction, AX will contain 0003h. When AL = 83h, AX will contain FF83h after execution of the CBW instruction.

The CWD instruction converts the value in AX into a value on 32 bits, of which the most significant word will be entered in DX. So if AX = 7311h, after CWD is executed, DX contains 0000h. When AX = A301h, DX is equal to FFFFh after CWD.

# 20.2 Conditional Jumps and Signed Numbers

Some conditional jumps are especially adapted to signed numbers. The mnemonic distinction between a test on signed numbers and a test on unsigned numbers is easy to remember. In the comparison of signed numbers, use the mnemonics whose names include the expressions "greater than" or "less than". For example, the following test executes a jump when AX is less than BX:

```
CMP   AX,BX

JLE   0110    (Jump if Less Than or Equal)
```

For unsigned numbers, the key mnemonics are those using above and below:

```
CMP   AX,BX

JBE   0110    (Jump if Below or Equal)
```

The CMP instruction is the same in both cases but the conditional jumps that follow are different. For example, with AX = F000h and BX = 2000h, the signed comparison is true (F000h represents -4096 in decimal, which is obviously less than the positive decimal value 8192). But the unsigned comparison is false (for JBE) because F000 in its unsigned format is equal to 61,440 in decimal which is not exactly less than 8,192 in decimal.

Start the SIGNEDN.DEM to become familiarized with unsigned numbers.

```
>>LOAD SIGNEDN.DEM <Enter>
```

Use the SIM calculator to produce the 2's complement of a number. This is performed either by subtracting a hexadecimal number from zero or by converting a negative decimal number into hexadecimal. Remember that there are no plus or minus signs in hexadecimal or binary base.

The most difficult part of assembly for many beginners is calculating on signed numbers. Fortunately, most assembly language programs do not require calculations on signed numbers. And when you do need them, all you need to do is to review this chapter.

## 20.3  Chapter Exercises

1)      Find the binary expression for:

        -12, -15, -22, -27, -38, -553

        Calculate this by hand without using the calculator.

2)      Write a program which multiplies -22h by -34h.

3)      Write a program to:

        a) Subtract 5 - 17 with the result in AX

        b) Convert the result into a word

# 21. Video Memory

The PC uses video memory (bit-mapped video), a modern technique that is both flexible and reasonably priced. Memory mapping fits into 4K of RAM that is used for a dual purpose. This video memory is a part of the memory block of the 80x86 which the central processing unit considers as a variant of RAM.

However, it's also an integral and vital part of the video circuits of the PC circuits that decide which dots on the screen are lit up and which are turned off. Furthermore, they constantly sweep the 4000 addresses of the circuit to ensure display on the screen. You just have to modify numbers stored in the video memory (or buffer) so that the video circuits instantly reflect these changes on the screen.

The PC uses two different methods for displaying data:

*   Text mode

*   Graphic mode (bit-mapped)

Most programs, including SIM, use the text mode. Entertainment software and many business and design applications use the graphic mode.

## 21.1 Video Adapter Cards

The *video adapter card* is the most common card used in a PC. Without this card you could not communicate with your computer because most PCs do not have chips or other built-in circuitry.

The video adapter card is plugged into one of the expansion slots on the data bus and passes on the digital information it receives from the data bus to the monitor through the monitor cable.

The card includes the video memory and the video controller. The video controller serves as a go-between for the processor, video memory, character generator and monitor. It communicates with the processor and the video memory through the data and address bus. Both the processor and the video controller access the video memory through a separate port.

Two types of cards include the:

- Text mode (also called character mode) constructs the display by using the built-in character set of the PC. As the name suggests, text mode can only display alphanumeric characters. It uses the MDA (Monochrome Display Adapter).

- Graphics mode is video graphics display which can include not only alphanumeric characters but free form graphics, designs and other images. This display requires a special graphics adapter. These adapters include high quality color card such as EGA (Extended Graphics Adapter) and VGA (Video Graphics Array). Another graphics card is the CGA (Color Graphics Adapter) which can also use both modes (character or graphic) equally well.

The *resolution* of a monitor is the maximum number of distinct pixels which it can display on the screen. The resolution is expressed as:

```
Number of horizontal pixels x Number of vertical pixels
```

The resolution improves as both numbers increase.

# 21.2 Text and Graphic Modes

There is similarity between displaying text on a monitor and displaying text on a printer. Both use specific codes to represent letters, numbers and punctuation marks. For a printer to print the letter A, you don't send the diagram of the letter A to it but rather the ASCII code for the letter A (41h). The printer recognizes this code as the letter A and prints it.

In the text mode, the presence of 41h in the video memory results in the letter A being displayed on the screen.

## 21.2.1 Attribute bytes

Each screen position has an attribute byte which indicates the color or display attribute of the character (underlined, blinking, inverse video, etc.). Therefore, two bytes are required for each position on the screen. This is a total of 4000 bytes of video RAM for a 25-line, 80-column monitor in text mode. *Video RAM* is the amount of RAM required by the video adapter to construct and maintain the full screen image of the video display.

The video RAM requirements are even larger for graphic mode where each dot is represented by 1 or more dots. A resolution of 640x200 pixels requires 16K.

The video buffer begins at address B000:0000 for monochrome screens and at B800:0000 for color screens. The two types of modes can therefore reside in the same PC without risk of addressing conflicts:

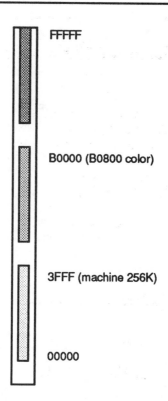

FFFFF

B0000 (B0800 color)

3FFF (machine 256K)

00000

The relation between the contents of the video buffer and the text on the screen is quite simple. As we mentioned earlier, each position on the screen requires two bytes in memory.

The first one identifies the character (for example, it contains the 41h which corresponds to the letter A). Since the entire byte is dedicated to character codes, the PC can display a maximum of 256 different characters. ASCII code only includes 95 characters, therefore IBM took the initiative to complete this set of characters by adding others.

These include figures or symbols that range from the little smiling face (code 01h or ☺) to musical notes (such as code 0Eh or ♫). They also include a series of single and double bars and angles that you use for drawing borders and boxes.

Examples of these include many of the tables and diagrams we include in this book such as the one below and on the previous page. With a little imagination, you can create quite impressive graphics using these additional ASCII codes.

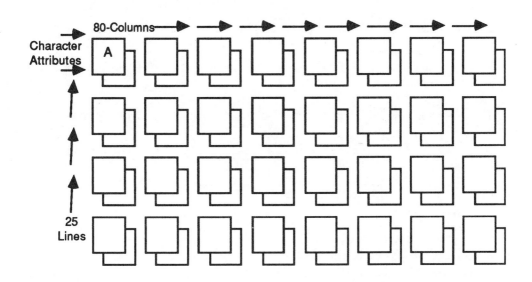

The second byte determines the attributes of the character. These attributes would determine whether it's displayed normally or highlighted, blinking, inverted video or in a combination of these characteristics. In the case of color graphic cards the attribute byte determines the color of the character.

## 21.2.2    Graphic mode

There are many applications which require the use of the graphic mode the color/graphic cards. For example, most CAD (computer aided design) applications require the higher resolution and picture quality.

Graphic mode stores the color of a screen pixel in one or more bits and then transfers the contents of video RAM directly to the screen. Therefore, a character generator is not used in the graphic mode. This has the advantage of not limiting us to the contents of the character set in ROM. You can draw anything on the screen, including alphanumeric characters as easily as graphs, charts, doughnuts, diagrams or other designs.

However, to do this requires as much as 16K of memory for the PC. It also requires time for the processor to change and rebuild the screen display.

## 21.3  SIM and Video Buffer Commands

Remember that you can read or write in video memory using SIM, so let's use SIM to work in the display modes.

The following table illustrates where video memory starts for a CGA and monochrome adapters:

| | |
|---|---|
| CGA card | B800:000 |
| Monochrome cards | B000:0000 |

The 0 offset of this memory corresponds to the upper left corner of the screen. When SIM is started, this position is occupied by the diagram of an upper left corner of a border. This symbol is coded by the value DAh. Let's see if this value is indeed at the correct address of the video memory. Type in:

```
>>D B000:0 L 1 <Enter>
```

**Note:**     If your computer has a CGA card installed, type B800 instead of B000 in this section and Section 21.4.

You'll find DAh is there. If we change this value, we'll modify what is displayed on the screen. Let's enter the ASCII value that we know so well of 41h:

```
>>E B000:0 41 <Enter>
```

The following byte corresponds to the attributes of the symbol for the upper left corner (07) by default. This produces a normal monochrome display. We can make the A blink by replacing the current attribute with 87h. This value activates bit 7:

```
>>E B000:1 87 <Enter>
```

# 21.4   Chapter Exercises

The second line on the screen starts at offset 160 (in decimal) because it must count 80 bytes for character codes and 80 bytes for the attributes. This corresponds to address B000:A0. The third line is at offset 320 (in decimal) or 140h.

To practice, write the initials of your name at the intersection of the 6th line (beginning at the top of the screen) and the 30th column. You should find offset (5 * 160) + (30 * 2) or 35Ch. For example, if your initials are J.O., you have to write:

```
>>F B000:35C L 4 4A 7 4F 7 <Enter>
```

The 7 that follows each byte dedicated to ASCII code means a normal display of the character.

Of course, you can be more original and display, for example, a series of little smiling faces:

```
>>F B000:0 L 1000 2 7 <Enter>
```

Use the DSCRN command to clear the screen:

```
>>DSCRN <Enter>
```

Next, move 4000 bytes of BIOS program into assembly language in the video memory:

```
>>M F000:E000 L 1000 B000:0 <Enter>
```

You see what happens when you confuse the meaning of bytes in the memory. BIOS bytes contain machine code that's incomprehensible for video memory which expects a series of various ASCII characters and their attributes.

**Exercise:**

1)      Make a program that enters HELLO on line 7, column 5 of the screen.

# 22. Address Modes

The quality of a processor isn't just in what it does (such as increment, subtraction and multiplication) but also by the way it does it. It's similar to a sporting event such as diving where there are points for effort and points for style.

For the processor, the points for effort correspond to the number of registers and the number of instructions that it has as well as its ability to execute mathematical operations. It gets points for style by the way it reads and writes to and from memory. Addressing techniques are commonly called *address modes*.

Address modes cannot determine the instruction to execute but the place where the processor has to read the number used by the instruction. In mnemonic syntax, when an operand isn't in a register, the address modes manage the location where the operand is located.

Intel considered address modes to be so important that it devoted most of the bytes to them. By adding an effective address byte to most of 80x86's instructions, Intel made them universal. This way you can execute increments, subtractions and multiplications in many different ways.

Until now, we haven't really used this powerful effective address byte but just limited ourselves to instructions where MOD = 11 (which limits the meaning of R/M to register). Now it's time to meet the other 23 combinations. This isn't as complex as you might think since it's not really about 23 different subjects.

The 80x86 uses a system of clever indexing by which R/M indicates which index register effectively points to the desired location and MOD gives information about the number of offset bytes (none, one or two [00, 01 or 10]). The only code that you don't use in this procedure is the offset follows of MOD=00 and R/M=110.

## MOD=00

When MOD=00, the three R/M bits specify the memory address (unless R/M = 110). How can three little bits represent a single memory location from among a million when we know for a fact that you need 16 bits to choose an address in a given segment?

The secret lies in the fact that R/M doesn't give the processor the operand location but is satisfied with telling it what it has to do to find it. R/M takes charge of selecting which register points to the desired location.

For example, when MOD=00 and R/M=100, the processor recognizes that the address of the memory location is in the SI register. The MOV3.DEM program contains a MOV REG,R/M instruction. Load this program by typing:

```
>>LOAD MOV3.DEM <Enter>
```

The program disassembles itself in the following way:

```
ssss:0100 8B04   MOV  AX,[SI]
```

```
|1 0 0 0 1 0 1 1|0 0|0 0 0|1 0 0 |
```

```
            D W  MD  REG   R/M

                      AX

                 [SI]
```

The brackets around SI mean that the MOV instruction doesn't move the contents of register SI to register AX, but from the memory location at the offset in register SI.

If you start this instruction, you'll see that when decoding the EA byte the form offset macro places the value of SI in AX.

Besides SI, which other register can you use here? Given that R/M can take 8 values, a well-informed reader would probably guess that it's possible to use any of the 16 data or index registers. That's logical but once again, it's not really true. Only index and base registers can be used. These include SI, DI, BP and BX.

The stack pointer isn't in this list because it has only one job which is managing the stack. Stacks are so important that it would be dangerous to let the SP (Stack Pointer) take part in effective addressing. BX replaces it as the fourth register that R/M uses. However, BX keeps its function as data register with indexing being its secondary activity.

Here's a table reviewing the relations between the value of R/M and the addressed register: index and base registers.

| R/M | Index Register |
|-----|----------------|
| 100 | SI |
| 101 | DI |
| 110 | BP *(except if MOD=00)* |
| 111 | BX |

You might notice that this table only contains four of the eight R/M combinations possible. Are the other combinations wasted? Not at all.

## 22.1 Double Indexing

Not only can R/M specify one of the four index registers, but it can also specify four complementary combinations of index registers. This is called double indexing. For example, the value 000 for R/M represents the BX/SI combination.

The following instruction:

```
0100  INC  BPTR [BX+SI]
```

specifies that BX and SI should indicate the offset where the byte to increment is located. This might seem odd at first, but makes sense when you think about index and base meanings.

A *base pointer* points to the base (or the lowest address) of a significant memory block. Therefore, an index register can point in this memory block. So the four combinations of double indexing correspond to four possible combinations between the base registers (BP and BX) and index registers (SI and DI).

| R/M | Combination |
|-----|-------------|
| 000 | BX+SI |
| 001 | BX+DI |
| 010 | BP+SI |
| 011 | BP+DI |

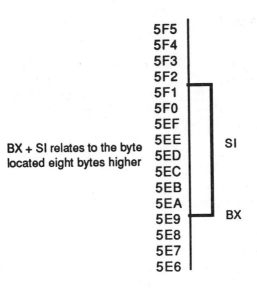

Load the MOV4.DEM file:

>>LOAD MOV4.DEM <Enter>

It will disassemble itself into an instruction on two bytes:

    MOV    AX,[BX+SI]

    | 1 0 0 0 1 0 1 1 | 0 0 | 0 0 0 | 0 0 0 |

                D W   MD   REG    R/M

                      (AX)

                  [BX+SI]

This instruction is executed almost identically to MOV AX,[SI] except that there is a second addition in X.

## 22.1.1    MOD: Offset Bytes

Now we've had some experience with what happens with two of the four possible values of the MOD field. We also know what happens with value 11 which causes EA to have nothing to do with memory (EA indicates registers). Until now we have only used the value 00 for MOD, a case where R/M proposes one of the eight indexing possibilities. What about MOD=01 and MOD=10?

When MOD=01, the instruction has a size of three bytes, including one offset byte following the EA byte.

**MOD=00**

```
    MOV   AX,[SI]
```

| 1 0 0 0 1 0 1 | 1 | 0 0 | 0 0 0 | 1 0 0 |

                  D W  MD  REG    R/M

                         (AX)

                    [SI]

**MOD=01**

```
     MOV    AX,[SI+60]
```

| 1 0 0 0 1 0 | 1 | 1 | 0 1 | 0 0 0 | 1 0 0 | 0 1 1 0 0 0 0 0 |

                  D W   MD  REG  R/M      60

                       (AX)

               [SI+nn]I

The offset byte is added to the contents of SI to generate the address of the operand. In this example, if we had 5000h in SI, the MOV AX,[SI+60] instruction would enter the word at offset 5060h in AX.

This offset byte serves as an extended sign before addition, and thus really represents a set of addresses located around SI (from 128 bytes before SI to 127 after it).

When MOD equals 10, two offset bytes are used to specify an address which the index register specifies.

## MOD=10

```
MOV   AX, [SI+F000]
```

| 1 0 0 0 1 0 |1|1|1 0|0 0 0|1 0 0|0 0 0 0 0 0 0 0|1 1 1 0 0 0 0 |

              D W  MD  REG   R/M      00           F0

                       (AX)

          [SI+nnnn]

In fact, the value of MOD is equal to the number of offset bytes of the instruction except in two specific cases:

- In the case where MOD=11. Then there is no need to take all this into account and R/M specifies a register.

- In the rare case when MOD=00 and R/M=110.

## 22.2   Chapter Exercises

Once you understand how to assemble these MOD-R/M combinations, it's better to have your PC do the work.

However, until you do understand the physical reality of the MOD and R/M fields, you could easily think it's quite arbitrary how the assembler rejects an ADD AX,[BP+BX] instruction although it accepts ADD AX,[BP+SI].

Go ahead and see if you can determine in which segments the offsets will be for each of these examples:

```
MOV   [SI],AX          =

MOV   [BP],AX          =

MOV   [BP+SI],AX       =

MOV   [SI 1022],AX     =

MOV   [SI+34],AX       =

MOV   [BX+DI+2233],AX  =
```

As a general rule, indexed EAs have their offset in the data segment. For example, MOV AX,[SI] transfers the word located at address DS:SI into register AX.

However, there are two exceptions to this rule:

- The stack segment is used each time that you deal with the BP (Base Pointer). This ability is exploited in stack oriented languages such as Pascal and C. So MOV AX,[BP] moves the word located at address SS:BP into AX. In principle, each of the two base registers point to a different segment: BP points to the stack segment and BX points to the data segment.

- You can bypass the implicit segment register, whether it's the SS or the DS, by adding a bypass prefix at the beginning of the instruction:

```
ADD SS:[BP+F000],100
```

adds 100h to the word at SS:BP+F000.

In the same way,

```
ADD CS:[BP+F000],100
```

adds 100h to the word at CS:BP+F000.

The MOV5.DEM demo file contains examples of several address mode permutations that can take MOV REG R/M. Start it to see how this works.

**Exercises:**

1)      What is the mnemonic that lets you transfer the contents of the DI register in the AX register?

2)      What is the mnemonic that lets you transfer the contents of AX in SI+36h?

# 23. The 80x86 Stack

A *stack* is a data structure (in some computers it's a part of the processor itself) where data is placed in a specific order. This order is usually the first items inserted are the last items removed.

Assembly language books generally compare the stack to the way food trays are distributed in cafeterias. The tray on the top of the stack (the first one that someone is going to grab) is also the last one that was put anywhere on the stack. On the other hand, the tray on the very bottom of the stack might stay there for several minutes if there aren't very many customers. This helps you to understand the computer (and accounting) notion of LIFO (Last In, First Out) data structures. There is also a FIFO (First In, First Out) structure called a queue.

## 23.1 POP and PUSH

Using a stack only requires these two instructions:

| PUSH |
| --- |

Use to "push" a tray or data on the top of the stack.

| POP |
| --- |

Use to "pop" a tray from the stack.

To work with the stack, you don't need commands like "Take the third element from the bottom" or "Put this one between the second and third elements from the top."

It doesn't matter whether there are five or 1500 trays in the stack when you send the POP instruction. The goal is only to "pick up" the last tray that was put there. When you place (or PUSH) a 4500h and then a 1000h on the stack, you'll get the last one back or the "1000h" when you execute a POP.

So now that we can handle how this works with a stack of "trays", what about a stack of numbers in a computer such as a PC or a compatible?

To start, consider the memory location stack:

| | |
|---|---|
| 9 | XX |
| 8 | XX |
| 7 | XX |
| 6 | XX |
| 5 | XX |
| 4 | XX |
| 3 | XX |
| 2 | XX |
| 1 | XX |
| 0 | XX |

To enter a number in the stack, you have to send this number to the address at the top of the stack. By definition, that's where the PUSH instruction sends numbers that are the object of the instruction.

But where's the "top?" The processors cannot even "see" a stack of numbers much less tell the top from the bottom. So they use a register called the stack pointer which always points to the top of the pile. Execution of PUSH and POP instructions consists of increments and decrements of this stack pointer to access the address it points to.

On the diagram on the following page, cell #6 is the top of the stack:

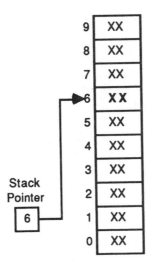

The PUSH instruction increments the stack pointer and enters the value specified by the instruction at the address the indicator points to.

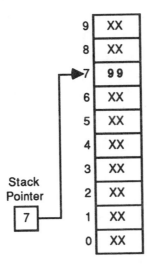

If AX contained "99" and we executed a PUSH AX instruction, the stack pointer would increment and "99" and would be entered in position #7.

It's certainly simple and efficient. But we'll give you one warning: In any stack, and especially in a stack like this one with only 10 elements, it's not wise to perform too many PUSHes and too few POPs. You would quickly make it move beyond its capacity. This is called a *Stack Overflow*. Therefore, you must carefully control what goes in and out of a stack.

## 23.2   The Stack In Detail

The stack in the 80x86 works more or less like the example in Section 23.1 with one important difference: It works in the opposite direction (bottom to the top). Although there are many reasons for stacking and unstacking only from top to the bottom, there is no technical reason the opposite cannot be done.

In this diagram of an 80x86 stack working backwards, 99 is at the top of the stack.

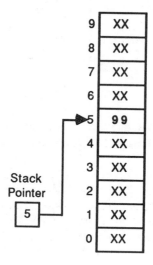

If you add a value to it (or PUSH), let's say 88, the stack pointer decrements (not increments) and "88" is placed in cell #4 and not in cell #6.

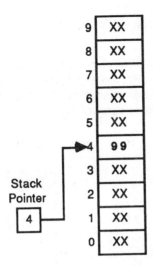

The 80x86 keeps a segment register for itself exclusively for managing the stack called the *SS register*. So the stack pointer has a 32-bit segment:offset structure capable of pointing to any address in the memory block.

To create a stack, programs begin by placing a value in the SS:SP. The SS:SP points to an address situated in a segment whose address is higher than the data and code segments (even though it isn't desirable to point in a "digital void"). The stack can be up to 64K long, although most programs are satisfied with a stack of several hundred bytes. When it starts, SIM places FFFEh in its SP register. FFFEh is then at the top of the memory and the stack has an exceptionally large size because of this.

## 23.3  Stack Instructions

The 80x86 uses four instructions to directly manipulate the stack: PUSH, POP, PUSHF (push flags) and POPF (pop flags). You probably won't be using PUSHF and POPF in the near future since the indicator register will detect problems. On the other hand, PUSH and POP are the ideal way to temporarily store values without needlessly occupying memory and using registers.

For example, let's say that CX contains the result of a calculation. Before being able to use this result, we temporarily need CX for another purpose, such as a counter during execution of a loop.

We can either save the contents of CX in a memory location (which means that you have to know what place is available in the RAM) or place the contents of CX in the stack. This last solution is usually the preferred one.

```
PUSH  CX

(executes the operation requiring CX)

POP   CX
```

In reality the PUSH CX instruction places the contents of CX in the memory in the same way as MOV [SI],CX. However, you will start to see the stack as something else, as if it were no longer part of RAM. It's a stack on which you place or from which you remove numbers without restraints specific to the memory. Observe that the 80x86 executes PUSHes and POPs 16 bits at a time. The result is that PUSH AX is possible but you can't do a PUSH AH.

### 23.3.1   Forms of PUSH and POP

PUSH and POP mnemonics are followed by 1-byte instructions for naming the register concerned by the operation with the stack, including segment registers. It's also possible to do PUSHes and POPs on memory locations with the address byte.

For example, "PUSH [F000]" reads the word located at address DS:F000, and then writes it at the top (remember that the "top" means the "bottom" here) of the stack (at address SS:SP-2). PUSH and POP R/M are only two of the three 80x86 instructions capable of moving a number from one memory location to another.

You might be saying that all this is very nice, but what are they used for? Well, you can use PUSH and POP to:

- Equalize two segment registers:

    ```
    PUSH    CS

    POP     DS
    ```

- Set and reset indicators that aren't tolerated by certain affectation instructions:

    ```
    PUSHF

    POP     AX      (AX contains the picture of the indicator)

    OR      AX,0004         (activates the parity indicator)

    PUSH    AX

    POPF    (now P is activated)
    ```

- Temporarily store values:

    ```
    PUSH    CX

    MOV     CL,4

    SHL     AX,CL

    POP     CX

    ADD     AX,CX
    ```

The STACK.DEM file gives examples of the use of the stack. Before starting this file, type the following to open a memory window at ssss:7F0.

```
>>DMEM 7F0 W <Enter>
```

The "W" argument forces SIM to open an 8-word instead of a 16-word window by default. Since the 80x86 executes PUSHes and POPs only on words, this is the logical way to see it at work. Next, enter 800h in SP. We have thus created a stack located at ssss:800. The first PUSH instruction will place a word at ssss:7FE.

Then load the STACK.DEM file:

>>LOAD STACK.DEM <Enter>

Now start the simulator by typing:

>>SIM <Enter>

and watch this window changing during the various steps of the execution of operations on the stack. The important macro stages are PUSH:REG and POP:REG.

The PUSH macro stage decrements SP by 2 and then writes the contents of the register at address SS:SP. The POP macro reads the word at SS:SP and increments SP by 2. You can also examine words at the top of the stack by doing a memory Dump from SS:SP. For example, if SP contains FF00h, then:

>>D SS:FF00 1 8 <Enter>

displays the four words at the top of the stack, with the one at the top in the first position.

# 23.4   Chapter Exercises

1)      Place the stack at address B800h. Do this with an assembly instruction.

2)      What is the mnemonic which lets you enter 55h on the stack? Execute the corresponding instruction.

3)      What is the mnemonic that lets you enter 67h on the stack? Execute the corresponding instruction.

4)      Restore the top of the heap in CX.

# 24. CALL and RET Instructions

Stacks are not used only to temporarily store values. In fact, they're more important because of how they are used in subroutines.

## CALL and RET instructions

The CALL and RET (return) instructions are the assembly language equivalents of the GOSUB/RETURN command in BASIC. Most programming languages have a form of these two instructions.

The CALL instruction is simply a JMP instruction where 80x86 begins by saving its current position so it can return to it. The "current position" is the value contained in the IP (occasionally in the CS). Any "saving" is simply done by PUSH which enters this value in the stack. You should understand that when we want to "return to it" this refers to a POP on the stack.

If you make the CALL to an address in the code segment (either Intrasegment or Near) then only the IP is entered in the stack. If it is executed on an Intersegment (or Far) the CS and IP registers are put in the stack in that order.

At the end of the subroutine, the RET instruction causes the stack to be read (POP) and the program picks up from the instruction right after the CALL. Far subroutines require a "FAR" RET to guarantee that the CS on the stack is read.

The CALL instruction has the same variants as JMP. You can call subroutines from and outside of the current code segment. You can express the destination address as a word included in the instruction or else it can be in a specific memory location (Call indirect). Since CALLs are generally executed at a distance above 128 bytes, they have no short format (an offset byte).

# 24.1   Traps and Overlaps

When you use the stack for temporary storage, you have to watch out that you don't alter the stack itself. This could very well jeopardize the return of the routine.

When you're in a subroutine after executing a CALL without a corresponding RET there are two possible things that can go wrong. You can either have execution of a PUSH on a number without carrying out a POP before the return or else execution of a POP without a PUSH beforehand.

Either way, the RET of the end of the subroutine causes a POP of the IP value somewhere in the memory but never at the routine calling for it. PUSHes and POPs that aren't counterbalanced are one of the best ways to lockup or crash assembly language programs.

## 24.1.1   Overlapping

The LIFO character of the stacks allows subroutine calls to overlap. The new return address is placed in the stack above the first return address of the preceding subroutine.

As soon as you encounter a RET, the return is done to the most recent CALL address. Subroutines can be fit together at almost infinite levels. However, most programmers are lost beyond the sixth level.

The CALL.DEM file illustrates one subroutine calling another. Load the CALL.DEm file by typing:

```
>>LOAD CALL.DEM <Enter>
```

Here, "RET to 30Bh" returns to the instruction after the last call. The subroutine located at 280h illustrates what you shouldn't do with PUSH and POP. When you come to the RET that ought to end the subroutine, instead of finding the return address in the word at the top of the stack, you find an SI value. That's not quite what you want. Try running this file and see what happens.

# 24.2 Indirect Calls

The last two CALLs for the 80x86 are indirect calls in their near and far formats. Let's take the intersegment format (or FAR) as an example.

## FAR

A normal CALL consists of five bytes with the last four bytes being immediate values to place in IP and CS. However, an indirect CALL is only an EA instruction letting the processor know the memory location where it should look for the words to put in IP and CS.

For example:

```
0100: FF1C    CALL  FAR [SI]
```

This instruction executes a jump to the address located in memory location DS:SI. The contents of DS:SI is put in IP. The following memory location contains what is placed in CS. "FAR", indicated by the disassembler, distinguishes this instruction from the one that uses the "near" format:

```
0100: FF14    CALL  [SI]
```

You can also call a subroutine at an address contained in a register:

```
CALL  SI
```

The JMP instruction has both near and far formats. Load the INDIRECT.DEM file:

```
>>LOAD INDIRECT.DEM <Enter>
```

At offset 200h is a six-byte table of vectors. Each is one word long, including the destination address of a JMP or CALL near.

```
0204: 0500

0202: 0400

0200: 0300
```

This table furnishes the destination address for the indirect CALL instruction of 106h while the loop is executed. With each execution of this instruction a different subroutine is called.

## 24.3 Chapter Exercises

1)    Write a program to:

> a) Enter 200h in SI
>
> b) Jump to the routine located at the address indicated in SI
>
> c) The routine located at the address specified in SI should enter 30h in AX and return

# 25. Working With Strings

There is a series of one-byte instructions known as *basic functions* that are available for the 80x86. We've have not yet discussed these instructions nor are they related to any instructions that we have discussed. However, if used effectively, they will produce shorter and faster routines.

We're dealing with key functions for processing strings of characters or practical functions for character string manipulations. They are even more efficient when you use them with the repeat (REP) prefix which was designed to be used with them.

## 25.1  What's a String?

Instructions for processing strings of characters are a useful tool in assembly language.

In 80x86 assembly language, a *string of characters* is a sequence of bytes or words in memory.

The instructions that we'll discuss will dramatically increase the speed of our program. In this chapter we'll discuss how to:

•    Move strings from one location to another (MOVSB and MOVSW)

•    Compare one string to another (CMPSB and CMPSW)

•    Search for a specific byte or word (SCASB and SCASW)

•    Read and write bytes or words in a string (LODSB, LODSW, STOSB and STOSW)

Before discussing each instruction in detail, let's look at what they have in common.

Each of these five pairs of basic instructions can either process a byte or a word. When you use these instructions, you just have to use the one with the "B" at the end of the mnemonic to process a byte or "W" to process a word. For example, MOVSB moves a string in memory byte by byte while MOVSW moves this string word by word.

The operands of these instructions are always the same. The SI register specifies the starting string and the DI register points to the destination string. The destination string is in the extra segment by default. The source string is in the data segment by default. However, you can modify this by using a segment override. Notice that if the two strings are in the same segment, you either have to use a segment override or initialize the DS and ES registers with the same value.

This addressing lets you, by default, use the SI register as a pointer for the source string and the DI register as pointer for the destination string. Strings can either be in the same segment or in different segments.

In the routine at the end of this section, we'll move a string from one segment to another. The DS and SI registers define the location of the source string. The ES and DI registers indicate the location where the string should be moved.

MOVSB moves a byte from the starting location to the destination location. The SI and DI registers are automatically updated so they point to the next byte of the string. Notice that MOVSW modifies the SI and DI registers so they point to the next word.

Automatic updating of the starting and destination pointers lets you manipulate long strings of characters by simply repeating the basic instructions several times. For this, you can use the REP code.

```
REP     MOVSB
```

The REP code repeats the instruction following this code as many times as are specified by the CX register. Each time the instruction is executed, the CX register is decremented by 1. When this register reaches zero, the 80x86 executes the next instruction. So we can use the CX register to indicate the length of the string to process.

With these instructions you can move a memory area from one address to another, compare two strings character by character, give a fixed value at a memory location or just look for a value in memory.

Let's illustrate how to substitute these instructions for the usual techniques of the 80x86 to save both memory space (by reducing the size of the program) and execution speed. One usual problem that we encounter in assembly languages is moving a memory block from one address to another. For example, here's a routine making the most of what we now know about the 80x86 for moving 100h bytes from offset 100h to offset 200h. We're not currently concerned with segments and assume that all the segment registers contain the same value:

```
[Initialize; Make SI = 100; DI = 200; CX = 100]

TOP:  MOV    AL,[SI]

      MOV    [DI],AL

      INC    SI

      INC    DI

      LOOP   TOP
```

Although this routine executes perfectly, we recommend using MOVS instead. It requires less code lines and executes much faster. MOVS is a one-byte instruction which takes care of 80% of the work all by itself.

**Note:**     Some assemblers let you get away with simply using the MOVS instruction, while others make you specify either MOVSB or MOVSW. With this or any of the other similar instructions we talk about in this chapter, you just have to follow what your 80x86 will allow you to do.

```
MOVS

1 0 1 0 0 1 0 W
```

MOVS moves the byte or the word to which DS:SI points to the address that ES:SI points to. Then, it increments SI and DI (twice when W = 1, once when W = 0). The mnemonic is MOVSB when W = 0 and MOVSW when W = 1. If you exclude PUSH and POP R/M, MOVS is the only 80x86 instruction that can move data from one memory location to another in one single action.

Here is our routine with MOVSB:

```
[Initialize; Make SI = 100; DI = 200; CX = 100]

TOP:  MOVSB

      LOOP   TOP
```

And for those of you who are never satisfied, you should know that nothing prevents you from going beyond this and getting rid of the LOOP.

## 25.2   The Repeat Prefix

```
REP

1 1 1 1 0 0 1 Z
```

The MOVS instruction preceded by the REP prefix corresponds to a one-instruction routine. The two bytes of the mnemonic REP MOVS create a loop whose counter is CX which by itself replaces all the lines of our preceding routine with the exception of the initialization.

```
[initialize]

REP    MOVSB
```

Load the REPMOVS.DEM file by typing:

```
>>LOAD REPMOVS.DEM <Enter>
```

This routine moves 30 bytes from xxxx:200 to xxxx:600. Other than the initialization sequence, it's only two bytes long.

```
REPMOVS.DEM

MOV    SI,200

MOV    DI,600

MOV    CX,30

REPZ   MOVSB

BRK
```

While observing the progress on the screen, keep your eye on the DS register which is used as a segment for the source register and ES for the destination. This is the only function dedicated to the ES (Extra Segment) in 80x86 assembly language. All the primitives of strings using DI use the ES register.

If we activate the W indicator of MOVS, we get the MOVSW (move string word) variant. MOVSW is only different from MOVSB in the fact that it moves words instead of bytes. To follow the movement, the SI and DI registers are incremented twice in a row. So if we had used MOVSW in our routine, we would have moved 60 instead of 30 bytes because each time a 16-bit word would have been moved.

**Note:**      SIM only accepts REPZ and REPNZ. It does not accept any other form (REP, REPE or REPNE).

# 25.3 Overwriting Problems

We can use REP MOVSB to overwrite values. This means moving a block of values in an area partially covering the area where the initial block is located (for example, moving 300h bytes from address 200h to address 280h). But if we use MOVSB as we've already done up to now, some bytes will be overwritten before being moved:

```
85   19   77   88   34   16   04   19   55   33   91   17   80 ... 31

 1    2    3    4    5    6    7    8    9   10   11   12   13 ... 16
```

Therefore, moving 8 bytes from address #1 to address #6 will result in serious problems. In fact, some addresses will be crushed before they can be moved, like the diagram above shows. When you have to move the initial contents of address #6, they will have already been replaced by the contents from address #1.

The trick is to start the execution of MOVSB from the end and not from the beginning. Think of it as working backwards, if you wish.

## 25.3.1 The Direction Pointer

To do that, of course you have to use the direction pointer. By setting "D", the index registers are decremented and not incremented which forces the strings to be processed from higher memory to lower memory. Check this on a piece of paper to see if it effectively resolves the problem. Except when the DF flag is indicated, CS is always decremented by repetitive primitives (REP MOVSB, etc.).

As you can see, the instructions for manipulating strings of characters offer many possibilities.

## 25.4   Other Basic Instructions

Now let's look at the other basic functions for processing strings of characters.

The basic instruction STOS enters the contents of the accumulator (AL for operations on bytes and AX for operations on words) in the destination string and then updates the destination pointer (DI). Therefore, STOSB will copy the contents of byte AL to the location in the string indicated by DI and STOSW will do the same thing with the contents of word AX. The starting pointer (SI) isn't used and therefore is not modified.

The REP STOS instruction is extremely useful for initializing memory blocks at a constant value. Remember that the destination string is always in the extra segment. STOS transfers the byte (or the word) from the accumulator into ES:DI. It's the best way to transfer a constant value in a memory location for entering a series of variables to zero or erasing the video memory, for example.

LODS loads the accumulator with DS:SI. It's the only basic instruction that doesn't have a REP prefix. The REP LODS instruction would result in permanently modifying the accumulator, which would overwrite the preceding contents every time.

LODS performs the opposite of STOS. LODS takes a byte or a word out of the source string and places it in the AL or AX register. Therefore, LODSB takes a byte in the string indicated by SI and puts it into AL, while LODSW does the same thing with a word by placing it in AX. The source string pointer, SI, is then updated. The DI register isn't used and remains unchanged. The LODS instruction is useful for syntactic analysis programs where you have to examine each string, one by one, in their order of appearance.

The scan instruction, SCAS, executes a subtraction between the contents of the AL (with SCASB) or AX (with SCASW) accumulator and the byte or word of the destination string. Then it modifies the state of several indicators to reflect the result of the comparison. Nothing is modified, except indicators and the DI register.

You can use this instruction to look for a specific character in a string. To do this, use the two prefix codes REPE (repeat if equal) and REPNE (repeat if not equal). These prefixes, like the REP prefix, cause the specified function to be repeated the number of times indicated by the CX register. Furthermore, these prefixes interrupt the repetition when the zero flag indicator (ZF) shows that the desired condition (equal or not equal) is achieved.

The basic instruction of comparison, CMPS, subtracts the destination byte or word from the starting byte or word and updates the different indicators according to the results of the comparison. Just like in the case of SCAS, the operands remain unchanged. Only the indicators and the DI and SI registers are modified.

You can use the CMPS instruction in conjunction with REPE to compare two strings and repeat the comparison until the difference shows up. You can also use it with REPNE to compare two strings until you discover an agreement.

CMPS and SCAS are the most versatile instructions of all. Combined with REP, they become powerful memory analysis tools. SCAS (scan string) covers a string of characters while comparing bytes or words that it contains with the accumulator. CMPS (compare string) compares two strings word by word, or byte by byte, whichever the case may be.

The prefix REP contains a "zero" pointer (don't confuse it with the zero flag ZF) which is only useful for CMPS and SCAS. When you use MOVS, STOS and LODS, this pointer plays no role. On the other hand, with SCAS and CMPS, it determines if the loop is ending or not (changing the state of ZF).

REP

1 1 1 1 0 0 0 1

To represent the state of this Z pointer, the prefix REP has two mnemonic appearances of REPZ and REPNZ which correspond to the operating codes F3h and F2h respectively. The SCAS or CMPS instructions also end when the contents of CX is equal to zero. This is valid in all cases.

**Note:**     As a reminder, SIM only accepts REPZ and REPNZ. It does not accept any other form (REP, REPE or REPNE).

# 25.5   Override Segments and Strings

You can add an override segment prefix to any basic function for manipulating strings. With this prefix, you disregard any data segment for the source string. However, you're not allowed to alter ES if you use it as a segment of a destination string. For example:

```
CS: MOVSB    moves a byte from CS:SI to ES:DI

CS: LODSB    loads AL from CS:SI

CS: STOSB    places AL at ES:DI - The override prefix can in no way
             place the destination string anywhere other than in ES
```

Start the SPRIM.DEM file by typing:

```
>> LOAD SPRIM.DEM <Enter>
```

The first three instructions illustrate how SCASB is used to find the end of a string of characters. The usual agreement here is to end each string of ASCII characters with a zero in memory. SPRIM.DEM does it at offset 200h. When the REPNZ SCASB instruction of 0108 ends, DI points to the byte that follows the final zero (at offset 228h).

Instructions located from 10B to 114h illustrate how SIM disassembles instructions with conflicting prefixes. When a prefix has no effect on the execution of an instruction, it isn't displayed with the instruction. For example, at 110h, the string of bytes F3 03 C3 (REP followed by ADD AX,BX) is simply disassembled into ADD AX,BX. However, the U (disassemble) command displays the hexadecimal value of the unnecessary prefix on the screen:

```
xxxx:0110:   F303C3        ADD     AX,BX
```

When we have multiple prefixes in an instruction, disassembling doesn't necessarily reflect their order in memory. At offset 10Dh, the segment diversion precedes the repetition prefix but in the assembly the former is in second position:

```
xxxx:010D:   2EF3A4        REPZ    CS:MOVSB
```

## 25.6   Basic Functions and Memory Mapping

The basic functions are well adapted to a rapid addressing of the memory mapped display. The code starting at 0116h writes a series of "happy faces" on the last two lines of the screen.

```
MOV     AX,B000     (B800 for color screens)

MOV     ES,AX       (establish possibility of addressing)

MOV     CX,A0       (write 160 words, 320 bytes)

MOV     DI,E60      (first address, line 23)

MOV     AX,0702     ("happy face" characters)

MOV     STOSW       (execution)
```

**Note:**      We have to resort to two MOV instructions to move an "immediate" value into ES because there is no form of MOV that lets you move an "immediate" value into a segment register.

## 25.7 Chapter Exercises

1) What is the most efficient sequence of mnemonics for transferring 100 bytes from memory address ssss:100 to ssss:400?

2) What is the most efficient sequence of mnemonics for transferring 200 bytes from address ssss:100 to address ssss:150?

3) Let's suppose that you have the string "THIS IS A STRING" in memory beginning at ssss:100h. You want to find the character "A" in this string. How do you go about it?

# 26. An Example Program

In this chapter we'll take all that we've discussed in previous chapters to create a real 80x86 program.

Let's pretend that we're going to write an accounting program for the Whatsit Company entirely in assembly language. The Whatsit Company wants its accounting program to include the age of each of its 256 salaried workers. The best way to solve this problem would be to use a table with one entry for each employee. Here's the way it could be created:

| # | Age | Name | Position |
|-----|-----|------------|------------------------------|
| 0 | 40h | Mr. Durand | President and General Manager |
| 1 | 20h | Mr. Martin | Head of Production |
| 3 | 3Ch | Ms. Emmons | Marketing |
| 255 | 10h | Abby | Student intern |

A table is as important in assembly language as in BASIC (similar to the importance of loops). A table in 80x86 assembly language is simply a sequence of memory locations. With an indexed set of addresses, we can create a table of variables in which each byte could be distinctly addressed.

We'll enter the table of ages at offset 200-2FFh. When the program needs to know the age of a given employee, it resorts to an index system based on the number of the employee. As long as the number doesn't exceed the 256 names and no employee is more than 255 years old, all you have to do is:

```
MOV  SI,# x      MOV  AL,[SI]
```

Now AL contains the age of the employee.

Now to complicate things, the Whatsit Company has to publish quarterly reports showing the total ages of all its employees. Not the average age, but the total sum of all the ages. We'll use the COUNTAGE.DEM routine to do this. Load COUNTAGE.DEM by typing:

```
>>COUNTAGE.DEM <Enter>
```

Then you can see the listing we've reproduced below:

```
CountAge.DEM

START     MOV   CX,100

          SUB   AX,AX

          MOV   BX,AX

          MOV   SI,200

          CLD

TOP:      LODSB

          ADD   BX,AX

          LOOP  TOP
```

CountAge goes over this table of ages with 100h elements (at 200h) moving from the bottom to the top while accumulating the totals in BX. The breakdown occurs in the CX register and the SI register serves as an index register.

The loop executes 256 iterations before the CX register is reduced to zero. You may want to change STEP to 4 and press the <Spacebar> to view each step of the COUNTAGE.DEM file. Now simulate COUNTAGE.DEM by typing:

```
>>SIM <Enter>
```

When SIM is completed, you can determine the average age of the employees of the Whatsit Company by dividing the total in the BX register by 256.

## More Challenges

The company has just informed you about its new policy for retirement pension payments. The amount payable each month by all of the employees less than 60 years old will now be doubled. Coincidentally, the youngest member of the administrative board is 60 years old. The overworked team from the data processing department has to modify the "deductions" part of this position.

Using the already existing table of ages, create a "retired" table based on the following data: If the employee benefits from the new retirement policy (59 or less), put his age in the table. If the employee doesn't benefit from the new policy (60 or older), the heading corresponding to his age in the new table has the number "0". As long as you're there, calculate the total number of employees that won't benefit from the new policy.

The table of ages is still at offset 200h. The new table will be at 300h.

```
BTABLE.DEM

START:    PUSH    DS

          POP     ES

          MOV     CX,100

          MOV     SI,200

          MOV     DI,300

          CLD

          REPZ    MOVSB

          SUB     AX,AX

          MOV     CX,100

TOP:      CMP     [SI],3C

          JL      SKIP

          MOV     [SI],00

          INC     AX

SKIP:     INC     SI

          LOOP    TOP
```

This program starts by copying the initial table of ages into the new table. It's customary to initialize the direction pointer before any base function because you usually cannot depend on the state of this pointer beforehand. One byte is a small amount to pay for this protection.

Then, with the help of the CX loop, we check each age we enter by eliminating everything equal to or above 60, while keeping track of the number of those eliminated (which are in AX). Now simulate the program. How many Whatsit employees are 60 or older? (Answer: 12 employees).

# 26.1 Bubble Sorting

Many programmers will have to write sorting programs or routines. The easiest technique is *bubble sorting*.

The principle of bubble sorting comes from champagne bubbles. The bubbles in champagne travel upwards with the lightest bubbles reaching the surface first. In a similar way, the smallest (or "lightest") numbers move towards the top in bubble sorting.

Here's how it works: You examine a series of numbers while comparing each number with the next one. If the first is larger than the second, you invert them so the smallest is on top. Then you compare this number with the one above it. At the end of the stack, the smallest number has been brought up to the top like a bubble that's lighter than the others. Then you start the process again, ignoring the number at the top since you already know it's the smallest. After you've gone through the stack a second time, you start over but this time you ignore the top two. And so forth.

After going "n-1" times through the list of "n" elements, you're finished.

Now let's execute a simple "bubble" sorting from a list with four elements. We'll have to make three passes (or 4 - 1). The first time through there are three comparisons, the second time two comparisons and the last time only one.

The arrow points to the lightest weight number being compared.

First pass:

           34

           19

           77

    ➙     22

Beginning at the bottom, compare 22 with 77. Since 22 is less than 77, invert the two numbers and place 22 above 77. The pointer moves up and we have:

34

19

→ 22

77

Compare 22 with 19. Since an invert is unnecessary the pointer moves up.

34

→ 19

22

77

Then compare 19 to 34. After that, you've finished going through the first pass. Now the smallest value is at the top of the list. Put the pointer at the bottom and start the process again.

19

34

22

→ 77

Compare 77 with 22. No inversion necessary. Move the pointer up.

19

34

→ 22

77

Compare 22 with 34. Do an inversion. This marks the end of the second pass. The first two numbers are at the correct location.

        19

        22

        34

→    77

We only have one comparison to execute: 77 with 34. There's no inversion necessary with these two numbers and this marks the end of the bubble sort.

One slight modification is all you need to sort in reversed order. In the next section we'll show a BASIC program which performs the same sorting.

## 26.2   Bubble Sort in BASIC

Let's write the same bubble sorting algorithm for the Whatsit Company in BASIC. The company wants to put out a sorted list of the ages of its 256 employees.

```
REM   AGES IN TABLEAGE(1)  -  TABLEAGE(256)

FOR COUNT = 255 TO 1 STEP -1

        (WORKING FROM BOTTOM TO TOP, COMPARE IN TABLEAGE THE NUMBERS BY
        PAIR AND INVERT IF NECESSARY)

NEXT COUNT
```

As for the loop:

```
FOR POINTER = 1 TO COUNT

 IF TABLEAGE(POINTER) < TABLEAGE(POINTER+1) THEN

        SWAP (TABLEAGE(POINTER),TABLEAGE(POINTER+1))

NEXT POINTER
```

One of the rare merits of "bubble" sorting is not having to check the top of the stack. That's why our loop goes to COUNT.

Here's the actual program in BASIC:

```
FOR COUNT = 255 TO 1 STEP -1

 FOR POINTER = 1 TO COUNT

  IF TABLEAGE(POINTER) < TABLEAGE(POINTER+1) THEN

        SWAP (TABLEAGE(POINTER),TABLEAGE(POINTER+1))

 NEXT POINTER

NEXT COUNT
```

All the same, such a routine in BASIC is extremely long, because, even for a small table, there are several comparisons and inversions to execute. For this list of 256 numbers, there are almost 32,000 comparisons and some 16,000 inversions.

The following is a slightly quicker routine:

```
BSORT.DEM

    START:  MOV     CX,FF           (255 times through)

            MOV     BX,200

    OUTER:  MOV     SI,0

    INNER:  MOV     AL,[BX+SI]

            CMP     AL,[BX+SI+1]

            JAE     NOSWAP          (same as JNC)

            XCHG    AL,[BX+SI+1]

            MOV     [BX+SI],AL

    NOSWAP: INC     SI

            CMP     SI,CX

            JNE     INNER           (same as JNZ)

            LOOP    OUTER

            BRK
```

We have two overlapped loops. The OUTER one uses CX and is used 255 times. It counts how many times the INNER one should be executed. The INNER one uses SI, starts at zero and works toward the top to end when SI reaches CX.

Start the BSORT.DEM by typing:

```
>>BSORT.DEM <Enter>
```

# 26.3 Privileged Mode

Until now you've only used SIM in its standard mode. Since it's almost impossible to crash or lockup the system in standard mode, it's excellent for beginners of 80x86 assembly language programming.

For example, in the standard mode you didn't have access to the GO command. When you use the GO command, a program in memory is executed not by the SIM but by the 80x86 itself. In *privileged mode*, typing GO instructs SI to load the 80x86 registers with the values from the corresponding simulated registers, and turns program control over to you. When SIM eventually takes over again, it displays its registers with the real values that the 80x86 registers contain.

To switch to privileged mode, type in the following:

```
>>PRIV <Enter>
```

The ">>" prompt in the Command Management Window is replaced with "—" (dash). This prompt shows you have complete control over the program. Of course this also means that even a small mistake could lockup or crash your computer. There are probably dozens of ways to lockup your program or to crash your system.

For example, if you were to type in the following (warning: this command intentionally crashes your computer):

```
—E 0000:20 FF <Enter>
```

Sometimes, pressing the <Ctrl><Alt><Del> key combination restarts the system. However, you may need to switch off your computer. Unfortunately, this is an example of how one small instruction can crash your computer to the point where even pressing <Ctrl><Alt><Del> cannot restart the system. You'll have to switch off and then switch on your PC.

We'll work in privileged mode from here on. The ability to write to any memory location is only one advantage of being a privileged user. You also have access to four new screen commands:

- G(o)

- SKIP

- O(utput)

- T(race)

## GO

The GO command provides you the option of specifying the address at which you want to turn command over to SIM. That's what we call "setting a breakpoint". The syntax is:

```
G [address...]
```

You can establish up to 10 breakpoint addresses. SIM takes control when you arrive at one of these addresses. For example, in the following command SIM takes control as soon as (and in case) CS:IP is equal to CS:345 or 60:21C:

```
—G 345 60:21C
```

Also, SIM automatically takes control when the program encounters a BRK instruction (opcode CCh).

With BSORT.DEM we want the 80x86 to execute the program until the point that it meets BRK at 11Ch. So we don't need to establish a "breakpoint". Now start the demo:

```
—G <Enter>
```

After this, it's really the 80x86 which executes the 32,000 odd comparisons and 16,000 inversions in BSORT.DEM. You can confirm this in the Status Area on the screen. It will show "80x86 Control". Did you notice the speed of the 80x86? What is the age of the youngest employee in the Whatsit Company? The age of the oldest?

You can modify BSORT so it executes in the video memory by entering DS on the segment address of the display buffer. Use either B000h for the monochrome screen or B8000h for the color screen. This will make the video display go totally bonkers.

## SKIP

SKIP, a form of GO, allows a step by step execution of your program, partially in SIM and partially in the 80x86 itself. If you want SIM to establish a "breakpoint" by itself just after the instruction at CS:IP, then start a SKIP without parameters.

SKIP is very useful for completely jumping a CALL. It can also quickly execute an operation on a long repetitive string. All executions can't undergo a SKIP. You can only perform CALLs, Soft interrupts (which we'll discuss soon) and base functions on strings.

# 26.4   Chapter Exercises

1)      Write a program to calculate the average of the first 255 bytes of the screen memory.

2)      Once you've calculated this average, write a routine that displays this value in the first 255 bytes of the screen.

# 27. Input/Output

## 27.1 Moving Beyond The 80x86

The 80x86, like the CPU of every computer, communicates with digits but we communicate by visual and verbal information. Input/Output (I/O) devices, such as monitors, printers, keyboard, mice, and others, allow us to communicate with computers. However, according to the strict meaning of 80x86 assembly language, I/Os are simply a memory addressing format.

The 80x86 executes I/O by writing numbers of 8, 16 or 32 bits at one of the 65,536 ports that are available to it. The term "port" is perhaps not the best of expressions. In reality, output towards a port is only a reference to a memory address, calling on the same series of data and address pins. From 80x86's point of view, the only difference between a memory reference and a reference to an I/O address is the way the pins act.

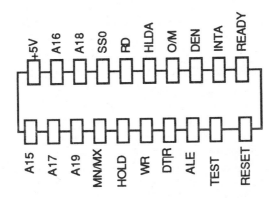

The different areas of memory and I/O ready to act to incoming information (address and data) during each read/write operation. The I/O pin determines which of the two is used.

If the I/O pin carries a signal, then the read/write operation will begin at the I/O peripheral and not in memory. For example, the keyboard is input port number 60h for the 80x86. When the CPU reads port 60h, it doesn't read RAM location 0000:0060; it reads the number returned by the keyboard in response to the user pressing a key. The keyboard has its own processor which is usually the Intel 8048.

## IN and OUT Instructions

IN and OUT are two instructions available to access the I/O ports of the 80x86. IN is used for reading (or input from a port) and OUT for writing (or output to a port).

IN and OUT instructions have two different formats. Both use the accumulator (AX or AL) to keep the value read or written on a port. If the number of the port is 255 or less, it can be entered in the second byte of the instruction:

```
IN fixed port

1 1 1 0 0 1 0 W     port #
```

For example, "IN AL,10" reads a byte on the 10h port and transfers it to the accumulator. If we set the word pointer, the instruction reads a word on this port and transfers it to AX.

To read a port with a number above 255, use the format using DX as a pointer:

```
IN variable_port

1 1 1 0 1 1 0 W
```

Here is an opcode using such an IN format:

```
IN    AX,DX
```

IN and OUT are both "hard" coded so they use the accumulator as a base register and DX as a port pointer. OUT instructions operates similarly:

```
OUT   FF,AL      (AL output in port 255)

OUT   DX,AL      (AL output in port # at DX)
```

You should know, however, that many processors manage without dedicated I/O instructions. These processors use *memory mapped* I/Os in which the peripherals of I/O are in normal memory blocks located far from RAM and ROM addresses.

The advantage here is that addressing modes is available for processing I/Os. If this technique had been used, every memory read/write instruction could be used as an I/O command. This places the full range of addressing modes for I/O problems available to you.

Without this advantage, the 80x86 programmer often has to call on three distinct functions to do what he can do elsewhere with only one function. However, it's not as restricting as it might appear.

The SIM screen has I(nput) and O(utput) commands which let you read/write ports at the rate of one byte at a time. For example, to read a byte in port 7FEh:

```
—I 7FE
```

The "O" command is reserved for privileged users because it commands the peripherals (like the disk controller) in a dangerous way, making them able to crash the system. For example, to write B6h in port 43h:

```
—O 43 B6
```

## 27.2 I/O On Your PC

With the exception of RAM and ROM, the 80x86 manages (controls and communicates with) the peripherals of the PC by an address of only one port. Let's take two particular peripherals, the speaker and the programmable timer, to see how the I/O screen instructions and ultimately programs in assembly language communicate with them.

### 27.2.1 Creating sounds

By manipulating the speaker output, you're able to program tones for warning messages or music for entertainment software. It's possible to even imitate the human voice, although this sound is similar to a robot.

The IBM-PC diagnostics diskette uses a specific series of "beeps" to alert you to a specific error. Beeps permit you to discover certain errors, for example if the video controller doesn't work, that cannot be displayed on the screen.

The speaker is controlled by the two least significant bits of an ordinary control port at address 61h.

```
Port 61h

x x x x x S S
```

The speaker has two execution modes *automatic* and *manual*. We'll discuss the manual mode (bit 0 = 0) first. Select this mode with bit "0".

An audible "click" is generated each time that bit 1 of port 61h is modified (or "toggled"). We can modify this bit by executing an OUT instruction on this port to give a new value to bit 1.

The other six bits execute a whole variety of functions and it would be iffy, and perhaps even dangerous, to change them while modifying the speaker bits. This requires some preliminary knowledge of the value of the other bits. Let's read the status of this port:

```
-I 61 <Enter>
```

This yields a value of 30h (00110000).

The six most significant bits are 010011 on our PC (this may be different for your PC). As we mentioned earlier, when you manipulate the speaker, it's important that the most significant six bits are unchanged when the value is written back to port 61h.

Therefore, to modify the speaker on our PC, we have to output 32h or 00110010. That means you send the six bits as they were and only modify bit 1. When you send 32h to port 61h a "click" is produced.

The click will not be sounded if 32h is sent a second time to this port because it's only produced by changing the speaker bit. To produce a second click you have to send a 30h:

```
—O 61 30 <Enter>
```

So creating sound effects and musical tones requires a programming which modifies hundreds, even thousands of times per second, the status of the speaker. It's a job worthy of assembly language:

```
Load SPEAKER1.DEM <Enter>

           MOV     DX,1000

TOP:       IN      AL,61

           AND     AL,FE

           XOR     AL,02

           OUT     61,AL

           MOV     CX,0010

DELAY:     LOOP    DELAY

           DEC     DX

           JNE     TOP

           BRK
```

Here we have an outer DX loop and an inner CX loop.

Here's the logic of the routine in pseudo code:

```
FOR N = 1 to 4096

     modify the speaker

     momentary pause (delay)

NEXT N
```

The outer loop (FOR N = 1 to 4096) indicates the number of times required to execute the "modify the speaker and delay" sequence and the duration of the sound. The inner loop (CX) manages the waiting time between each modification, and, therefore, the frequency of the sound.

The four instructions executing the modification are very important. The INs read and transfer the contents of port 61h in the AL register where we can modify them. The AND instruction (FEh in AL) erases bit 0 without affecting bits 1 to 7. "XOR AL,02" inverts bit 1 without affecting the other bits. And the OUT produces the click.

To illustrate what "XOR AL,02" does, let's suppose that an IN has transferred 4Eh to the AL register:

```
        01001110      4Eh

XOR     00000010      02h

        01001100      4Ch
```

You recall that the Boolean "not OR" (XOR) function produces a 1 if, and only if, its two inputs are different. When you execute an XOR on a zero byte, the byte is not modified. If you execute an XOR on a byte composed only of 1s, all the bits are inverted.

We can combine these effects by mixing 0s and 1s. If you place one or several set bits in the XOR mask, then only these bits are inverted. The same "XOR AL,02h" instruction will later produce 4Eh again.

```
        01001100      4Ch

XOR     00000010      02h

        01001110      4Eh
```

The AL register now contains a value to send into 61h to cause a click. The DELAY loop causes a short delay in looping back until the CX register is at 0. Larger values in CX produce longer delays and therefore lower notes. Next, we decrement the DX register to indicate that we have executed the loop once. When DX is finally at 0, the program arrives at BRK (Break).

If you execute this program on SIM, it doesn't produce anything resembling a sound because the clicks are too distant. Type GO so the true 80x86 executes the program to produce a sound.

Experiment by modifying the delay constants in CX. Try to create the loudest and softest sounds possible.

# 27.3   Generating Better Sounds

## 27.3.1     The timer

Bit 0 of port 61h is an electronic switch linking the speaker to the internal clock of the PC. If you flip this switch by writing "1"s in the speaker bit and the timer bit, the two are linked together. According to the frequency of the internal clock, you produce an appropriate sound.

```
Port 61h

x x x x x x S T    (S = SPEAKER, T = TIMER)

—O 61 4F <Enter>
```

This sound only stops when you erase bit 0:

```
—O 61 4E <Enter>
```

This ability would be rather useless if there were no way to modify the frequency of the timer to change the sound we generated. Fortunately we have 65,536 frequencies at our disposal by addressing our outputs towards a different couple of ports whose function is to manage the timer. We know that port 61h manages the speaker. Ports 42h and 43h manage the frequency of the timer. You begin by transferring a starting value to the master port (43h). If you send the starting value B6h to this port, the timer is in a mood to accept a new frequency through port 42h.

However, the format of the frequencies isn't as simple as you might wish for. Instead of simply having to send a value of "440" (decimal) to produce 440 cycles per second (or 440 Hz), we have to use a divisor. The internal clock produces a frequency equal to 1,190,000 divided by the value that we furnish.

For example, to get a frequency of 440 Hz, you must find a value so that dividing 1,190,000 by this value results in 440. In other words, you need to divide 1,190,000 by 440 (the result is 2704 decimal or A90h). Timer divisors have 16 bits, and since port 42h only consists of one byte, the timer expects to receive the divisor as two bytes with the lowest significant byte first.

## 27.3.2    Sounds with SIM

The next three commands produce a frequency of 440 Hz with the timer:

```
—O 43 B6 <Enter>
```

—O 42 90 <Enter>     (least significant byte of A90h)

—O 42 A <Enter>      (most significant byte of A90h)

For the speaker to give a sound at 440 Hz, you only have to link the speaker to the timer:

—O 61 4F <Enter>

SPEAKER2.DEM uses the timer to produce a continuous sound that's higher and higher pitched. This starts with a significant value (which produces a very low sound) and then continually decrements this value to produce a higher and higher sound. Start with 1,190,000/65,536 (or about 18Hz) to arrive at 1,190,000/60 (about 20,000 Hz) which is the limit of what humans can hear.

```
START   IN    AL, 61

        OR    AL, 3

        MOV   BL, AL

        MOV   DX, FFFF

        MOV   AX, B000

        MOV   ES, AX

        MOV   AL, B6h

        OUT   43, AL

TOP:    MOV   AL, DL

        MOV   ES:[2], AL

        OUT   42, AL

        MOV   AL, DH

        MOV   ES:[0], AL

        OUT   42, AL

        MOV   AL, BL

        OUT   61, AL
```

```
            MOV     CX,100

DELAY:      LOOP    DELAY

            DEC     DX

            JNE     TOP

            MOV     AL,BL

            AND     AL,FC

            OUT     61,AL

            BRK
```

In SPEAKER2.DEM, the 2 bytes of the value in DX are written in the video memory each time the timer is modified.

**Note:**        Don't forget to change the value of the segment in ES if you have a color screen.

Type in the following to execute the program:

  –G <Enter>

Then experiment by modifying the value in the CX register.

## 27.4 Chapter Review and Exercises

The 80x86 uses IN and OUT instructions to manage all the subsystems of the PC, which essentially include display, readers, series and parallel communication ports. Most peripherals are managed by a controller card.

For example, the NEC PD745 controls the disk drives. If you examine the disk drive controller card, you'll probably see a 40-pin IC dominating all the chips. That chip is the NEC PD745. The Motorola 6845 controls video memory and screen displays. A 8048 microprocessor manages the keyboard.

You can program each of these peripherals using the OUT and IN instructions. The 80x86 can set and clear these peripherals with the OUT instructions. Instead of waiting until the disk drive head is on track 7 and the diskette is at a specific sector, the 80x86 indicates what it wants to the disk drive controller. It then takes care of other tasks until the controller indicates to the 80x86 that it has completed its task. Then an IN instruction can read the appropriate information.

Of course, most of these functions could have been accomplished by the 80x86 itself. However, by delegating these jobs to others, the 80x86 can devote itself more to the program.

**Exercises:**

1) What's an I/O port?

2) What is the mnemonic that lets you read a byte at the keyboard?

3) What's the mnemonic that lets you send a byte to the speaker port?

# 28. The 80x87 Math Co-processors

The one area where the set of 80x86 instructions cannot excel is when performing operations on real numbers with a floating decimal point. Any value with a decimal is enough to affect the 80x86. This is a serious handicap for the 80x86 since we often use these types of numbers. If you can't calculate with a floating decimal point, 5 divided by 2 gives 2, Pi ($\pi$) equals 3 and the 80x86 ignores any remaining numbers.

The problem isn't with the capacity of the 80x86 because it is possible to execute floating decimal point operations with 80x86 instructions. Any BASIC programmer knows that executing "PRINT 3.1 * 64.777" gives a real result. The problem is that to do this, it has to execute hundreds or even thousands of instructions.

So to multiply 3.1 by 64.777 you need a assembly language program with around a hundred bytes. Then the program takes 3 to 4 milliseconds to execute (four milliseconds equals 1/250th of a second). Although this may not seem to be very long, you should understand that the 80x86 does a single simple multiplication a hundred times faster than that.

You'll start losing milliseconds and eventually larger mathematical applications can take several days to complete. The 80x87 is a math co-processor which can execute such operations 200 times faster. The 80x87 only needs 20 microseconds (and not milliseconds) to execute a problem similar to 3.1 * 64.777.

If a co-processor can perform that fast, why hasn't Intel done this with the 8088? There are two reasons:

- At the time the 80x86 was released, it wasn't technically possible because the 80x86 contains only 20,000 transistors while the 80x87 is more complex with 60,000 transistors.

- Many applications (word processing, for example) don't require the power of the 80x87 and it would require valuable space in the 80x86 that can be better used for other tasks.

Therefore, Intel gave the ESC command to the set of 80x86 instructions. This meant the 80x86 could be used with a co-processor such as the 80x87. Your computer could execute operations with a floating decimal point (in simple and double precision) simply by adding an 80x87 co-processor.

**Note:** The newest member of the 80x86 family is the 80486 processor. It has a built-in math co-processor.

241

## 28.1   How the 80x87 Co-processors Work

The 80x87 manages floating decimal point instructions by looking for the instructions executed by the 80x86. When the 80x87 encounters an instruction that it should execute, it "steps in" and begins to work on it.

Seeing that both processors can work at the same time, they have to be synchronized. The WAIT instruction of the 80x86 takes care of this synchronization. The 80x87 is linked to the 80x86 in such a way that, when the NDP is busy carrying out a floating decimal point operation, the "test" input of the 80x86 is inactive.

WAIT stops the processing of the instruction in action in the 80x86 until the "test" input becomes active, which tells the 80x86 that the 80x87 instruction has finished. The 80x86 can also make sure that the 80x87 has finished an operation before trying to give it another one to execute. This prevents the 80x86 from accessing data stored by the 80x87 before the end of the instruction.

The processor and co-processor only communicate through external signal lines, such as the "test" input. The 80x86 cannot read the internal registers of the 80x87 and vice versa. All the data that moves from one to the other must be entered in memory that is accessible to both processor and co-processor.

However, since addressing registers are in the 80x86, it's difficult for the 80x87 to effectively address the memory by using the same addressing modes as the 80x86. To let the 80x87 address the memory by using 80x86 addressing modes, both processors are set to work executing the floating decimal point instruction.

The set of 80x86 instructions contains an Escape (ESC) instruction which isn't executed in the 80x86. In a system without a 80x87, ESC is identical to NOP (No Operation) except that it takes longer to execute. However ESC instructions include lots of addressing information. They have a MOD-R/M byte for calculating the address.

Even though ESC acts like the 80x87, the 80x86 calculates the effective address. With this, it reads in memory but it doesn't use the data. Otherwise, if the MOD-R/M byte specifies a register of the 80x86 and not an operand in memory, no reading is carried out in memory.

Under this system, the 80x87 constantly watches over what the 80x86 executes. As soon as the 80x87 sees an ESC (Escape to external device), it enters into play. The last three bits of the primary operation code are combined with the secondary operation code to define the operation. MOD and R/M give the memory location where the action occurred.

```
ESC    operation,register/memory

1 1 0 1 1 n n n  MOD  n n n  R/M
```

Let's take, for example, the 80x87 instruction FMUL [SI], which the 80x86 recognizes as "ESC 01,[SI]".

FMUL [SI] orders the 80x87 to multiply a number with a floating decimal point at DS:SI (4 bytes in memory) by the value with a floating decimal point at the top of its internal stack. 80x86's work is done when it has read the byte of the effective address.

Although the 80x87 can execute up to 50,000 multiplications with a floating decimal point, if you insert an 80x87 into your PC, there's no guarantee that all your applications will be 100 times faster. Software and other applications must be specifically written to use the 80x87. You won't gain anything if your application doesn't support 80x87 instructions.

For example, when BASICA was released, no one anticipated a math co-processor. So BASICA continues to process floating decimal point operations itself whether you have an 80x87 or not. However, most current languages use the 80x87 co-processor.

A problem appears when you write programs using the set of 80x86 instructions if you use the IBM Macro Assembler. It doesn't have the mnemonics for 80x87 instructions. To use them, you must form instructions using operation codes WAIT and ESC. The best way to do it is to use a set of macro instructions which let you define the instructions of the 80x87. We'll discuss macro instructions later.

# 29. Interrupts

Interrupts are an important part of 80x86 operations. An *interrupt* is a signal from a peripheral device or a request from a program to perform a specific function. When an interrupt occurs, the current program is temporarily suspended and an *interrupt routine* begins execution to handle the condition that caused the interrupt.

The interrupt process is essential in any data processing system. As you'll see, it is also essential in the PC. This process lets the input/output devices communicate with the 80x86. It's a subject that we'll develop in detail because managing interrupts comes completely within the framework of programming in assembly language.

Peripherals generally cause interrupts. These are called *hardware interrupts*. For example, the keyboard sends an interrupt signal each time that you press a key. The keyboard interrupt tells the 80x86 that it has to temporarily suspend its current activity and read the character corresponding to the key which was just pressed. The suspended program then continues after completion of the interrupt routine.

Two of the 80x86's 40 pins are interrupt lines that let the peripherals call the 80x86. These two pins are so important as register pointers that they're called INTR (Input Request) and NMI (non-maskable interrupt).

At the end of each instruction, the 80x86 verifies whether this signal is on the pin. If it is, then the 80x86 executes a subroutine to call the program intended to deal with the needs of the peripheral that's calling. These programs are interrupt functions or call routines. In the event that the 80x86 is busy with a necessary job that it cannot interrupt, an interrupt pointer reset pointer is used so the 80x86 doesn't have to answer the call.

The NMI pin announces calls that won't wait, for example when a memory chip breaks down. It's an INTR that cannot be "masked". What good is it to continue if a part of memory suddenly fails? Some systems (but not the PC) have a NMI control in their electrical supply. So any lack or alteration on the sector is indicated to the processor so it interrupts everything, closes the files in progress and stops.

# 29.1   Interrupt "Masks"

*Interrupt masks* are bits which let the programmer determine what conditions will produce an interrupt and which will be managed in other ways. These bits are called interrupt masks because you can use them to mask, or to prevent, the call of an interrupt.

Start SIM and press <I> to send a signal to the INTR pin. Press <I> again and the signal is cleared. Load the INT.DEM file:

```
—LOAD INT DEMO <Enter>
```

to read the routine.

```
STI

ADD      AX, BX

ADD      BX, CX

JMP      0101

BRK

BRK

BRK

PUSH     AX          (store AX)

MOV      AX, [200]   (load "rhythm box" counting)

INC      AX          (increment)

MOV      [200], AX   (new safety)

POP      AX          (restore AX)

IRET                 (return to the interrupt program)
```

INT.DEM consists of two programs.

The first program is a simple loop which constantly adds the same registers. Beginning with a "PUSH AX" we have a program that manages interrupts. We're going to interrupt the loop in order to make SIM execute the program code.

Before executing this routine, you must define the type of interrupt that we want to start (with a value from 0 to 255) by pressing the <I> key. To do this we use the SIM "INTR" command. We'll use a weak interrupt value in order to avoid all conflict with a significant value that might be stored in low memory (especially those that could break down the system if they were modified). Let's take interrupt 60h.

```
—INTR 60 <Enter>
```

Use DSTAT to make sure that the value of the interrupt is indeed 60h:

```
—DSTAT <Enter>
```

Next, we have to put the correct values in the 60h interrupt vector that begins at address 60h * 4 of segment 0000, that is, at address 0000:180. Specify the interrupt routine. First give the offset:

```
—E 0:180 0A 01 <Enter>
```

Next enter the segment at memory location 182h. Be very careful to type it using LSB,MSB notation (least significant bit,most significant bit). For example, if ssss gives 1823h on your computer, do this:

```
—E 0:182 23 18 <Enter>
```

Put SIM in STEP=3:

```
— STEP 3 <Enter>
```

and simulate several hundred instructions with:

```
—SIM 300 <Enter>
```

**Note:**     Press the <Spacebar> when necessary.

Press the <I> key to call an interrupt. If the interrupts are set (pointer established), after execution of the present instruction the simulator makes a successive PUSH of FL, CS and IP in the stack. Then it reads the type of interrupt. This is managed according to the INTR command of the simulator. In this example we've called interrupt 60h.

The 80x86 automatically gets <I> back from the keyboard buffer during the response process to the interrupt thereby preventing any other interrupt from being prompted by a new interrupt, unless we expressly want it. For example, the keyboard interrupt routine can interrupt a printer routine. Press the <I> key again to clear the interrupt.

SIM determines the address of the printer routine by multiplying the type of interrupt by 4 and then loading CS:IP from the offset address of the newly created 0000 segment. At the end we're in the printer routine program at ssss:010A. In this example, the printer routine is near the interrupt program but often in reality this is not the case. Most routines are in BIOS or high memory.

This interrupt routine is a simple software timer. Let's imagine a quartz oscillator outside the 80x86 managing an interrupt 70 times per second. If the interrupt routine (in the "background") increments a 16-bit memory location with each interrupt, we have indeed created a software timer pulsating every tenth of a second. Every program, whether it's a main program or in the background, can "tell the time" by reading the value at address 200h.

All interrupt routines must end with an IRET instruction. IRET terminates the execution of an interrupt routine and then continues the execution of the program at the location following the interruption. After erasing CS:IP from the stack, it also erases the pointers. When the pointers are erased, interrupts are automatically reset.

## 29.1.1    Multitasking Work

Interrupts let a single processor work as though it processed several programs simultaneously. It does this by moving between the programs several times a second.

In this case, it's absolutely essential to save carefully and then restore each register of the interrupted program and even to make sure that all the tasks are executed in definite memory locations. Of course, this form of multitasking reduces the execution speed. Most of the time, however, the processor only waits instruction. So a rather powerful processor can simultaneously process hundreds of independent tasks.

# 29.2 Non-Maskable Interrupts

A *non-maskable interrupt* cannot be disabled by the STI instruction. The SIM "N" instruction can call a non-maskable interrupt.

| N                    instruction |

The N instruction produces a result similar to INTR except that here you cannot "mask", or hide, the interrupt and it's a matter in all cases of interrupt 2. Unless you change interrupt 2, you will only get the execution of a DOS routine. Try using the instruction. As soon as SIM reacts press <N> again for the interrupt (otherwise you'll produce a series of useless interrupts).

## 29.2.1  Processing a keystroke

Since your PC keyboard is controlled by interrupts, software and applications do not verify what keys are pressed. When you press a key, the PC immediately "listens" and the keyboard identifies the key and a signal is generated on the INTR pin of the 80x86.

After finishing the task in progress, the 80x86 calls the appropriate interrupt routine to read and enter the code of the key in a buffer. After that, the 80x86 returns to its previous tasks. Therefore, even the interrupted program isn't aware of the interruption much less that an ASCII value has just been placed in a keyboard buffer.

Programs requiring keyboard input read this buffer (which is in the BIOS memory at 40:0) rather than the keyboard itself.

Let's look at this process in more detail. The Intel 8259 (which controls programmable interrupts) generates the INTR signal. The 8259 also furnishes the number identifying the type of interrupt. This is an important bit of information so the 80x86 "jumps" to the "key has just been struck" routine rather than to "character arriving at series output," or "finished reading disk," etc.

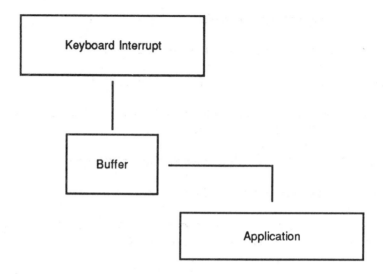

This is what happens when you press the <\> (backslash) key :

1.      <\> key is pressed.

2.      The 80x86 identifies the keystroke and produces a code unique to that key. (In this case <\>= code 43h.)

3.      Keyboard sends 43h to E/S port 60h.

4.      Signal generated on the 8259 interrupt controller input 1 (we'll discuss this in the next section).

5.      The 8259 interrupt controller verifies that a priority interrupt isn't active. If so, it begins verifying again until the priority interrupt is cleared.

6.      When cleared, the 8259 generates an INTR.

7.      The processor suspends the processing in progress.

8.      The processor recognizes this interrupt (unless the interrupts are cleared, in which case nothing happens).

9.      The processor enters the CS and IP pointers in the stack.

10.     The processor requests information from the 8259 as to which peripheral caused the interrupt.

11.     The 8259 responds with peripheral #9.

12.     The processor reads the interrupt routine address in vector 9.

13.     Keyboard routine reads the number of the key on the E/S port.

14.     Keyboard routine translates the number of the key into ASCII characters according to the code and <Ctrl>, <Alt> and <Shift> keys.

15.     Keyboard routine places the ASCII character in the keyboard buffer.

16.     Keyboard routine informs the 8259 that it is done.

17.     Interrupt routine executes the IRET instruction to return control to the suspended program and clears the pointers as well as IP and CS of the stack.

This process is repeated every time that you press a key.

Although the 80x86 is fast, it's possible to lose characters when the keyboard buffer overflows. "Overflows" means that you try to put in more characters than the buffer can contain and occurs when you fill the buffer faster than your application uses or "reads" the contents. When the program interrupt determines the buffer is full, it sends a warning beep. Any keys you press after the warning tone are lost since the interrupt program is not able to load it in the buffer.

# 29.3 The 8259 Interrupt Controller

We cannot discuss interrupts without discussing the 8259 because it controls programmable interrupts. Each of the five peripherals capable of generating interrupts (timer, keyboard, disk controller, parallel interface and serial interface) is connected to one of the eight inputs of the 8259. Only one output connects the 8259 to the INTR pin of the 80x86.

Interrupts 08H to OFH are generated by the 8259 interrupt controller. This chip receives all interrupt demands within the system first. It determines the *priority* in which multiple interrupt requests must be executed. The interrupt with the highest priority passes through the INTR line to the CPU.

Priority lets you deal with the case where two peripherals (a keyboard and a disk, for example) simultaneously request an interrupt. Since the very idea of interrupts is to allow peripherals access the 80x86 at the same time they need it, we have to have a coherent system to decide who has the priority and make certain that everyone else will be served later on.

A maximum of eight interrupt sources (devices) can be connected to the 8259. Each device is assigned a different priority. The IBM-AT has two 8259 interrupt controllers so it can control a maximum of 16 interrupts.

The 8259 is *programmable* because the 80x86 can control the responses of the 8259 by using OUT instructions.

The 8259 timer chip receives 1,192,180 signals every second from the oscillating quartz crystal. After 65,536 of these signals, it triggers a call of interrupt 8 which is transmitted by the 8259 to the CPU. The frequency of this call is separate from the system clock, this interrupt is used for timekeeping. BIOS points the interrupt vector of this interrupt to its own routine (called 18.2 times per second). A time counter increments every second and disables the disk drive motor if disk access hasn't occurred within a certain time period.

# 29.4   The Timer Interrupt

It's possible to make keyboard and timer interrupts visible by placing the stack in video memory. If we type GOTO to a program at the moment when SS:SP points to the video memory, the PUSHes caused by the timer and keyboard interrupts appear as characters.

First load SS:SP with the address of the last character position of the first display line. This will be either B000:9E if you have a monochrome monitor or B800:9E if you have a color monitor.

Next, write an infinite loop.

```
0100    STI            (sets interrupt flag [IF])

0101    INC  AX

0102    INC  DX

0103    JMP  0101
```

Start the program with GO. Press any key to view a rapid series of stack manipulations as soon as you press the key. Now the only way to exit the program is with the <Ctrl><Alt><Del> key combination.

## 29.5   The TRAP Bit

The TRAP bit in the flag register is important when discussing interrupts. When the TRAP bit is set to 1 in the flag register it simulates a hardware interrupt. This interrupt allows the user to trace the execution of every instruction to determine changes in register contents or the instructions executed.

Instead of waiting for the 8259 to provide it with an interrupt type number, the 80x86 automatically knows when it encounters a type 1 interrupt. So after executing PUSHes for FL, IP and CS, the processor enters interrupt 1 in CS:IP at address 00004-00007.

Since interrupt 1 is rarely executed in application programs, DOS sets the vector of interrupt 1 to an IRET instruction. If a program accidentally sets the TRAP bit, it only slows the execution of the program. Therefore, interrupt 1 is most useful in utility programs such as DEBUG which allow program execution in *trace mode* (execution of each instruction in slow mode).

It's occasionally difficult to set the TRAP bit because there is no "STT" (Set Trap flag) instruction. The following is one way to set the TRAP bit:

```
PUSHF

MOV     BP,SP

OR      [BP],100H

POPF                    (remove flags from stack)
```

The problem is that TRAP bit is now set but the processor jumps to the next instruction. Unfortunately, this isn't one the user gave it but one from Debugger. What we need to use for the TRAP bit flag (TF) to simulate a program is an instruction able to clear the pointers and change IP and CS so they point to the user's program.

Let's try "POP CS:IP" or Pop the Flags. We've just seen IRET (return from interrupt). Remember that IRET does two things at a time. Here's a summary of what you can do to use the TRAP bit flag in a useful way of step by step execution.

First, place the five following words at address SS:SP of the user program, on what will be the true stack when we load the true SS and SP registers of the 80x86 in the user's SS:SP values (you therefore save a part of the user registers):

```
FL   (with TF set)

CS

IP

DS

SI
```

Next we load the user registers, except those already in the stack, into the processor. The reason why we have placed DS and SI on the stack is simple. We can then use them to load the other registers.

Now we have to subtract "10" from SP (SP = SP - 2 bytes) in order to place SI on top of the stack. After clearing the SI and DS registers, we have a processor containing only user program registers with the one exception of CS:IP (we're still executing our code in SIM and not in the processors) and its pointers (including a dangerously activated TF flag). However, the stack conditions are ready for an IRET instruction.

The TF flag only acts after the instruction following IRET, particularly after a user program instruction. The TF flag passes control to the address that interrupt vector 1 points to. This is where we're waiting with a program to carefully save the values if its registers (CS, IP and FL) are already in the stack. These registers will be replaced with those called by DEBUG. After the values that the user registers contain are displayed, the CPU appears to stop after it executes each instruction.

You can observe this using SIM. Open a window to see the five words right above the present SS:SP value. Every time that SIM executes a GO command or a SKIP (which uses similar processes to exchange registers), the contents of SI, DI, IP, CS and FL are entered in these five words in memory.

Most utility programs such as DEBUG don't use this TRAP bit as an example because they use it themselves. To see this for yourself, do a Dump of DEBUG. You won't be able to read your screen and there is nothing to confirm that the TRAP bit exists.

```
AX=0000 BX=0000 CX=0000 DX=0000 SP=FFFE BP=0000 SI=0000

DI=0000

DS=253A ES=253A SS=253A CS=253A IP=0100 NV UP PL NA PO NC
```

Rather than providing the values of each of these flags, DEBUG only provides 2-letter mnemonic codes:

| Flag | Clear | | Set | |
|------|------|------|-----|-----|
| Overflow | NV | (no overflow) | OV | (overflow) |
| Direction | UP | (direction up) | DN | (down) |
| Interrupt | DI | (disable interrupt) | EI | (enable interrupt) |
| Sign | PL | (plus) | NG | (negative) |
| Zero | NZ | (not zero) | ZR | (zero) |
| Aux. Carry | NA | (not aux. carry) | AC | (aux. carry) |
| Parity | PO | (parity odd) | PE | (parity even) |
| Carry | NC | (not carry) | CY | (carry) |

| **T** | **trace command** |
|---|---|

Besides simulation, SIM can do a step by step TRAP bit. The Trace command (T) uses the TRAP bit in the 80x86 to execute a program step by step like DEBUG would. The final result of a trace is identical to that of a SIM execution.

# 29.6   Error In The 8088

In this section we'll discuss a rather subtle problem in the way some 8088 processors handle interrupts. In certain cases, the 8088 can store bytes into RAM without warning or it may attempt to store an interrupt return address in ROM. A system crash occurs when the routine attempts to return control to the calling program.

For example, suppose we're executing a program. Every keystroke from the keyboard is accompanied by a type 9 interrupt. More than a thousand timer interrupts (type 8) occur every minute. Suppose a program that we've just loaded creates a new stack during its initialization. Establishing a new stack means giving new values to SP and perhaps even to SS.

```
Before (former stack):  SS:SP = 1000:0100

              MOV   AX,2000

              MOV   SS,AX

              MOV   SP,FF00

After (new stack):  SS:SP = 2000:FF00
```

Let's assume that the timer interrupt points right after our MOV SS but before the MOV SP. The stack at this very moment is at 2000:100 which is a memory location that could be a part of an application or a part of DOS. The system randomly enters three words at 2000:FA-FF. After the interrupt, the 8088 turns control back to the program and everything appears quite normal. But six memory bytes have just been lost.

The solution, according to Intel, is to clear the interrupts for any instruction after a MOV to a segment register.

A MOV instruction to any segment register forces the 8088 to disregard interrupts as long as an instruction hasn't been executed. Unfortunately, this solution won't work if you modify a stack by first moving the stack pointer.

You can quickly determine if the 8088 processor in your computer has this problem. The following routine tests your 8088 by using the SIM "T" command. First type these three lines to create a test routine:

```
0100    MOV   SS,AX

0102    MOV   SP,BX

0104    BRK
```

Now let's go through this step by step:

```
—T <Enter>
```

If CS:IP comes back while pointing to BRK at 104h, instead of MOV SP,BX at 102h, you have a corrected 8088 processor. The MOV SP,BX instruction seems to have been jumped because the TF flag interrupt cannot take place before a complete instruction has been executed after the MOV to a segment register. In reality, MOV SP,BX has indeed been carried out.

If you have an earlier version of the 8088 processor, you see the execution of the instruction at 0102h. Any program will work safely with the older 8088. You have to take one precaution and clear the interrupts during an operation on the stack:

```
CLI                  (clear the interrupts)

MOV   SS,AX          (establish new stack)

MOV   SP,BX

STI                  (reactivate the interrupts)
```

## 29.6.1    Does the 8088 modify SIM?

Now "simulate" this routine. Try to interrupt the MOV to a segment register. SIM simulates the modified version of the 8088 and so it only reacts after execution of a complete instruction.

# 29.7   Software Interrupts

A *software interrupt* is an interrupt or interrupt request called by a program using the INT instruction. Each of the 256 existing interrupts can be called using the INT instruction.

The INT instruction includes the number of the interrupt to be signalled. For example, the instruction to call interrupt 5 (for a screen dump) appears as INT 5. Let's review this CALL format.

An indirect call transfers control to the effective address. For example, after saving IP and CS, CALL FAR[SI] transfers the word at DS:SI to the IP and transfers the word at DS:SI+2 to the CS register, and then makes a jump to CS:IP (CS=SI+2, IP=SI). The INT instruction does something similar but here the pointers also go onto the stack and use an IRET, instead of a RET, to come back.

```
INT type specified

1 1 0 0 1 1 0 1     type #
```

Let's consider the INT 17 instruction. After reading and decoding the operation code, the processor reads the number of the kind of interrupt. Beginning at this stage everything takes place like it would for a hardware interrupt. The next stage is the first instruction of the routine located at the address specified by the 17h interrupt vector.

In a PC, the software interrupt is essentially used to execute a BIOS or DOS function. We'll see that more in detail in the next chapter.

# 29.8 Special Interrupts

### Interrupt 3 (breakpoint)

While other interrupts are called with a two-byte instruction, interrupt 3 is called by a one-byte instruction CCH. This is another instruction reserved for writing debugging programs. In assembly it's known as:

```
INT 3
```

Execution of the CCH operation code forces the processor to do a type 3 interrupt. You can use INT 3 when you want to execute a program to a certain instruction and then stop and display the current register contents.

For example, by using the SIM GO command combined with a break (let's say G 110), here's what happens:

SIM replaces the byte located at CS:110 with a CCH after first saving the contents of CS:110 so it can later replace it in CS:110. Then SIM turns control over to your program by placing the contents of the simulator registers in those of the true 80x86. When your program encounters the INT 3 that we put in CS:110 (or any other INT 3), SIM takes over control. We planned to have interrupt vector number 3 point to a SIM address.

### Interrupt 4 (INTO)

INTO (INTerrupt on Overflow) is a one-byte instruction that causes a interrupt 4 every time that the overflow pointer is positioned, which is very useful for processing signed numbers.

The call occurs when the overflow bit in the flag register is set during the execution of the INTO instruction. This may occur during math operations (such as with the MUL instruction) that cannot be represented by within a specific number of bits.

### Interrupt table

The following table shows the significance of BIOS and DOS interrupts in the control and use of the PC:

| Interrupt | Purpose |
|-----------|---------|
| 00 | Division by zero |
| 01 | TRAP bit (single step) |
| 02 | NMI (Error in RAM chip) |
| 03 | Breakpoint (CCH) |
| 04 | Numeric Overflow |
| 05 | Hardcopy |
| 06 | Reserved/Unknown instruction *(80286)* |
| 07 | Reserved |
| 08 | Timer |
| 09 | Keyboard |
| 0A | Reserved/2nd 8259 *(AT)* |
| 0B | Serial interface 1 |
| 0C | Serial interface 2 |
| 0D | Hard disk |
| 0E | Disk drive |
| 0F | Printer |
| 10 | Video functions (BIOS) |
| 11 | Determine configuration (BIOS) |
| 12 | Determine RAM storage size (BIOS) |
| 13 | Diskette/Hard drive functions (BIOS) |
| 14 | Access to serial interface (BIOS) |
| 15 | Cassette/enhanced functions (BIOS) |
| 16 | Keyboard sensing (BIOS) |
| 17 | Access to parallel printer (BIOS) |
| 18 | Call of ROM-BASIC (BIOS) |
| 19 | BIOS system boot of <Ctrl><Alt><Del> |
| 1A | BIOS Read time and date (BIOS) |
| 1B | Break key not activated (BIOS) |
| 1C | Called after every INT 08 (BIOS) |
| 1D | Address of the video parameter table (BIOS) |
| 1F | Address of the character bit pattern (BIOS) |
| 20 | Terminate program (DOS) |
| 21 | Call DOS function |
| 22 | Address of DOS / end of program routine |
| 23 | Address of DOS / <Ctrl><Break> routine |
| 24 | Address of DOS error routine (DOS) |
| 25 | Read diskette/hard drive (DOS) |
| 26 | Write diskette/hard drive (DOS) |
| 27 | DOS end program and remain resident |
| 28-3F | Reserved (DOS) |

Interrupts 0 to 4 have the same function in every 80x86 computer. Interrupts 8 to F are inputs of the 8259 interrupt controller.

## 29.9   Starting the Reset Cycle

The control pin called the Reset determines what values are in the registers when you switch on your PC.

### 29.9.1   Reset

The only way to send a signal to the Reset pin is to turn on the computer. Only a few milliseconds after you switch it on, the AC current sets the Reset signal. The same Reset signal is installed each IC, from the 80x86 to the most simple.

When the 80x86 receives a Reset signal, the pointers are put at zero, which clears the interrupts and the TF flag. The DS, ES, SS and IP registers are cleared. The value FFFFh is placed in the CS register.

That's why the processor has to read and execute the instruction at address FFFF:0000. If you disassemble this address in high ROM, you'll find a long JUMP to the beginning of the BIOS of your system (F000:E05B on our IBM).

This routine starts a long series of tests and beginning tasks which go from the simple test of the processor (a number is sent into all the registers to verify that they are functioning properly) to determining the configuration of the system and memory size.

Except for memory tests which are particularly long, this routine only takes a few seconds. Finally, the routine attempts to place the "Boot" area of the A: disk drive into RAM to give control to this disk drive.

The routine for starting as well as the initial jump to F000:FFF0 must be in ROM. When you switch on the computer, the contents of the RAM is only gibberish. That's why you always find a small amount of ROM at the top of the 80x86 memory block.

Note:      The reset caused by the <Ctrl><Alt><Del> keys has absolutely nothing to do with the 80x86 Reset pin. A reset from the keyboard is the result of a BIOS keyboard routine. When a bad program happens to clear the interrupt mechanism of the keyboard (for example, by affecting interrupt 9 or by entering into an infinite loop with cleared interrupts), any attempt to reset from the keyboard (warm start) will not work.

# 29.10 Chapter Exercises

1)     What's an interrupt?

2)     Interrupt 16h, function 2 (AH=2) will return the keyboard status in AL. Bits 5 and 6 of AL represent the status of the <NumLock> key and <CapsLock> respectively (1=ON). How could we test the status of the <NumLock> key?

# 30. DOS

By itself the PC cannot do too much for you because on its own it's capable only of asking for a DOS disk. You've read and heard a lot of information concerning DOS and might be wondering just what DOS means. DOS is acronym for Disk Operating System and is the foundation for your communication with the PC.

DOS (also called PC-DOS, MS-DOS and other forms of DOS) is a rather complex set of programs in 80x86 assembly language that give us a certain control over our computers.

DOS has two parts:

- It's a set of external routines (DISKCOPY, FORMAT, CHKDSK) executing useful disk and file management functions.

- DOS is actually a program located in memory every time you switch on your PC. It's in fact the definition of a "boot" that you load DOS and start it.

This second part is what we'll discuss in this chapter. Most users only know the user-interface of DOS or the part of DOS which loads and executes programs. However, DOS does more than simply loading and executing programs. It's also a software buffer between applications and hardware.

| Software and Programs | DOS | Hardware |
|---|---|---|

DOS requires a large number of different routines (called *functions*) to accomplish its tasks. All of these functions are available to both the user and to DOS.

# 30.1 Calling a DOS Routine

You call a DOS routine by loading the number of the function that you want to execute in AH (and in other registers as well according to the kind of call) then by executing a software interrupt 21h (INT 21).

For example, use DOS function number 2Ah to determine the date.

Let's see what the DOS technical reference manual tells us about this function:

    2A to get the date

Return the date to CX:DX. Use CX for the year (1990-????), DH for the month (1=Jan, 2=Feb, etc.) and DL for the day.

To read the date system, this following program works:

```
GETDATE

MOV     AH,2A

INT     21

BRK
```

When DOS completes the requested function and returns to your program (following INT 21) the CX and DX registers contain the date. Using a DOS function is an important exception to the rule that says that a programmer in assembly language must know all the details. We don't know and we don't really pay any attention to how DOS determines the date.

Assemble and execute the two instructions of the GETDATE program. Use the SKIP command to jump the INT 21 mysteries.

When CS:IP points to an interrupt, an intersegment call, or a string, then SKIP puts a breakpoint right after the instruction in progress if this instruction is INT 21. Then:

    -SKIP TVC turns control back to 104h

Values returned in CX and DX represent the date. For example, let's suppose that CX:DX returns with "07C7:010F" as a value. This gives 7C7h as the year and the first month, 15th day (F) or January 15, 1991.

If you're curious, simulate a call of a DOS function at the place of the SKIP. After PUSHing all your registers in the stack, you see DOS fall into an "internal" stack. Try to execute some tests on the function numbers (note that they might be too large) and if you remain long enough you see DOS turn control over to a BIOS routine which reads the addresses of the clock.

Fortunately you don't have to trace the function each time that you call back your program.

DOS is used on all 80x86 computers and any program that uses DOS functions will work without any modification on each of them. Programs structured in this way see the same DOS regardless of the computer they're working on whether it's an IBM PC or compatible. The routines themselves may be different but results from the DOS functions are consistent.

# 30.2 The I/O Screen

One criticism of the DOS routines is the slowness at which characters are displayed on the screen. That's why quite often programmers write their own character display routines which are faster than those in DOS.

Load the CHARIO.DEM by typing:

```
-LOAD CHARIO.dem <Enter>
```

This demo lets you view the slow performance of DOS functions compared to user-defined screen routines. After the program has loaded, examine the listing in the Disassembly Area.

First, call the DOS function 2000 times in a loop. Next, the character in DL (02h) is displayed normally. The character backspace moves the cursor one place to the left and replaces it with a blank space and stops.

Then, CHARIO.DEM enters "happy faces" 2000 times on the screen with a string repetition prefix.

Divide this program into two parts. First, enter a breakpoint after the MOV AX,B000 instruction. If your computer has a graphic color adaptor, change this to MOV AX,B800. Then run the program. On our computer, DOS needs several seconds to fill the screen with characters. Now execute CHARIO.DEM from BRK. You will notice that it's very fast.

# 30.3 DOS Programs

In this section we'll discuss how DOS loads and executes programs, what the .COM or .EXE extension indicate and the difference between a .COM and an .EXE file.

COM    represents "compiled" or "command" programs. These are programs which are translated and compiled.

EXE    represents executable programs. These programs can use the entire MS-DOS memory area and can be located anywhere in memory.

BAT    represents batch files and refer to multiple MS-DOS commands that are stacked together.

If you type the following DOS command:

```
A>CHKDSK <Enter>
```

DOS first searches for files CHKDSK.COM, CHKDSK.EXE or CHKDSK.BAT in that order.

Let's suppose that it finds CHKDSK.COM. The bytes that make up this program are read from the disk using the same I/O disk function calls as any other program. These are loaded word by word into the memory beginning at the top of DOS in the part called *user area* or the address of the area for application programs.

In reality, they are loaded 100h bytes higher. The first 100h program segment bytes are reserved for the program just about to be executed and make up the Program Segment Prefix (PSP). The PSP is an area reserved for the programmer. Useful data can be entered there such as a program protection routine.

Next the processor turns control over to the first byte of CHKDSK.COM by a jump to offset 100h in the program segment.

At the very instant of this first jump to 100h, all the segment registers contain the address of the program segment. SP can contain any value as long as SS:SP doesn't point outside of the RAM.

When CHKDSK finishes, it turns control back to DOS by a standard end of program mechanism. Then DOS displays its prompt.

The LOAD command in SIM does more than move bytes from the disk to the memory. It simulates DOS itself by loading .EXE and .COM files in memory. It also constructs the program segment prefix.

DOS is divided into a resident part and an external part which could be overridden by other programs. Here's how it works:

When a program such as CHKDSK is executed, the DOS routines which display the DOS prompt on the screen, analyze keystrokes, process batch files (.BAT) and so forth are actually useless. The DOS prompt is "A:>" (the A is replaced by the current disk drive). We currently only need the part of DOS which is concerned with function calls.

DOS includes command processing routines in the COMMAND.COM file. These routines places it in the high memory (RAM) when the system is started. The COMMAND.COM is active when the DOS prompt appears on the screen. It executes your commands or displays an error message to the DOS commands that you're typing on the keyboard.

When a program doesn't require a large amount of RAM it works even better. COMMAND.COM will then remain high in memory. But if the space it's occupying is needed, the program that you're going to load in memory assumes this location and overwrites COMMAND.COM.

When execution of the program has ended, the resident part of DOS verifies the area where COMMAND.COM should be. If it finds anything other than COMMAND.COM there, it reloads COMMAND.COM in this area.

Check it out for yourself. From SIM, load a byte in high RAM and then exit SIM. You'll hear the disk drive because the COMMAND.COM load operation is in progress. The DOS control concerning the presence of COMMAND.COM in memory is so precise that you only need to modify a single byte so that DOS reloads the file in memory.

COMMAND.COM is the only component of DOS that appears in the disk directory. The resident part of DOS put in memory at the moment DOS is loaded (and which "resides" there until you switch off the computer) also consists of two parts called IBMBIOS.COM and IBMDOS.COM.

Of course, these files are on the diskette but with a special "hidden files" status which means that the DIR command doesn't read them or more precisely doesn't "see" them.

# 30.4 .EXE Files

.EXE programs have an advantage over .COM programs because they're not limited to a maximum 64K for code and data. An .EXE program contains separate segments for code, data and stack which you can organize into any sequence. Unlike a .COM program, an .EXE program loads into memory from disk and undergoes processing by the EXEC function and then finally begins execution.

The disadvantage for .EXE programs is that they have a more complex internal structure than .COM files. The .EXE program is composed of a LINK program (header) and loader. The loader constitutes the largest part of the file and consists of a sequence of bytes.

The LOAD program places a data structure at the beginning of every .EXE file containing, among other data, the address of all segments. It contains the addresses of all memory locations in which the segment address of a certain segment is stored during program execution.

Unlike .COM files, .EXE programs are not limited to loading at a specific memory location. They can be loaded into any desired location in memory as long as the memory is a multiple of 16.

The LOAD program also includes a "relocation" table used to modify addresses in the executable module according to the address segment where the program is at the moment it's started. Addresses modified during this "relocation" process, which takes place when file .EXE is loaded, cannot be modified later on simply because this relocation information then disappears. That's why SIM doesn't even attempt to save an .EXE file.

The EXE loader attempts to reserve the maximum number of paragraphs by determining the total program size based on the number of the individual segments of the .EXE program. If this is not possible, the loader attempts to reserve the remaining memory which must be at least as large as the number of *paragraphs* (1-6 bytes).

Note:     You can ensure compatibility with future DOS versions, an EXE program should terminate by calling interrupt 21H function 4CH.

# 30.5  BIOS

BIOS is an acronym for *Basic Input Output System*. It's a program permanently stored in ROM of your PC and is available without an operating system disk. For example, it performs the internal self test of the computer (counting up the memory available, and testing for connected peripherals such as disk drives). It also triggers the search for the operating system (MS-DOS) on the disk in the drive.

BIOS is located in 8K of ROM addressable at F000:E000. BIOS routines execute the following functions:

- Auto-test and loading DOS

- Software logistics for:

  communication port

  keyboard

  floppy

  parallel printer

  video display

- Configuration analysis system

- Controlling other functions such as time and date and screen display.

## 30.5.1    What does BIOS do that DOS cannot?

Remember that DOS operating systems work on any series of compatibles. Some of these computers are almost identical to the IBM PC while others are so different that they use custom terminals and 8-inch diskettes. The one item that compatibles always have in common with the IBM PC is the operating system and a processor from the 80x86 family.

The BIOS routines are standardized. This lets you develop programs on one particular PC and have the program run on another compatible PC. Neither the hardware or BIOS need to be completely compatible.

DOS itself calls on BIOS routines. Calling DOS function 2 (character display) always ends by calling a BIOS routine to finally display the character. The only reason that DOS displays so slowly is that it has to take several detours.

For example, let's take the BIOS video display routines. Along with being slow, the DOS functions for the video display are extremely limited. At the most, all you can do is send a character to the screen. The following is a list of what you cannot do with DOS system calls:

• Modify the form of the cursor.

• Selectively making different parts of the screen file by initializing the display (for example, having a mono card and a CGA card set at the same time).

• Executing bit map graphics.

However, BIOS screen output functions are more versatile and powerful. You should refer to *PC System Programming* by Abacus for detailed information on BIOS and BIOS functions. A complete BIOS assembly source listing is given in the IBM Technical Reference Manual. This manual is worth its price just for you to get this listing.

Now load BIOS.DEM file by typing:

```
-LOAD BIOS.DEM <Enter>
```

The first BIOS call sends a character to the printer. The second causes a display area to file. Use the SKIP command to execute high-speed BIOS calls.

## 30.6  Chapter Exercises

1)  Modify your answer of question #2 in Section 29.10 to read the status of the keyboard and display an "N" if the <NumLock> key is on and a "C" if the <CapsLock> key is on.

# 31. Additional Instructions

In this chapter we'll discuss several little known yet useful instructions and prefixes for 80x86 assembly language programming. We'll also discuss a few instructions and prefixes you should avoid using.

## 31.1    NOP (No Operation Instruction)

In this section we'll discuss one instruction which does absolutely nothing; it doesn't point to any pointers, doesn't change any register and doesn't modify the memory. This is the NOP (No Operation, or operation code 90h) instruction. The only result after a NOP execution is that the instruction counter (IP) is incremented to the next instruction.

So why use such an instruction? NOP is used to create a pause in a loop and even more important, to "hold" space in a program (a debugging technique).

Here's a debugging routine:

```
ssss:0100    E8FD0E    CALL    1000
ssss:0103    EAFA1E    CALL    2000
ssss:0106    EAF72E    CALL    3000
```

Once you've determined that the second subroutine (CALL 2000) doesn't work, you can quickly test the third subroutine by inserting a series of NOP instructions between the first and third subroutine:

```
ssss:0100    E8FD0E    CALL    1000
ssss:0103    90        NOP
ssss:0104    90        NOP
ssss:0105    90        NOP
ssss:0106    EAF72E    CALL    3000
```

When we execute this routine, we move directly from the subroutine at 1000h to the subroutine at 3000h. Notice that there is a large difference between NOP (operation code 90h) and undefined operation codes (F6h and 8Ch, for example). The 80x86 will do nothing if it encounters these op-codes.

### 31.1.1    NOP is an "XCHG AX,AX" instruction

While we were writing SIM we realized that NOP is actually an "XCHG AX,AX" instruction. If you force the processor to load and execute a 90h operation code, NOP merely exchanges the AX registers. And the result, of course, is a loss of time.

The loss of time generated by NOP leads us to talk about timing loops. You may consider that one of the reasons for writing in assembly language is for the fast execution speed. However, sometimes it's useful to know the execution time of a given instruction. The unit of measure of time for the 80x86 is the instruction cycle.

For a standard IBM PC with an 8080 processor, this cycle represents 0.210 microseconds (approximately 1/5th of a millionth of a second). Many instructions require one or two cycles for execution. But in general, the number of cycles required for execution increases as the number of read/writes increase.

For example, INC BL requires 3 cycles, INC BPTR requires 20 cycles and INC BPTR ES:[SI+BP+F000] requires 29 cycles. This should suggest to you that when speed is a critical element, enter your important variables in registers.

Multiplication and division instructions are among the slowest. They require up to 275 cycles for execution. However, this high number of cycles is for another reason. The 80x86 cannot directly execute multiplication and division operations. Instead, the 80x86 uses an internal program which breaks the problem down into a series of additions and subtractions.

SIM doesn't show these difficulties. Its operations occur from a simple addition or subtraction macro. You should consider the slow speeds of these operations when you write your own programs. If you can bypass them by using a more efficient algorithm, do so.

# 31.2   Combining Prefixes

## 31.2.1    LOCK prefix

This is the last of the three prefixes of the 80x86. It's at the same time the most general prefix and, in the PC, the most useless. When you enter the LOCK prefix (operation code F0h) in front of an instruction, the processor pin with the same name is set during the whole operation. It's intended for multiprocessor environment programming in which several 80x86s must share the same memory space.

If you put the LOCK prefix before a memory referencing instruction, no other processor can access the memory during the execution of that instruction.

Like any other prefix, you can use LOCK without danger even when it's not necessary (for example, when you put a LOCK in an instruction that doesn't address the memory).

You can also combine the three prefixes. For example, by combining the following four bytes, you can modify the performance of the base function MOVSB (move string byte-by-byte):

```
F4     2E:    F2     A4
LOCK   CS:    REP    MOVSB
```

LOCK sends a signal to the LOCK pin for the duration of the instruction. The segment override modifies the DS source segment to CS. Remember that you cannot use ES as destination segment in base functions. REP activates the looping properties of MOVSB in the normal way.

Notice that you're free to repeat a prefix as many times as you want in an instruction. The 80x86 will take an instruction without caring about how many prefixes you give it.

## 31.2.2    Prefix Order

The order for placing prefixes depends on the interrupt. If an interrupt intervenes during execution of an instruction then the order for placing prefixes is important but if an interrupt doesn't intervene then the order is not important.

Here's a 3-byte instruction which moves a string with the CS register as the source segment.

```
2E     F2     A4
CS:    REP    MOVSB
```

However, if an interrupt intervenes (which is almost inevitable since this kind of repetition easily takes a full second to execute and that's more than enough time for a timer interrupt to point), the address put onto the stack is the one that precedes the instruction itself. In the case of a REP CS:MOVSB, the override segment address is on the stack.

CS:IP is cleared from the stack and returns to the calling address of the instruction when you return from the interrupt. The instruction using a REP CS:MOVSB is now CS:MOVSB (it's normal for the repetition prefix to be eliminated so as not to repeat the instruction again) and the repetition prefix (REP) is then lost forever. If, however, we entered the instruction CS: REP MOVSB, the CS override prefix would have been cleared after the instruction was executed.

As a result, the instruction becomes REP MOVSB and the processor doesn't recognize where it's at because the CS has disappeared. It will most likely address a undefined area which will stop or crash the program.

Once again the answer is to reset the interrupts in such an instruction, even though we don't advise you to reset the interrupts for very long time. The 80286 and 80386 get around this problem by making sure that the address entered in the stack during an interrupt is the one of the first prefix.

## 31.2.3    NEG

NEG (negate) subtracts either its registers or memory arguments from 0:

```
NEG  register/memory

1 1 1 1 0 1 1 W  MOD  0 1 1   R/M
```

Execution of NEG AX when AX = 17Ch results in AX=FE84h.

```
NEG 17Ch
= 2's complement of 17Ch
= 00000001 01111100
= 11111110 10000011 + 1
= 11111110 10000100
= FE84h
```

## 31.2.4    XLAT

XLAT (translate) is an instruction that requires a large amount of effort to use. Although a useful instruction, you can get the same result with many other instructions which are faster and more efficient.

```
XLAT
```

```
1 1 0 1 0 1 1 1
```

XLAT lets you translate an 8-bit code into another code. It's normally used to translate ASCII into EBCDIC (the ASCII equivalent on large IBM machines).

The value of AL is used as an index in a table beginning at DS:BX. The byte read in the table is placed in AL. For example, if BX = 1000h and AL = 41h ("A" in ASCII) and at offset 1000h in the current data segment we have a 256-byte ASCII to EBCDIC translation table, then execution of the instruction without XLAT argument places byte number 41h (located at 104h) from the table into AL. This value would be the EBCDIC equivalent of "A".

Load XLATNEG.DEM and start it to see a demo of XLAT and NEG.

## 31.2.5 LEA

LEA (Load Effective Address) is an EA instruction which takes care of determining an effective address. However, instead of reading and writing this address, it places the offset calculated in a register. For example, if BP = 3222h and SI = 2000h:

```
0100  LEA   AX,[BP+SI]
```

places 5222h in AX, without doing anymore. Location SS:5222 is neither read from nor written into.

```
LEA  register,register/memory
```

```
1 0 0 0 1 1 0 1  MOD  REG   R/M
```

LDS (Load Data Segment [DS] register) and LES (Load Extra Segment [ES] register) are variations on effective addresses. LDS loads a 32-bit pointer in memory in the specified register and in DS. LES does the same thing for ES. The pointer consists of two segment and offset words located somewhere in memory:

```
LDS  register,memory
```

```
1 1 0 0 0 1 0 1  MOD  REG   R/M
```

If BP = 3222 and SI = 2000, then:

```
LDS  CX,[BP+SI]
```

reads the word located at SS:5222 and puts it in CX. The word at SS:5224 goes into the data segment. LES does the same for EA. LES and LDS let you quickly define any memory location. You're actually moving a string when you use these instructions in a row:

```
        CS:[F000] = SI,DS;  CS: [F004] = DI,ES

LDS   SI,CS:   [F000]      setting up DS:SI
LES   DI,CS:   [F004]      setting up ES:DI
MOV   CX,200
REP   MOVSB
```

LDSLEA.DEM contains examples of LEA, LDS and LES.

## 31.2.6   HLT

HLT (Halt, operation code F4h) is an exotic instruction for controlling the progress of the program. The program stops at the location of the HLT instruction. The processor then must wait for a hardware interrupt with CS:IP pointing to the instruction that follows the HLT.

When an interrupt is finally executed, the CS:IP in the stack doesn't point to the HLT but to the next instruction. This way when you return from the interrupt the processor continues as if nothing had happened.

## 31.2.7   WAIT

After reading the one-byte WAIT instruction (wait for a test signal), the processor waits to execute the next instruction until detecting a signal on the Test Pin.

WAIT is used to keep the 80x86 synchronized with a co-processor, usually an 80x87 co-processor. WAIT is important because the 80x86 reads instructions faster than the 80x87 can execute them. For example:

```
FMUL   [SI]     (since ESC  01,[SI])
FDIV   [DI]     (since ESC  06,[DI])
MOV    AX, [BP]
```

As soon as it sees the first instruction, the 80x87 multiplies a floating value of 4 bytes in DS:SI by the number at the top of the internal stack. It no longer bothers with anything else before finishing this operation (around 100 cycles). So it doesn't notice the FDIV instruction that follows.

We'd recommend that you be careful and enter a WAIT in front of every 80x87 instruction. WAIT is often called FWAIT (all 80x87 mnemonics begin with an "F") to emphasize the fact that it's for the 80x87 (Float Wait).

```
FWAIT
FMUL    [SI]
FWAIT
FDIV    [BP]
```

Load the demo HLTWAIT.DEM. The two instructions will only stop when you specify the appropriate instruction so the processor takes over control again. HLT waits for an interrupt, either a NMI or an INTR.

WAIT waits for a signal on the Test Pin of the 80x86. Use the "T" command to simulate the 80x87. You're free to interrupt a WAIT, but after leaving the service routine in progress, you'll still be in WAIT because the address of the WAIT instruction is the one that's entered in the stack.

At offset 200h of HLTWAIT.DEM we have a sequence of 253 stops. If we enter the IP at 200h and perform GO to 300h, the processor takes an infinite time (almost 14 seconds) to wait for the break point at 2FFh. This is because each HLT takes the processor into a loop in which all it does is verify the interrupts. In a standard PC, the clock interrupts arrive every .005 seconds without failing. When the clock service routine has ended, the IP is advanced to the next HLT. It takes about 14 seconds to process 254 HLTs to the break point.

## 31.2.8   AAA, AAD, AAM, AAS, DAA and DAS

These six "calibrating" instructions take the value in AX and modify it according to a certain number of ASCII or BCD mathematical rules. BCD arithmetic (Binary Coded Decimal) is a variation of binary and decimal mathematics. A BCD numeral places two decimal numerals in a byte, one numeral per nibble. Thus, "0110 1001" would be the BCD equivalent of 69.

This BCD notation is a real plus since it can avoid rounding errors when you want to represent decimal fractions in binary. At the risk of shocking readers who have training in accounting, it's impossible to represent "$1.31" in binary form. You can come close to being precise, to the millionth or billionth of a cent, but never absolutely precise.

## 31.2.9   LAHF/SAHF

The LAHF (Load AH register with Flags) and SAHF (Store AH into Flag register) instructions are used to translate an 8080 assembly program to an 80x86 assembly program. Several CP/M programs written for the 8080 and upgraded for the 80x86 include many LAHF/SAHF instructions.

LAHF places the SF, ZF, AF, PF and CF flags into specific AH bits. SAHF does the same thing in the opposite direction. These five pointers have their equivalents in the 8080.

You probably won't be using LAHF/SAHF much in 80x86 assembly language because most of the time, while the 80x86 program is syntactically correct, it cannot execute correctly. You may spend more time debugging the 80x86 version than writing a completely new 80x86 program.

# 31.3 Chapter Exercises

1)      Make a program with three instructions that really don't do anything.

2)      Do a routine that gives the negative equivalent of a positive number.

# 32. Writing In Assembly Language

In this chapter we'll show you how to write 80x86 programs. Until now we've only used SIM's LOAD command for the programs. We'll start out by developing the program idea and follow the steps necessary to create an executable program.

Although there are hundreds of different applications that we could program, the trick is to find one that is difficult enough to challenge you, but not so hard to discourage you.

We'll write a program to help play music with the keyboard of our PC. We'll create an ASCII organ.

This is what we want the program to do: Striking a key should produce a sound. To do this we'll link the sound to the ASCII value of the key. The higher the ASCII value, the lower the pitch will be. Since this is a sample program, we won't worry about controlling the duration of the sound. Therefore each sound will have the same duration. We'll exit from the program by pressing the <Esc> key.

We recommend breaking the problem into a series of steps. For our first sketch, let's write the program in a "language" that is a compromise between plain English and 80x86 assembly language. We'll call it *psuedo-code*:

```
ASCII ORGAN

START :     READ A KEY
            IF KEY = "ESC" THEN END
            GOSUB BEEP
            GOTO START
```

The next stage requires us to change this into something closer to assembly syntax. For now we'll use labels so we won't need to enter into real addresses.

```
        START:      CALL      GETKEY
                    CMP       AL,1Bh
                    JNE       SKIP
                    INT       20h

        SKIP:       CALL      BEEP
                    JMP       START

        GETKEY:     MOV       AH,7
                    INT       21h
                    RET

        BEEP:       MOV       BL,AL
                    MOV       AL,B6h
                    OUT       43h,AL
                    MOV       AL,0
                    OUT       42h,AL
                    MOV       AL,BL
                    OUT       42h,AL
                    MOV       AL,4Fh
                    OUT       61h,AL
                    MOV       CX,FFFFh
                    REP       LODSW
                    MOV       AL,4Ch
                    OUT       61h,AL
                    MOV       AH,7
                    MOV       DL,Eh
                    INT       21h
                    RET
```

As you can see, we're using normal writing techniques "from the top to the bottom," a technique that is even applied to higher level languages (top-down programming). The professional programmer starts with the general and then moves to the specific.

The program is easy to follow through the main loop. At this point we don't need to know how to execute the BEEP to understand the logic of the program.

To see if it executes, call the GETKEY subroutine. This subroutine returns the value of any key that's struck to AL. By definition, nothing happens as long as we haven't struck a key. Therefore, we verify whether it's the <Esc> key (ASCII code 1Bh) in which case we exit the program. If not, we call the BEEP subroutine which plays a sound according to the ASCII value of the key struck.

The BEEP subroutine is a modified version of SPEAKER2.DEM. In programming, try to save as much work as you can. Store the value of the key struck in register BL because we need AL for outputs.

We send a 16-bit divisor after notifying the timer to remain to finalize the frequency. This creates a link between the timer and the speaker. Now use a loop to cause a small delay. The delay is the result of creating the LODSB instruction 65,536 times which requires about a quarter of a second. After this delay, we break the timer/speaker connection and send a graphic of the note to the screen using DOS routine 21h.

We must use DOS to load the ASCII Organ I program. You exit the ASCIIORG program by pressing <Esc> which makes it easy to return to DOS. This is accomplished by using software interrupt 20h.

## 32.1 Assembly by Hand

Our program in its present form isn't yet a true assembly language program. The 80x86 cannot process a "CALL BEEP".

Before we can execute our program, we must assemble it to machine language:

```
100 :   E8  0B  00        START :    CALL   GETKEY
103 :   3C  IB                       CMP    AL, 1Bh
105 :   75  02                       JNE    SKIP
107 :   CD 20                        INT    20h
109 :   E8  07  00        SKIP :     CALL   BEEP
10C :   EB  F2                       JMP    START
10E :   B4  07            GETKEY :   MOV    AH, 7
110 :   CD                          INT    21h
112 :   C3                          RET
113 :   8A  D8  :         BEEP :     MOV    BL, AL
115 :   B0  B6                       MOV    AL, 0B6h
117 :   E6  43                       OUT    43h, AL
```

Assembling each instruction in object code can be a difficult and time consuming job. You must constantly refer to a manual, calculate the displacement values of conditional jumps and replace the labels with addresses. After doing this for awhile, learning assembly language will seem like pure nonsense.

The SIM assemble command (A) will help if your program is less than 30 bytes. However, if your program is more than 30 bytes, even with the help of SIM, it becomes a monumental task.

Once the source program is translated into a series of bytes (called an *object program*), we must enter it into the computer and hopefully not losing a single byte or transforming CALLs into IRETs during the process.

As you've guessed, *"assembling"* is an easier and more efficient way to do this. Fortunately, software is available which converts assembly language into machine language. The most popular assembler for PC users is the *Macro Assembler* from Microsoft. The same program is available from IBM as the *IBM Macro Assembler*.

**Note:**    The term "MACRO" is a "plus" included with most Assemblers. Therefore, the expression *Macro Assembler* is usually abbreviated to simply *Macro*.

The Microsoft Macro Assembler might be too powerful for beginner programmers. The numerous commands may be too confusing for what you need. After reading the first few pages in the manual about formatting lists, you may notice that only two or three instructions are enough for assembling a simple program.

If you use the Microsoft Macro Assembler while you're still a novice, it's like putting a Corvette engine into a Ford Escort. The problem is (and it's a big one) that no one that we know of has created an Assembler that's simple and easy for a novice to use.

The success of your first program depends largely on your ability to ignore the commands and features that you don't need and to recognize those that you do need.

It's not necessary for you to have a copy of either the Microsoft or IBM version of the Macro Assembler to follow along with us through the rest of this chapter. However, if you want to become more experienced with writing in assembly language, we recommend using an assembler.

## 32.2   The Source File

Since the Macro Assembler cannot understand your program listing as it now appears, you'll need to use a *program editor* to create a source file. You can use the DOS editor called EDLIN for some programs. However, we don't recommend EDLIN unless it's your only alternative. There are several other editors that are far more user-friendly, such as VEDIT, KEDIT, EC and the Professional Editor from IBM or Norton. You can even use word processors if they have the capability to save your programs as ASCII files.

The following is a source listing of ASCIIORG.ASM which we've created with a word processor in ASCII format:

**ASCII Organ**

```
;ASCII Organ

          code      segment
          org       100h
          assume    cs:code

timer     equ       42h
speaker   equ       61h

start:    call      getkey          ; store key pressed in AL
          cmp       al,1bh          ; escape?
          jne       skip
          int       20h
skip:     call      beep            ; if not escape, beep according to
          jmp       start           ; value in AL, and return

getkey:   mov       ah,7            ; prepare for interrupt
          int       21h             ; execute DOS function 7
          ret                       ; return with key in AL

beep:     mov       bl,al           ; store key in BL
          mov       al,0b6h         ; prepare timer for
          out       timer+1,al      ; accepting new division
          mov       al,0            ; send 0 as LSB
          out       timer,al        ; of the new divisor
          mov       al,bl           ; and key value
          out       timer,al        ; like MSB
          mov       al,4fh          ; start sound by linking the
          out       speaker,al      ; speaker and timer
          mov       cx,0ffffh       ; pause
          rep       lodsw           ; while the note is played
          mov       al,4dh          ; stop by cutting the connection
          out       speaker,al      ; between speaker and timer
          mov       ah,2            ; prepare for DOS output function
```

```
          mov     dl,0eh          ; (out) character to send
          int     21h             ; symbol of the note to the screen
          ret

code      ends
          end     start
```

Since learning to use the Microsoft Macro Assembler often requires weeks of reading and practicing, we'll only discuss the most important points. Each line of assembly language can include the following elements:

- label

- mnemonic

- operand(s)

- comment

The fact that the mnemonics aren't limited to 80x86 instructions, assemblers are very useful but they're also quite complicated. Because of this a mnemonic can represent one of the 12 *pseudo operation codes* (also called *pseudo ops* or *directives*). Therefore, they're special mnemonics which aren't actually instructions but rather commands addressed to the assembler.

Unlike SIM, the Macro Assembler assumes all numbers to be decimal unless otherwise indicated. One of the most common mistakes in assembly programming is forgetting the "h" after a hexadecimal number. Although it may not seem too serious, forgetting the "h" means that "INT 21" becomes "INT 15h". This example now shows you have created a request from the BIOS cassette routine.

If a hexadecimal number begins with a letter, you must place a "0" (zero) at the beginning. So, "MOV AL,B6h" confuses the Macro Assembler because it doesn't know that "B6h" is a number. Instead the Macro Assembler assumes its a label and it doesn't recognize it. Therefore, use the form "MOV AL.0B6h".

The semi-colon (;) is the equivalent of the REM in BASIC. It indicates that a comment follows. The Assembler ignores everything following the semi-colon so be certain not to include any instructions following a semi-colon.

The numerous empty lines (blank spaces) in ASCII Organ I make the program easier to read and has no affect on the Macro Assembler (blank lines are ignored), although this may not be true for other Assemblers.

Labels such as SKIP and GETKEY must be followed by colons (:).

The Macro Assembler refers to psuedo-ops as *directives*. We discussed earlier that instructions give directions to the 80x86 processor. The directives give directions to the assembler. They specify how the assembler is to generate the object code at assembly time.

ORG (origin) instructs the Assembler to start at 100h instead of zero. This directive is necessary because we want ASCII Organ I to be a .COM program. DOS always loads .COM files at offset 100h of the program segment.

The EQU (equates) directive lets you assign a value to labels. This is similar to constants in higher languages. After an EQU directive, we can refer to the timer value by using the word "TIMER" rather than the obscure expression 42h. Also, we can address port 43h with the expression "TIMER+1" and leave the difficult task of calculating to the Assembler.

EQUs let you create a source code that's easier to understand not only while you're writing the program but also for making future changes.

# 32.3  Segment/Ends

The .CODE directive (when used with .MODEL) indicates the start of the code segment and thereby defines a logic segment. In the OASCII Organ I program we called this segment "CODE". Since we've entered all our "CODE SEGMENT" and "CODE ENDS" in brackets in the program, each byte produced during the assembly will be entered in the "CODE" logic segment. The file produced by this assembly contains this information, which lets us combine this data with another logic segment having the same name but created by another assembling process. At the start, the same value in CS lets us access the two logic segments.

The ASSUME directive determines which segment register is referenced by the code that this assembling process produces when it starts. So ASSUME CS:CODE directs the assembler to act as if this value were in CS.

You'll understand the tricks of the "directives" with practice. You can use the following outline for your programs until you understand directives more completely:

```
        (put the EQU here)

code    segment
        org     100h
        assume  cs:code,ds:code,es:code,ss:code


start:

        (put your program here)

code    ends
        end     start
```

## 32.4   Assembling ASCIIORG.ASM

The next step, once you've completed the source listing, is to instruct the assembler to translate into object code. Small programs like ASCII Organ I require only a few seconds to assemble.

Microsoft Assemblers are available in two different formats. One format has a MACRO capacity (MASM.EXE) and the other one (ASM.EXE) does not include the MASM.EXE. The advantage of ASM.EXE is that you can use it on a 64K computer. In this section we'll use ASM.EXE instead of MASM.EXE.

Type ASM.EXE at the DOS prompt (or MASM.EXE if you're using that version):

```
C>ASM ASCIIORG <Enter>
```

The assembler starts by asking several questions:

```
Microsoft (R) Macro Assembler Version 5.10
Copyright (C)Microsoft Corp 1981, 1988  All rights reserved.

Object filename [ASCIIORG.OBJ]: _
```

It wants to know the name that we'll give to the object file that we'll create. You can accept the default, ASCIIORG.OBJ which appears in brackets, by pressing the <Enter> key.

Next, it asks you the name you want to give to the source listing (.LST) file. The assembler produces a source listing of the program with the coding in front of each line. You should not forget the headings including page numbers, date and time.

The assembler displays NUL.LST as the default. By accepting this as the default (Press <Enter>), the assembler produces no source listing. You must provide a name if you want to produce a .LST file. It's logical to use the name of the selected OBJ file, for example, ASCII Organ I. You do not need to type the extension, the assembler adds .LST:

```
Source listing [NUL.LST]: ASCIIORG
```

Next the assembler asks you if you want a cross reference file. This file is helpful for debugging your program. We'll assume there are no programming errors, so accept NUL.CRF by pressing <Enter>:.

```
Cross-reference [NUL.CRF]: _
```

**Note:**     "NUL" is a filename exclusively reserved for use by DOS. Never give the name NUL to one of your files or you'll create a "null" file. That means it doesn't exist.

Try experimenting by using the COPY command from DOS to create a file named NUL:

```
C>COPY TEST.TXT NUL.TXT
              1 file copied
```

Everything seems to function normally. But if you enter a DIR, you'll realize that no file has been created.

You only need a few seconds for the assembler to finish. You get the following message:

```
47930  +  409409  Bytes symbol space free

        0  Warning Errors
        0  Severe Errors
```

There may be different values next to the "Bytes symbol space free" depending on your system. However, there should be no severe errors or other errors.

In most of your assembler work, things won't be this simple. If you create your own program (or copy one of the listings in this book or a listing published in a magazine), you'll discover several errors in pressing keys, incorrectly written mnemonics, hexadecimal numbers without their required "h" and obvious logic errors.

The best advice that we can give you for getting programs that work perfectly is to remember that there will always be errors in your programs. Don't be surprised if a program works the first time you assemble it but doesn't work a second time. The process of debugging a stubborn program can require more time than writing the program itself.

During the assembling process, the Assembler created two files called ASCIORG.LST and ASCIORG.OBJ. As we've already said, ASCIORG.LST is a listing of the assembling process. This listing repeats everything that ASCIIORG.ASM contains and includes the new listing. We've deleted the comments only for clarity.

```
Microsoft (R) Macro Assembler Version 5.10        10/3/90 21:13:43
                                                  Page    1-1


                                 ;ASCII Organ

0000                                 code     segment
0100                                 org      100h
                           assume  cs:code
```

```
 = 0042                      timer   equ     42h
 = 0061                      speaker equ     61h

0100  E8 010E R      start:  call    getkey
0103  3C 1B                  cmp     al,1bh
0105  75 02                  jne     skip
0107  CD 20                  int     20h
0109  E8 0113 R      skip:   call    beep
010C  EB F2                  jmp     start

010E  B4 07          getkey: mov     ah,7
0110  CD 21                  int     21h
0112  C3                     ret

0113  8A D8          beep:   mov     bl,al
0115  B0 B6                  mov     al,0b6h
0117  E6 43                  out     timer+1,al
0119  B0 00                  mov     al,0
011B  E6 42                  out     timer,al
011D  8A C3                  mov     al,bl
011F  E6 42                  out     timer,al
0121  B0 4F                  mov     al,4fh
0123  E6 61                  out     speaker,al
0125  B9 FFFF                mov     cx,0ffffh
0128  F3/ AD                 rep     lodsw
012A  B0 4D                  mov     al,4dh
012C  E6 61                  out     speaker,al
012E  B4 02                  mov     ah,2
0130  B2 0E                  mov     dl,0eh
0132  CD 21                  int     21h
0134  C3                     ret

0135                         code    ends
                             end     start
```

Segments and Groups:

| N a m e | Length | Align | Combine | Class |
|---|---|---|---|---|
| CODE . . . . . . . . . . | 0135 | | PARA | NONE |

Symbols:

| N a m e | Type | Value | Attr |
|---|---|---|---|
| BEEP . . . . . . . . . . . . . . | L NEAR | 0113 | CODE |
| GETKEY . . . . . . . . . . . . | L NEAR | 010E | CODE |
| SKIP . . . . . . . . . . . . . . | L NEAR | 0109 | CODE |

```
SPEAKER  . . . . . . . . . . . .      NUMBER  0061
START  . . . . . . . . . . . . .      L NEAR  0100   CODE

TIMER  . . . . . . . . . . . . .      NUMBER  0042

@CPU . . . . . . . . . . . . . .      TEXT  0101h
@FILENAME  . . . . . . . . . . .      TEXT  asciiorg
@VERSION . . . . . . . . . . . .      TEXT  510


        40 Source  Lines
        40 Total   Lines
        12 Symbols

    47908 + 289671 Bytes symbol space free

         0 Warning Errors
         0 Severe  Errors
```

The left column gives the product of the real work of the assembler, the conversion of the source text into binary numbers. These numbers, with some useful codes in them, are the ones which make up the ASCIIORG.OBJ file.

Notice that the EQU, SEGMENT and ASSUME directives haven't produced any binary code. Remember that the 80x86 doesn't know any ASSUME instruction.

## 32.5   Linking

The ASCIIORG.OBJ file contains the binary product of the assembly. However, this file cannot be used since DOS can neither load it nor execute it. We still must go through two more stages. The first is linking.

LINK (which is on your DOS diskette) is a useful part of DOS and continues the work started by the Assembler. It reads the ASCII.OBJ file to create an "executable" (.EXE) file. LINK can "link" several .OBJ files into only one .EXE file and that's why it's called a *link editor*. You could be even more exact by saying that it's an *automatic link editor*.

You can try it by typing the following:

```
C>LINK ASCIIORG <Enter>

IBM Personal Computer Linker
Version 3.1 (C)Copyright IBM Corp 1987

Run File:     [ASCIIORG.EXE]
List File:    [NUL.MAP]
Libraries:    [.LIB]
```

Press <Enter> three times to accept the defaults. This produces an executable ASCIIORG.EXE file. We won't currently require a listing of the link editing (NUL.MAP) or the "Libraries". We'll discuss these later.

You'll probably see the following error message:

```
Warning : No STACK segment.
```

However, we can ignore this error message for now.

LINK produces an ASCIIORG.EXE file. We discussed in an earlier chapter that the .EXE files are assembly language files which DOS can execute. However, if you now load the ASCIIORG.EXE file, it will only work if you do not press <Esc> (for exiting the program). If you do press <Esc> you'll crash or lockup the system. Therefore, there is a second operation we must perform before the file can be executed successfully.

We wanted ASCII Organ I to be a .COM program. This is a simpler format for a program in 80x86 assembly language working under DOS even though it has to have an extra operation to create it.

We'll need to use the DOS command EXE2BIN to translate the .EXE file into a .COM file. The term EXE2BIN means EXE "to" BINary (the "2" for "to" is a useful trick for naming files):

```
C>EXE2BIN ASCIIORG ASCIIORG.COM <Enter>
```

It requires very little time for the ASCIIORG.EXE (approximately 50 bytes) to translate into the ASCIIORG.COM file. Then we finally have a file that DOS can execute without any problems.

Verify this yourself at the DOS prompt by typing:

```
C>ASCIIORG <Enter>
```

Press a few keys on the keyboard to create the different sounds. Press the <Esc> key to return to DOS.

Although all the demonstration files that you've loaded so far are routines exclusively in 80x86 assembly language, we didn't write them to be entered by DOS in memory. If, for example, you change the name of BSORT.DEM to BSORT.COM and then start BSORT.COM, DOS is forced to enter this program in memory and give it control of your computer. However, it will be the last operation your system executes before it crashes.

Let's summarize the cycle of "assembly code" transformation to "bytes loadable in memory." We started with a text file ASCIIORG.ASM which represents a form of 80x86 instructions capable of producing sounds on your PC. We've divided the file into three programs. The result of each one produces a file used upon entry for the following one and the final result is a .COM file that DOS can process. DOS loads the bytes which format the program and tells the 80x86 to point to the first address of the program.

```
ASM    →    OBJ    →    EXE    →    COM    →    into memory
assemble    link         EXE2BIN    load
```

This process is perfectly adapted to an automatic execution with a .BAT file. Let's create a ALC.BAT file (Assemble, Link, Convert):

```
ASM %1;
LINK %1;
EXE2BIN %1 %1.COM
```

Then type in the following under DOS:

```
C>ALC ASCIIORG <Enter>
```

to get in sequence:

```
C>ASM ASCIIORG
C>LINK ASCIIORG
C>EXE2BIN ASCIIORG ASCIIORG.COM
```

With the semi-colon at the end of each instruction, you can ignore the questions of the assembler and linker and accept the parameters by default. However, you'll probably use these parameters with more advanced programs.

You may have considered that the ASCII.ORG program would have been easier to create in in BASIC. However, what if we program a version of ASCII Organ I which is difficult to execute in BASIC or even Pascal? For example, what about a resident version which functions in the background and behind a current application? This version could generate sounds from BASIC or even during a DOS execution (for example, during formatting) every time that the user presses a key.

Now finally here's a problem worthy of assembly language. The ASCII organ program will emit a sound every time a key is struck on the keyboard however this must be independent of the program in memory.

The difference with this program is that the frequency of the sound not only depends on the key struck, but unlike the earlier version, the pitch is linked to the scan code of the key and not to its ASCII value. As the value of the scan code increases, the pitch decreases. Also, we do not control the duration of the sound. Of course, we're reserving <Esc> as the key to exit and return to DOS.

We recommend using an editor to write AO2.ASM to follow these steps:

The A02 program consists of two independent programs sharing the same .COM file. Here we have an initializing program and a service interrupt routine. This is in fact a routine located above that of the keyboard.

## ASCII Organ II

```
; ASCII Organ II (Version 2: bypasses DOS)

timer   equ     42h
speaker equ     61h
sponmsk equ     4fh
spofmsk equ     4ch
settim  equ     0b6h
termkey equ     1
keyport equ     60h
```

```
doscall macro   x
        mov     ah,x
        int     21h
        endm

pout    macro   x,y
        mov     al,y
        out     x,al
        endm

code    segment
        org     100h
        assume  cs:code

start:  jmp     begin           ; bypasses variable storage

;---- Variable storage ----

msg     db      'Attention: <ESC> to quit$'

oldvect dd      0               ; define double word (4 bytes)
                                ; for storage...
; Start of Program

begin:  mov     dx,offset msg
        doscall 9
        sub     ax,ax           ; establish addressing area
        mov     ds,ax           ; interrupt vector
        mov     si,9*4          ; mov si,36
        mov     cx,4            ; 2.0 makes a call here
        mov     di,offset oldvect
        cld                     ; in precaution
        rep     movsb
        push    cs              ; set DS = CS
        pop     ds
        mov     dx,offset kbdintarget
        mov     al,9            ; make interrupt 9 point
        doscall 25h             ; to kbdintarget
        mov     dx,offset lastin + 5
        int     27h             ; end, make resident

; execute with each stroke of a key

kbdintarget:
        sti                     ; timer interrupt
        push    ax              ; save ax
        in      al,keyport      ; read key
        cmp     al,80h          ; key > 80h?
        jnb     exit            ; if yes, jump...
        cmp     al,termkey      ; <esc> key?
        je      lastime         ; if yes, jump...
        push    ax              ; store key
```

**301**

```
            pout    timer+1,settim
            sub     al,al           ; let AL = 0
            out     timer,al        ; send divisor, LSB first
            pop     ax              ; MSB of divisor=value of key
            out     timer,al        ; timer controls tone
            pout    speaker,sponmsk ; play note

            mov     ax,2000h        ; wait loop
repeat:     dec     ax
            jne     repeat

            pout    speaker,spofmsk
            jmp     exit

lastime:                            ; resume keyboard vector
            push    ds              ; store all registers in stack
            push    es              ;
            push    si              ;
            push    di
            push    cx
            push    cs
            pop     ds              ; let DS = CS
            sub     ax,ax           ; establish addressing area
            mov     es,ax           ; interrupt vector
            mov     di,9*4          ; move program storage
            mov     si,offset oldvect ; into int. vector area
            mov     cx,4
            cld
            rep     movsb           ; return former keyboard interrupt
            pop     cx              ; vector and registers
            pop     di              ; in order opposite of push...
            pop     si
            pop     es
            pop     ds

exit:       pop     ax
lastin:     jmp     [oldvect]       ; jump former rout. keyb. int.

code        ends
            end     start
```

# 32.6  Macros

We mentioned earlier how difficult it is to program immediate outputs on a port. In reality, in order to send an 8-bit number to a port we first must put the immediate value in AL and then execute the OUT instruction.

Assembly Macros let us create our own output instructions.

```
POUT          MACRO   X,Y
              MOV     AL,Y
              OUT     X,AL
              ENDM
```

These four lines define a new mnemonic for the Assembler. This new mnemonic is a macro named POUT (port output). From now on, when the Assembler sees the mnemonic POUT mnemonic, followed by two numbers separated by a comma, it will replace it with two lines of 80x86 assembly language. It generates an immediate move (MOV) into AL and an output on a port by using the values specified by the X and Y as arguments.

For example, POUT 43h,0b6h becomes:

```
MOV AL,0B6h
OUT 43h,AL
```

POUT doesn't let you save anything in assembly language but you'll notice how it simplifies writing the source program. It's useful to have within easy grasp some clear way to output a value to a port. Macros let you redefine 80x86's instructions for your own personal use.

The DOSCALL Macro provides us with a tailor-made 80x86 instruction to manage DOS function calls. DOSCALL 2 produces the following assembly code:

```
MOV AH,2
INT 21h
```

# 33. Data and The Assembler

The AO2.COM program starts with a jump (JMP) beyond the storage area. This is a classic procedure in .COM files. We recommend entering any data at the beginning of the program to make the program listing easier to read. However, we cannot put this data at the very top of the program because DOS gives control to the first byte of the file and there's an advantage to the first byte being an 80x86 real instruction. The answer is to make a JMP past the data storage area.

AO2.ASM uses a pair of new directives defining data storage areas called DB and DD.

DB (define byte) instructs the assembler to assign one or several bytes. A processor cannot live on assembly language code alone. Sometimes it has to have data to process.

```
msg       db       'Attention: <Esc> to quit$'
```

This statement tells the assembler to define the ASCII string within the quotes and associate the first byte of this string with the label MSG. The dollar sign ($) specifies the end of the string. Later, our program will display this message on the screen.

```
oldvect    dd       0  ; define double word (4 bytes)
```

This statement tells the assembler to set aside a doubleword (DD - for defining two adjacent words). These bytes are initialized to a zero value and the label OLDVECT is associated with the first byte of the doubleword.

The main ASCII Organ II program starts at the label BEGIN. After calling the DOS function to display our message on the screen, this program recopies the actual contents of interrupt vector 9 (keyboard INT) in the OLDVECT data area. Thus, you save the contents of interrupt vector number 9, so you can restore it to the original when the program finishes processing.

# 33.1 Offset Operator

```
mov     di,offset OLDVECT
```

This statement instructs the assembler to generate a MOV DI instruction using an immediate value that is the offset to the label OLDVECT. Here the "offset" operator is used to return the desired value. In this case a value of 130h is returned as the immediate value of the MOV DI instruction.

The previous keyboard interrupt vector points into the BIOS (F000:E987 on our computer) unless you have an alternate keyboard management program (for example, like ProKey) resident in memory. In that case, interrupt vector 9 points to RAM.

After saving the keyboard vector, we use DOS function 25h to modify the value of this vector. To do this, the address of the new keyboard interrupt processing routine is specified in AL. This is mandatory when you use function 25h.

Later versions of DOS (3.0 and higher) provide a similar function for reading interrupt vectors. By using this function, we can avoid moving strings but that would have certainly prevented our program from working on earlier versions of DOS (since these versions don't have this function).

Now let's look at the tricky part of our program. We must turn control over to it. But we don't want to give up the memory space that our program is occupying. In DOS terms, we want a "resident in memory" program.

Interrupt 27h (this has nothing to do with function 27h) turns control back to DOS but forces it to load the new .EXE and .COM files above the memory location occupied by ASCII Organ II. This memory location is reserved for us unless we restart the system. The area of reserved memory depends on the value in DX.

We've reserved an area for storing miscellaneous data at the end of the program. You never know; it might come in handy. The label ENDOFPROG makes one more byte in the program. After INT 27h is executed, the main part of the program is forgotten.

# 33.2 Keyboard Interrupt Routine

Now the vector for interrupt 9 points to KBDINTARGET. This means that every time a key is struck our program is given control before the BIOS routine.

However, every time that it assumes control, you must be careful not to change the contents of the registers. If you modify a register without having first saved its value, you'll risk crashing the system. Imagine the reaction of ASCII Organ II if it suddenly finds itself faced with a value of AX other than the one it has just put there.

The only register that we must save is the AX register. The first thing that our keyboard routine does is reset the interrupts. This is wise since priority interrupts, like the timer, must be capable of functioning when needed. Our new keyboard routine is in the same situation as any program which handles keyboard interrupts. It doesn't know and doesn't want to know if it has been interrupted.

After saving the contents of AX, we read the scan code of the keyboard port. This code remains in AX, which means that any routine that accesses it will read this value. This is essential if we don't want ASCIIORG to interfere with the operations of any subsequent keyboard routines.

```
CMP     AL,80h
```

This statement leads us to the topic of *key coding*. The keyboard generates not only a code each time a key is struck, but also every time that a key is released. Any scan code larger than 80h represents one of these "release" codes. For example, the <Ctrl> key has a code value of 1Dh (0001 1101) and a release code of 9Dh (1001 1101). Since we only want one BEEP and not two, each time that a key is used, we must be sure that the code is less than 80h. If not, we jump to the label EXIT.

Next, we must consider the possibility of interrupting the program by pressing a key. The TERMKEY (key for terminating) was initialized to a value of "1" at the beginning of the program. This label is the code of the <Esc> key. If this code is detected, a jump to the label LASTIME is made which restores the initial value of the keyboard interrupt vector. It's important now to save and restore each register used by this routine. The exception to this is AX which has already been saved.

If the <Esc> key is not pressed, a note is played by using the most significant byte of the code of the key as timer divisor. Our instructions are similar to those we used in the ASCII Organ I and don't require any further comments here. However, be careful not to use any registers other than AX. If you use DX without first saving it, you'll be heading for a disaster when you return to the program that was functioning before you called ASCII Organ II.

When we arrive at the label EXIT, we restore register AX and then execute an indirect JMP to the beginning of the original keyboard interrupt routine. Control returns to the program interrupted by the IRET instruction.

```
jmp     [oldvect] ; jump former routine keyboard int.
```

This statement shows the difference between the classic Assembler and a nonsymbolic assembler like the one SIM has. The assembler knows that it has to generate a "far" jump even if this isn't explicitly written, because OLDVECT is defined as a double word. If we had reserved a 4-byte area using two DW (define word) pseudo-ops instead of the single DD pseudo-op, a "near" JMP would have been generated since a DW defines a single word.

# 33.3    Return to ASSUME

ASSUME CS:CODE informs the assembler that all the references are to be relative to the code segment, which means that the assembler will generate a prefix override segment for each instruction containing a label in the segment CODE. Without this, the assembler would generate instructions relative to DS by default.

In the initialization part of the program, this isn't necessary because when DOS turns control over to a .COM file, the registers are already identical. But in the keyboard interrupt part of our program, DS contains a value set by the interrupted program and not by the segment value of ASCII Organ II. So if we attempt to address an area of data in CODE by using DS, goodness only know where we'll go to look for our byte. The indirect JMP, for example, needs an override prefix segment value when the address to which you jump is defined as OLDVECT.

## 33.3.1    An improved version

Here's a third version of ASCIIORG, although from a technical point of view, ASCII Organ III sounds more like a juke box than an organ. AO3.ASM is a program generated by interrupts dependent on the timer (upper case "T") and not on the keyboard.

**ASCII Organ III**

```
; ASCII Organ III

timer   equ     42h
speaker equ     61h
sponmsk equ     4fh
spofmsk equ     4ch
settim  equ     0b6h
keyport equ     60h

doscall macro   x
        mov     ah,x
        int     21h
        endm

pout    macro   x,y
        mov     al,y
        out     x,al
        endm

code    segment
        org     100h
        assume  cs:code,ds:code
```

```
start:  jmp     begin               ; bypass variable storage

;----- Music data -----

song    db      17,4,16,4,15,4,16,4,17,4,17,4,17,8
        db      16,4,16,4,16,8,17,4,19,4,19,8
        db      17,4,16,4,15,4,16,4,17,4,17,4,17,4
        db      17,4,16,4,16,4,17,4,16,4,15,4

;----- Timer divisor data (Pitch) ------

;               C-1 D-2 E-3 F-4 G-5 A-6 B-7 C-8 D-9 E-10 F-11
divsors dw 0000,9121,8126,7239,6833,6088,5423,4832,4560,4063,3620,3417
;               G-12 A-13 B-14 C-15 D-16 E-17 F-18 G-19 A-20 B-21 C-22
        dw      3044,2712,2416,2280,2031,1810,1708,1522,1356,1208,1140
;               D-23 E-24 F-25 G-26 A-27 B-28
        dw      1016, 905, 854, 761, 678, 604

;----- Variables ------

notecnt dw      0                               ; counter for notes
played
beatcnt dw      0                               ; counter for beats
tbtn    dw      0                               ; n beats

;----- Initialize ------

begin:  mov     al, [song+1]                    ; length of first note
        cbw
        mov     tbtn,ax
        call    playnot                         ; begin first note
        mov     dx,offset target1c
        mov     al,1ch                          ; get timer interrupt
        doscall 25h
        mov     dx,offset lbyte+1
        int     27h                             ; end, make resident

;----- target for interrupt 1Ch ------

target1c:
        push    cs                      ; synchronize execution time
        pop     ds
        inc     beatcnt
        mov     ax,tbtn
        cmp     ax,beatcnt              ; end of note?
        je      in2                     ; yes, jump next note
        iret                            ; no...
in2:    cmp     notecnt,(offset divsors - offset song) / 2
        jne     in3                     ; if not equal continue
        mov     byte ptr target1c,0cfh
        iret
```

```
; to play following note

in3:      push    si                      ; store ds,dx,ax
          inc     notecnt                 ; advance to next note
          mov     beatcnt,0               ; reset beatcount=0
          mov     si,notecnt
          shl     si,1                    ; 2 elements for each note
          mov     al,[si+offset song+1]   ; duration of the note
          cbw
          mov     tbtn,ax
          call    playnot
          pop     si
          iret


playnot:  mov     si,notecnt
          shl     si,1
          mov     al,[si+offset song]     ; AL = number of note
          or      al,al                   ; force pointers
          jnz     pn1                     ; note 0 is a pause
          pout    speaker,spofmsk
          ret
pn1:      cbw                             ; AH in one byte
          mov     si,ax
          shl     si,1                    ; divisor table
          pout    timer+1,settim
          mov     ax,[si+offset divsors]
          out     timer,al
          mov     al,ah
          out     timer,al
          pout    speaker,sponmsk
lbyte:    ret

code      ends
          end     start
```

This program plays complete tunes and not just random sound while the computer can concentrate on other tasks. A priority interrupt is incorporated in the BIOS Timer service routine. It communicates with the 80x86 at a rate of 18.2 times per second. Thanks to the fact that the programmable timer (lower case "t") isn't greedy, it has virtually no effect on the performance of your computer.

The program no longer depends on the keyboard routine like AO2. One of the last instructions in the timer routine is INT 1Ch. Vector 1Ch normally points to an IRET instruction, which means that it does nothing.

ASCII Organ III, during initializing, forces interrupt 1Ch to point to the beginning of ASCII Organ III itself. As soon as it's done, our ASCII Organ III takes control 18.2 times per second.

# 33.4 Song Format

Each note in the ASCII Organ III program is represented by a pair of note/duration bytes which are in the "SONG" notes table. The notes are numbers from 1 to 28 representing the white keys on a piano keyboard from 2 octaves over middle C to the B located 4 octaves above that. Note "0" doesn't produce any note, but is used for tests. Notes are specified according to normal musical notes of A through G.

Since we're using the timer interrupt, our unit of time is an 18th of a second. For example, a duration of "4" produces a sound of 4/18 seconds (or, more accurately, 4/18.2 seconds).

To play the scale of C major starting with C, with a duration of a half second for each note followed by a 10 second pause, your data table is:

```
SONG    DB      15,9,16,9,17,9,18,9,19,9,20,9,21,9,22,9
                0,180,15,9,16,9,17,9,18,9,19,9,20,9,21,9,22,9
```

The PLAYNOT subroutine translates numbers corresponding to each note into appropriate divisors and sends everything to the timer.

This routine shifts the binary value of the note one position to the left (or multiplication by 2) to determine the correct divisor. For example, note "15, C" is represented by the divisor located at the 30th byte in the table. If you send this value in the timer, it produces a sound of 522 Hz (or C).

AO3.ASM has three variables named NOTECNT (pair note/duration during execution), BEATCNT (how many beats the note lasted during execution) and NBTN (total duration of the note in number of beats).

The action really begins at label TARGET1C. One of the advantages of our timer addressing system is that it foresees saving the initial contents of DS, AX and DX in the stack, which lets them be modified without fear of losing anything. When our program executes an IRET to BIOS, these registers are restored just before the final IRET turns the control over to the interrupted program.

When TARGET1C gets control, a note has been played during the last 18th of a second. So we increment the BEATCNT variable, which takes into account the duration of the notes. Next we compare it to TBTN (Total Beats of the Note) to see if there's a reason to stop it. If the results aren't equal, we haven't finished with this note and we do an IRET which restarts the sound.

If TBTN is different from BEATCNT, there are two possibilities. Either we're at the end of a note or at the end of the song. The total number of notes in the tune is calculated at the time of assembling by the expression:

```
(offset divisors - offset song) / 2
```

If the song is finished, we write an IRET (opcode CFh) and the address of TARGET1C, which amounts to not executing this program anymore. If that's the case, we increment the note counter, erase the beat counter, enter in TBTN the number of beats that the new note requires and then play the music.

## 33.5  Dump .ASM

DUMP.ASM is a routine similar to the SIM Dump. However, instead of displaying the contents of memory, it displays the contents of files on the disk. When you type:

```
C>DUMP SAMPLE.TXT <Enter>
```

SIM displays the SAMPLE.TXT file in a hex and ASCII format. If the file that you want to examine does not exist, an appropriate message is displayed on the screen. The file must be present in the current directory.

### DUMP.ASM

```
; DUMP.ASM: Dump Utility

; ------Macros-------------------------

doscall macro    x
        mov      ah,x
        int      21h
        endm

outchar macro    x
        mov      dl,x
        doscall 2
        endm

code    segment
        org      100h
        assume   cs:code,ds:code
start:  jmp      begin

; ------Variables----------------------

fcount  dw       0
eofflag db       0
fnfmsg  db       'File not Found$'
hexchar db       '0123456789ABCDEF'

; ----- main loop -------------

begin:  mov      dx,5ch          ; fcb prepared by DOS
        doscall 0fh              ; open file
        cmp      al,0ffh         ; if ffh then
        jne      d1              ; file not found
        mov      dx,offset fnfmsg
        doscall 9                ; display message
        jmp      exit            ; end
```

```
; if file is present begin by reading
; data in DTA at offset 80h

d1:     mov     dx,5ch
        doscall 14h             ; read data block (128 bytes)
        cmp     al,1            ; if end of file
        je      exit            ; end
        cmp     al,3            ; if partial block
        jne     d2              ; display file and end
        inc     eofflag
d2:     call    outrec          ; display 128 bytes of DTA
        cmp     eofflag,1       ; EOF?
        jne     d1              ; if not, jump to top
exit:   int     20h

outrec  proc    near
        mov     bp,80h          ; bp points to beginning of DTA
or1:    call    outcnt
        call    outhex
        call    outasci
        outchar 13
        outchar 10
        add     bp,16           ; position base pointer
        add     fcount,16       ; and file counter
        cmp     bp,100h         ; finished after 128 bytes
        jne     or1
        outchar 13
        outchar 10
        ret
outrec  endp

outcnt  proc    near            ; outcnt displays the memory address
        mov     ax,fcount       ; in hex as MSB LSB:
        mov     al,ah           ; switch for display
        call    outbyte
        mov     ax,fcount
        call    outbyte
        outchar ':'             ; separate with :
        outchar ' '
        ret
outcnt  endp

outhex  proc    near            ; outhex displays a hex dump
        mov     si,0
oh1:    mov     al,[bp+si]      ; read byte
        call    outbyte         ; and display
        outchar ' '
        inc     si
        cmp     si,8            ; add extra space between
        jne     oh2             ; bytes 7 and 8 for clarity
        outchar ' '
```

```
oh2:    cmp     si,16           ; if si = 16 then return
        jne     oh1
        outchar ' '             ; separate with a space
        ret
outhex  endp

outasci proc    near            ; outasci displays the ASCII characters
        mov     si,0            ; prepare oa1 loop
oa1:    mov     dl,[bp+si]      ; read character
        and     dl,7fh          ; set MSB = 0
        cmp     dl,20h          ; if char can be printed then
        jae     oa2             ; jump to oa2
        mov     dl,'.'          ; else print
oa2:    doscall 2               ; print character
        inc     si
        cmp     si,16           ; when performed 16 times, end
        jne     oa1
        ret
outasci endp

outbyte proc    near            ; output char. to screen
        mov     bx,offset hexchar
        push    ax
        and     al,0f0h
        mov     cl,4
        rol     al,cl
        xlat                    ; translate into hex
        mov     dl,al
        doscall 2               ; display
        pop     ax
        and     al,0fh
        xlat                    ; translate into hex
        mov     dl,al
        doscall 2               ; display
        ret
outbyte endp

code    ends
        end     start
```

This listing illustrates how to fit Macros together. For example, the OUTCHAR Macro calls the DOSCALL macro. The OUTCHAR ':' line generates these three instructions:

```
        mov     dl,3ah      (3Ah = ASCII code for :)
        mov     ah,2
        int     21h
```

The PROC/ENDP directives let you structure these subroutines by defining the beginning and ending addresses.

## 33.5.1    Help From DOS

This program uses a series of routines furnished by DOS every time that it loads an .EXE or .COM file in memory. When these are loaded, DOS creates a 256K program segment prefix starting at offset 0 of the program segment. The address of this segment is entered in the 80x86 segment registers.

At offset 5Ch of the program segment, DOS enters a *File Control Block (FCB)*. The FCB provides the DUMP.COM with data about the file whose contents will be displayed.

FCBs are data structures of data (less than 30K) that serve as information exchange centers between DOS and your program. Each file destined to be read or written absolutely has to have its FCB. For example, to read the TEST.TXT, you create a FCB containing information necessary to DOS for localizing this file. This information includes the name of the file, its extension and eventually the reader and/or directory where it's located.

## 33.6 How DUMP.COM Works

DUMP.COM doesn't prompt you for the filename as it starts. Instead you must specify the filename on the command line when you start the program. DOS enters everything it finds on the command line after the word DUMP at offset 80h of the program segment prefix. Therefore, if you type:

```
C>DUMP TEST.TXT <Enter>
```

DOS puts "TEST.TXT" in the segment prefix for this DUMP program:

```
154F:0080 09 20 74 65 73 74 2E 74 78 74 0D 00  . TEST.TXT ...
154F:0090 00 00 00 00 00 00 00 00 00 00 00 00  .............
154F:00A0 00 00 00 00 00 00 00 00 00 00 00 00  .............
```

The first byte represents the number of characters (9) on the command line following the word DUMP. A carriage return (0Dh) is at the end.

DUMP only has to read starting at offset 80h to identify the file to be used. In fact it doesn't have to read the filename at all. DOS has already copied the text at offset 80h to address 5Ch of the FCB.

When data is read from or written to a disk, DOS uses a Disk Transfer Area (DTA) to store that data. The address of the default DTA is found at offset 80h of the PSP. We'll use this DTA to read 128 bytes of data from the file.

Before DUMP.COM takes control, these following conditions must be met:

Segment registers ES, CS, SS and DS must contain the segment address of the program. At offset 5Ch of the program segment is an entry containing the filename specified when the DUMP is started. The DTA is at offset 80h.

If you take the trouble to start DUMP.COM with SIM, you'll note that it offers the same functions as under DOS. Type the following:

```
>>LOAD DUMP.COM TEST.TXT <Enter>
```

You see that you haven't only loaded DUMP.COM in memory but also that DOS has created an FCB containing the name DUMP.COM at address ssss:80. SIM, also puts the parameters that are passed to it at address 80h. Start everything from DOS:

```
C>SIM DUMP COM TEST.TXT
```

and you get the same result. It was essential if we wanted SIM to be a tool for debugging programs.

The first thing that we ask DUMP.COM to do is open the file specified at offset 5Ch of the FCB. We open the FCB to verify the existence of this file and prepare DOS for read/write operations.

The files are opened by calling DOS function Fh. To specify the file to open, registers DS:DX must point to an unopened FCB. Then you search the directory for the desired file. AL returns "FF" if the file isn't found. Otherwise it returns "0".

If the Fh function returns a FFh in AL, the file does not exist. In our case, the file does exist, but we still have some housekeeping to do – the size of the file, the date of the last debugging, etc.

Before calling function 14h, we must make sure that DS:DX points to the open FCB. This function reads the data into the DTA.

If we're at the end of the file, then AL returns one of the two following values:

• 1 means that the record is empty.

• 3 means that a part of a record has been read and that the remaining bytes contain all zeros.

AL=0 if the transfer is successful.

After it reads 128 bytes of data from the TEST.TXT file, DUMP.COM checks to see if the file is empty (AL=0), in which case the program is done. If not, it verifies whether it's the last record and whether it has to display the remainder as zeros (AL=3) in which case it sets an indicator.

The subroutine OUTSEC (Output Sector) writes the contents of the data that we have just put in the DTA in a classic DUMP format. First this routine displays the word FCOUNT on the screen. The routine OUTBYTE converts the binary to ASCII format.

OUTBYTE displays the byte contained in AL as two ASCII characters that are the hexadecimal representatives. Here we use a method of looking for things in a table, each nibble being used into the table HEXCHAR. Here the clever XLAT is used.

OUTHEX is a loop based on the SI counter, which reads 16 data bytes in the DTA and calls the subroutine OUTBYTE to carry out the tough work. OUTASCII does the same thing for the ASCII part of DUMP.COM. After masking bit 7 and verifying that the character is displayable (greater than or equal to 20h), it sends it to the screen.

We've come to the end of our discussion of assembly language. Now all that's left is for you to practice. Good luck!

# Appendix A: The Simulator

The simulator is the part of SIM which executes the 80x86 machine language. It's able to detect and refuse to execute any undefined operation code. While working in normal mode, any attempt to write in memory outside of the user area or directly to the ports is prohibited and terminates the user program.

To start the simulator, type the following at the command prompt:

```
>>SIM <Enter>
```

To end the simulator, press the <Q> key to return to DOS.

### The Command Management Window

When the simulator is started, each instruction simulated is displayed and described in the Command Management Window.

The first line consists of the mnemonic of the instruction being executed. The EA byte modifies the instruction line as the instruction reads and processes information.

The "Macrostep" and "Microstep" lines describe the actions which SIM is about to take.

For teaching purposes, the instructions are divided into somewhat larger steps (macro and micro). Any complex action composed of several operations and using several registers (like PUSH:REG, for example) is carried out stage by stage. This way you can easily follow its mechanism. However, so as not to discredit SIM's adaptability of use, this mode is an option that you can omit as soon as you understand how these operations are carried out.

The STEP instruction lets you choose the level of the simulation. STEP=2, for example, pauses before executing each macrostep and displays the important stages of executing the instruction but it doesn't describe the detail of transfers and incrementing of the instruction pointer.

Here's the function of the different STEP settings:

| STEP= | Effects |
|-------|---------|
| 4 | Lowest detail level. Pauses between instructions, macro and micro stages, elementary read/write stages and between each phase during interrupt verification. |
| 3 | Pauses between instructions, macro and micro stages. |
| 2 | Pauses between instructions and macro stages. This is the ideal STEP setting for learning to use SIM. |
| 1 | Pauses between instructions only. |
| 0 | No pauses. |

During a simulation, the following instructions are used to control the operation:

| | |
|---|---|
| `Spacebar` | To request or cancel pause. |
| `1` - `9` | Establishes SIM execution speed of the simulation. Press <1> for the fastest execution speed and <9> for the slowest execution speed. |
| `N` `I` `T` | Press these keys to change the status of the corresponding input pin:<br><N>=NMI      <I>=INTR      <T>=TEST |
| `C` | Press this key to use the calculator (during a pause). Press <Esc> to return to the pause. |
| `Ctrl` `P` | Sets and resets the printer. When the printer is set, PR is displayed on the status line. The status of the processor is printed at the end of each instruction SIM executes. This includes the next disassembled instruction. |
| `Esc` or `Ctrl` `C` | Ends simulation and returns to the Command Management Window. |

## About simulation

When a nonprivileged user simulates writing to protected memory or to a port, the simulator ignores these requests, restores the registers, terminates the simulator and returns to the command prompt. Likewise, when an undefined instruction is encountered the simulator stops with CS:IP pointing to the undefined instruction (certain instructions are undefined as long as an EA byte has been read and decoded, such as JMP FAR SI and LEA AX,BX).

## Limits of the 80x86 Simulator

80x86 SIM is a tool for teaching machine language programming. It's also a tool for a final checkout of programs. However, it isn't an exact copy of the internal functions of the 80x86 because SIM could arrive at the same results by other paths.

Our objective in creating SIM was to develop a training tool that would make understanding 80x86 instructions easier. However, we decided against using simulations which were more like the 80x86 in favor of others somewhat less exact but more useful for teaching purposes.

A simulator of the 80x86 that perfectly reflects techniques for manufacturing and setting up microprocessors would be an ideal tool for a course about how to set-up processors but not for studying how to program these microprocessors.

A true 80x86, for example, uses the signals which determine the addresses for reading and writing data. It would be useless to simulate these signals and it might possibly confuse the user.

The real 80x86 uses a buffer. The processor sometimes sometimes "pre-fetches" up to 4 bytes in advance of reading an operation code and carrying out the task. In SIM, the read/decode cycle of the operation code is less complex. SIM presents all at once the instructions with complex micro-codes (MUL, DIV) rather than displaying a complex of displacements and additions.

SIM is written in MS-Pascal and in assembly language. The part written in Pascal does most of the work. It is helped by assembly routines for mathematical instructions and functions closely related to the machine (for example, transmitting to the 80x86 the registers of the simulator during a GO instruction).

SIM displays certain information about its status on the screen. For example, at the moment of an interrupt control, the program verifies the video memory to know if the arrow towards the top points to the NMI and INTR pins. Therefore, SIM might give a strange result if the program being executed made it write on its own screen.

## SIM and the 80x86 processors

The members of the 80x86 microprocessor families are very similar. The 8088 and the 8086 for example are almost identical except that the 8086 writes to and reads from memory one word per cycle while the 8088 requires two cycles.

## SIM and the 80286

The 80286 is an 8086/88 which incorporates supplementary chips. For example, the 8086/88 requires a programmable 8059 interrupt controller while the 80286 has it built-in.

The 80286 is upward compatible with the 8086/88, which means that programs written for the 8086 work without modifications on the 80286. The opposite isn't true. The 80286 includes several new instructions and new addressing modes.

New instructions:

```
PUSHA        (Push all general registers)
POPA         (Pop all general registers)
BOUND        (check array index for value out of range)
INS          (input string from port)
OUTS         (output string to port)
ENTER        (execute calling sequence for high level language)
```

New addressing modes:

```
PUSH immediate
IMUL immediate
SHL (count immediate)
```

Other differences for the 80286 include:

- Word write at offset FFFFh

  When the 8086/88 writes a word in a segment at offset FFFFh, the least significant byte goes to offset FFFFh and the most significant byte goes to offset 0. The 80286 writes one byte at offset FFFFh and the other one at the address following the end of the segment.

- Nondefined operation codes

  The 80286 executes a type 6 interrupt when it encounters operation codes 63h-67h, F1h, FEh xx111xxx and FFh xx111xxx. In this case, SIM stops executing and returns to the control screen with the CS:IP pointing to the invalid instruction.

- Operation code 0Fh

  When the 8086/88 encounters 0Fh, it executes a POP of the word at the top of the stack in CS. The 80286 executes a "non valid instruction exception."

- Shifting and rotating values greater than 31

  Before executing a shift or a rotation by a value found in the CL register or an immediate value, the 80286 performs an AND operation on this value with 1Fh, limiting the displacements to less than 32. The 8086/88 doesn't have this limitation.

- The locking prefix (LOCK)

  The 80286 doesn't activate the LOCK signal if the processor isn't ready to execute the locked instruction. The 8086/88 activates the LOCK signal immediately after executing the prefix.

- Moving interrupted strings

  When the 8086/88 is interrupted during a repetitive string movement, the return address, placed in the stack, points to the last instruction prefix preceding the string primitive itself. If the string primitive initially had more than one prefix, the extra prefixes aren't re-executed after the interrupt.

  On the other hand, an 80286 interrupt produces a PUSH from the address of the first prefix, so the rest of the chain processing is correctly carried out after the interrupt.

- Errors of division on wholes

  The 8086/88 results in an overflow if the absolute value of a quotient is greater than 7FFFh (for a 16-bit division) or 7Fh (for an 8-bit division). On the other hand, the 80286 increases the valid quotient to 8000h or 80h respectively.

- Operation code ESC

  The 80286 can be programmed to cause a type 7 interrupt each time an Escape instruction (ESC) is executed. The 8086/88 doesn't have this ability.

- Addressing Mode

  The 80286 doesn't require extra clock cycles to carry out effective address calculations.

- Multiplication and Division Speed

  The 80286 executes multiplications and divisions on whole numbers more than three times faster than the 8086/88.

# Appendix B: Error Messages

If the following messages are displayed:

*Bad Address*

*Bad Base*

*Bad Command*

*Bad Count*

*Bad Flag*

*Bad List*

*Bad Port Number*

*Bad Range*

*Bad Register*

*Need Value*

*Value Out of Range*

there are syntactical errors in your instructions.

*Bad .EXE Signature*

The loading routine has found something other than the word 544Dh at the top of the file.

*Can't Create File*

DOS hasn't been able to finish the file creation system call. Verify the space remaining on the disk or diskette.

*CS Changed Since Load*

CS was modified after the last time a program was loaded in the memory. The file you now save will also be modified and probably not work the way it should.

*Disk Full*

The file cannot be entirely saved because the disk is full. Either use another diskette or delete unnecessary files.

## *File Length (BX:CX)=0*

SIM uses BX-CX as a 32-bit value to contain the size in bytes of the file to save. If this value is equal to 0, no saving is authorized.

## *File Not Found*

The file to load can't be found. Verify whether the file doesn't load from another directory or disk drive. In that case, don't forget to specify the name of this disk drive in front of the name of the file. Remember that SIM doesn't accept DOS 2.0 paths.

## *File too Large*

According to the directory data or heading data of an .EXE file, the module to load is too large to be entered between CS:100 and the top of RAM.

## *Load into Protected RAM*

The value contained in the CS register has been modified after the program has started, or after the NEW instruction has started and now points to an address considered dangerous. A nonprivileged user cannot load files in protected memory.

## *Need Filename*

The SAVE instruction requires a filename when no file has been loaded beforehand in the memory.

## *No RAM for PSP*

CS:00 points to a memory area of less than 256K for establishing the program segment prefix.

## *Privileged user modes*

The OUT, SKIP and GO instructions are only available in "privileged user" mode.

## Calculator errors

### *Divide by zero*

This message is entered when you try to divide by zero.

### *Overflow*

The result of the operation is greater than 7FFFFFFFh (2,147,483,647) or less than 800000000h (-2,147,483,648).

## Assembly errors

*Bad Mnemonic*

The assembler is unable to locate the instruction selected in the mnemonics table (for example, "SEI").

*Bad Operand*

The assembler hasn't found any operand corresponding to a given mnemonic.

*Jump Out of Range*

A conditional jump cannot do branching greater than 127 bytes forward and 128 bytes backward (example: 0100:JNZ 0F00).

*Operand Out of Range*

The assembler received an inappropriate numerical operand (for example: INT F00).

*Unexpected Operand*

The operand appears to be correct but it lacks a character on the right (example: CLC [SI]).

# Appendix C:  ASCII Table

| Dec | Hex | Char | Dec | Hex | Char | Dec | Hex | Char | Dec | Hex | Char |
|-----|-----|------|-----|-----|------|-----|-----|------|-----|-----|------|
| 0 | 00 |  | 32 | 20 |  | 64 | 40 | @ | 96 | 60 | ` |
| 1 | 01 | ☻ | 33 | 21 | ! | 65 | 41 | A | 97 | 61 | a |
| 2 | 02 | ● | 34 | 22 | " | 66 | 42 | B | 98 | 62 | b |
| 3 | 03 | ♥ | 35 | 23 | # | 67 | 43 | C | 99 | 63 | c |
| 4 | 04 | ◆ | 36 | 24 | $ | 68 | 44 | D | 100 | 64 | d |
| 5 | 05 | ♣ | 37 | 25 | % | 69 | 45 | E | 101 | 65 | e |
| 6 | 06 | ♠ | 38 | 26 | & | 70 | 46 | F | 102 | 66 | f |
| 7 | 07 | • | 39 | 27 | ' | 71 | 47 | G | 103 | 67 | g |
| 8 | 08 | ◘ | 40 | 28 | ( | 72 | 48 | H | 104 | 68 | h |
| 9 | 09 | ○ | 41 | 29 | ) | 73 | 49 | I | 105 | 69 | i |
| 10 | 0A | ■ | 42 | 2A | * | 74 | 4A | J | 106 | 6A | j |
| 11 | 0B | ♂ | 43 | 2B | + | 75 | 4B | K | 107 | 6B | k |
| 12 | 0C | ♀ | 44 | 2C | , | 76 | 4C | L | 108 | 6C | l |
| 13 | 0D | ♪ | 45 | 2D | - | 77 | 4D | M | 109 | 6D | m |
| 14 | 0E | ♫ | 46 | 2E | . | 78 | 4E | N | 110 | 6E | n |
| 15 | 0F | ☼ | 47 | 2F | / | 79 | 4F | O | 111 | 6F | o |
| 16 | 10 | ► | 48 | 30 | 0 | 80 | 50 | P | 112 | 70 | p |
| 17 | 11 | ◄ | 49 | 31 | 1 | 81 | 51 | Q | 113 | 71 | q |
| 18 | 12 | ↕ | 50 | 32 | 2 | 82 | 52 | R | 114 | 72 | r |
| 19 | 13 | ‼ | 51 | 33 | 3 | 83 | 53 | S | 115 | 73 | s |
| 20 | 14 | ¶ | 52 | 34 | 4 | 84 | 54 | T | 116 | 74 | t |
| 21 | 15 | § | 53 | 35 | 5 | 85 | 55 | U | 117 | 75 | u |
| 22 | 16 | ▬ | 54 | 36 | 6 | 86 | 56 | V | 118 | 76 | v |
| 23 | 17 | ↨ | 55 | 37 | 7 | 87 | 57 | W | 119 | 77 | w |
| 24 | 18 | ↑ | 56 | 38 | 8 | 88 | 58 | X | 120 | 78 | x |
| 25 | 19 | ↓ | 57 | 39 | 9 | 89 | 59 | Y | 121 | 79 | y |
| 26 | 1A | → | 58 | 3A | : | 90 | 5A | Z | 122 | 7A | z |
| 27 | 1B | ← | 59 | 3B | ; | 91 | 5B | [ | 123 | 7B | { |
| 28 | 1C | ∟ | 60 | 3C | < | 92 | 5C | \ | 124 | 7C | | |
| 29 | 1D | ↔ | 61 | 3D | = | 93 | 5D | ] | 125 | 7D | } |
| 30 | 1E | ▲ | 62 | 3E | > | 94 | 5E | ^ | 126 | 7E | ~ |
| 31 | 1F | ▼ | 63 | 3F | ? | 95 | 5F | _ | 127 | 7F | Δ |

| Dec | Hex | Char | Dec | Hex | Char | Dec | Hex | Char | Dec | Hex | Char |
|-----|-----|------|-----|-----|------|-----|-----|------|-----|-----|------|
| 128 | 80 | Ç | 160 | A0 | á | 192 | C0 | L | 224 | E0 | α |
| 129 | 81 | ü | 161 | A1 | í | 193 | C1 | ⊥ | 225 | E1 | β |
| 130 | 82 | é | 162 | A2 | ó | 194 | C2 | ⊤ | 226 | E2 | Γ |
| 131 | 83 | â | 163 | A3 | ú | 195 | C3 | ├ | 227 | E3 | π |
| 132 | 84 | ä | 164 | A4 | ñ | 196 | C4 | ─ | 228 | E4 | Σ |
| 133 | 85 | à | 165 | A5 | Ñ | 197 | C5 | ┼ | 229 | E5 | σ |
| 134 | 86 | å | 166 | A6 | ª | 198 | C6 | ╞ | 230 | E6 | μ |
| 135 | 87 | ç | 167 | A7 | º | 199 | C7 | ╟ | 231 | E7 | τ |
| 136 | 88 | ê | 168 | A8 | ¿ | 200 | C8 | ╚ | 232 | E8 | Φ |
| 137 | 89 | ë | 169 | A9 | ⌐ | 201 | C9 | ╔ | 233 | E9 | θ |
| 138 | 8A | è | 170 | AA | ¬ | 202 | CA | ╩ | 234 | EA | Ω |
| 139 | 8B | ï | 171 | AB | ½ | 203 | CB | ╦ | 235 | EB | δ |
| 140 | 8C | î | 172 | AC | ¼ | 204 | CC | ╠ | 236 | EC | ∞ |
| 141 | 8D | ì | 173 | AD | ¡ | 205 | CD | ═ | 237 | ED | Ø |
| 142 | 8E | Ä | 174 | AE | « | 206 | CE | ╬ | 238 | EE | ∈ |
| 143 | 8F | Å | 175 | AF | » | 207 | CF | ╧ | 239 | EF | ∩ |
| 144 | 90 | É | 176 | B0 | ░ | 208 | D0 | ╨ | 240 | F0 | ≡ |
| 145 | 91 | æ | 177 | B1 | ▒ | 209 | D1 | ╤ | 241 | F1 | ± |
| 146 | 92 | Æ | 178 | B2 | ▓ | 210 | D2 | ╥ | 242 | F2 | ≥ |
| 147 | 93 | ô | 179 | B3 | │ | 211 | D3 | ╙ | 243 | F3 | ≤ |
| 148 | 94 | ö | 180 | B4 | ┤ | 212 | D4 | ╘ | 244 | F4 | ⌠ |
| 149 | 95 | ò | 181 | B5 | ╡ | 213 | D5 | ╒ | 245 | F5 | ⌡ |
| 150 | 96 | û | 182 | B6 | ╢ | 214 | D6 | ╓ | 246 | F6 | ÷ |
| 151 | 97 | ù | 183 | B7 | ╖ | 215 | D7 | ╫ | 247 | F7 | ≈ |
| 152 | 98 | ÿ | 184 | B8 | ╕ | 216 | D8 | ╪ | 248 | F8 | ° |
| 153 | 99 | Ö | 185 | B9 | ╣ | 217 | D9 | ┘ | 249 | F9 | • |
| 154 | 9A | Ü | 186 | BA | ║ | 218 | DA | ┌ | 250 | FA | · |
| 155 | 9B | ¢ | 187 | BB | ╗ | 219 | DB | █ | 251 | FB | √ |
| 156 | 9C | £ | 188 | BC | ╝ | 220 | DC | ▄ | 252 | FC | ⁿ |
| 157 | 9D | ¥ | 189 | BD | ╜ | 221 | DD | ▌ | 253 | FD | ² |
| 158 | 9E | ₧ | 190 | BE | ╛ | 222 | DE | ▐ | 254 | FE | ∎ |
| 159 | 9F | ƒ | 191 | BF | ┐ | 223 | DF | ▀ | 255 | FF | |

# Appendix D:  SIM Instructions

| A | Assemble in memory |
|---|---|

**Syntax:**

```
A[address]
```

**Description:**

Assembles instructions directly in memory. Press <Ctrl><C> to exit.

**Example:**

```
A CS:100
```

| BASE | Modifies the calculating base of the registers |
|---|---|

**Syntax:**

```
BASE reg|* HEX|BIN|DEC
```

**Description:**

Specifies whether the contents of the registers are displayed in hexadecimal, binary or decimal according to your choice. When you've selected the hexadecimal base for 16-bit registers, the simulator doesn't break them down into two 8-bit ones. If you type "*" instead of "reg," the base is modified for all the registers.

**Examples:**

```
BASE * HEX
BASE CH BIN (register CH is displayed in binary)
```

| BIG | Changes size of the Processor Area and the Disassembly Area |
|---|---|

**Syntax:**

```
BIG
```

**Description:**

Switches between a large Processor Area with a small work screen display and a small processor with a large work screen.

**Example:**

```
BIG
```

## C — Compares two memory areas

**Syntax:**

```
C area address
```

**Description:**

Compares the contents of two memory areas. Displays the address of each byte which is different. Differences are displayed as: adrs1:diffadrs1 diffadrs2:adrs2.

**Examples:**

```
C DS:100 L 300 CS:100
C 100 200 500
```

## CALC — Activates the calculator

**Syntax:**

```
CALC
```

**Description:**

Activates the calculator to perform the four basic mathematical operations. The calculator can also be activated during a simulation by pressing the <C> key if you're in WAIT. The base can be in hexadecimal (H), binary (B) or decimal (D).

**Note:** No matter what the display mode is (decimal, hex or binary), calculations are always performed in decimal mode.

Entries can be done using two formats:

```
N1 operator N2
```

Where N1 and N2 are whole numbers written in the selected calculating base and the operator is one of these four operations: +, -, /, *.

```
N1
```

Where N1 is a whole number written in the selected base. This format is reserved for conversions. Negative values are displayed as a 32-bit value (2's complement). The maximum positive value is 7FFFFFFFh and the maximum negative value is 80000000h.

**Example:**

```
CALC
```

333

**Errors:**

*Overflow*

The result of an operation is greater than 7FFFFFFFh or less than 80000000h.

*Divide by zero*

The N2 operand in the division is equal to 0.

## CASE
Switches between upper and lowercase letters

**Syntax:**

    CASE

**Description:**

Displays letters as either uppercase letters (capitals) or lowercase letters.

**Example:**

    CASE

## CLEAR
Clears flags

**Syntax:**

    CLEAR flag

**Description:**

Clears the setting of the flag. You can omit the "F" part (flag) of the name of the flag.

**Examples:**

    CLEAR TF
    CLEAR Z

## D
Displays the contents of the memory

**Syntax:**

    D [address]

**Description:**

Displays 128 bytes of memory beginning at address x.

    D area

Displays all the bytes in area x.

**Examples:**
```
D CS:100
D CS:100 L 500
```

## DSCRN                                    Redisplays the screen

**Syntax:**
```
DSCRN
```

**Description:**

Redisplays the SIM screen taking into account the settings of DMEM, BIG and CASE

**Example:**
```
DSCRN
```

## DMEM                                        Displays memory

**Syntax:**
```
DMEM address|OFF [W]
```

**Description:**

Opens or closes a memory window at address x. The OFF parameter closes the memory window and enlarging the disassembly window. The W parameter causes the memory to be displayed word by word. If W is not present, memory is displayed byte by byte.

You can display two distinct 16-byte areas. To display a second area type DMEM a second time.

**Examples:**
```
DMEM SS:FFF0  W
DMEM OFF
```

## DSTAT                                   Displays the current status

**Syntax:**
```
DSTAT
```

### Description:

Displays the following information:

1. Top of DOS (addresses segment where SIM is loaded)
2. The size of the user area
3. The INTR value selected

### Example:

DSTAT

---

## E
Enters data in the memory

### Syntax #1:

E address

### Description:

Enters data directly in memory. The dash (-) decrements the address counter. You can increment using the <Enter> key without changing the value of the address. Press <Ctrl><C> to end this operation.

### Syntax #2:

E address list

### Description:

Enters a list of bytes at address X.

### Examples:

E CS:0100
E CS:0100 01 02 03 04

---

## ERASE
Erases the screen

### Syntax:

ERASE

### Description:

Erase the screen. You can later use DSCRN to redisplay the screen.

### Example:

ERASE

## F
Fills an area

### Syntax:

```
F area list
```

### Description:

Fills memory beginning at *area* with a *list* containing data values. Be careful of overlapping memory areas. FILL terminates if you attempt to write in a critical memory location in nonprivileged mode.

### Example:

```
F 100 L 500 1 2 3 4 5
```

## G
Go (turns control over to the 80x86)

### Syntax:

```
G [address]
```

### Description:

Turns control over to the 80x86 and lets you start your programs or your applications. Control goes back to the simulator when CS:IP = the address that you have indicated in the GO command or when your program comes upon a BRK instruction (INT 3, opcode CCH) or when your program normally ends (call system 20h). The message "80x86 Control" displays on the error line.

You can specify up to 10 breakpoints (BRK) in the GO command. The GO command will not let you send a trap flag to the 80x86 flag register.

### Examples:

```
G 4000
G DS:333 CS:101
```

## I
Input port

### Syntax:

```
I addr
```

### Description:

Reads a byte on the port at *addr z*.

### Example:

```
I 3F8
```

337

## INTR
Defines an interrupt priority

**Syntax:**

```
INTR num
```

**Description:**

Defines an interrupt of type *num* to be simulated by the signal on the INTR pin.

**Example:**

```
INTR 9
```

## LOAD
Loads file into memory

**Syntax:**

```
LOAD filename [name of file]
```

**Description:**

Loads the *filename* in memory and creates a program segment prefix at CS:0000. If you specify a second filename, this name is entered in the FCB located at CS:5C. BX:CX contains the length of the file. The DTA is entered at CS:80. If the filename has an .EXE extension, then the file is reloaded and CS, SS, IP and SP assume the values of the headings.

The file extensions must be specified. The filenames can also be specified when you load SIM:

```
C>SIM filename 1 filename 2
```

Here *filename 1* is placed in memory and *filename 2* is treated as a FCB located at CS:5C.

**Examples:**

```
LOAD PROG13.DEM
LOAD WS.COM TEST.COM
C>SIM WS.COM TEST.TXT
```

## M
Moves an area in memory

**Syntax:**

```
M address len area
```

## Description:

Moves the memory block at *area* to *address*. The memory block is *len* bytes long.

## Examples:

```
M CS:100 L 500 SS:1000
M 100 500 800
```

| NEW | Replaces SIM default values |
|-----|-----------------------------|

## Syntax:

```
NEW
```

## Description:

Restores initial SIM values. If a filename was intially loaded when SIM was started, the file is reloaded.

## Example:

```
NEW
```

| O | Sends a byte to the port indicated |
|---|------------------------------------|

## Syntax:

```
O addr value
```

## Description:

Outputs *value* to port at location *addr*. Only for privileged users.

## Example:

```
O 3F8 CC
```

| PRIV | Go into privileged mode |
|------|-------------------------|

## Syntax:

```
PRIV
```

## Description:

Sets SIM for privileged mode. You cannot write in memory or execute GO, SKIP, T or O instructions unless SIM is set for privileged mode.

## Example:

```
PRIV
```

---

## Q
Quit

**Syntax:**

Q

**Description:**

Exit SIM and return to DOS.

**Example:**

Q

## REGISTER
Assigns a register

**Syntax:**

reg value

**Description:**

Loads register *reg* with the date *value*. A "Range error" message appears if *reg* is an 8-bit register and *value* is greater than 256.

**Example:**

IP   100

## S
Search memory

**Syntax:**

S addr len list

**Description:**

Searches memory beginning at *addr* for data value *list* which is len bytes long.

**Examples:**

S CS:100 L 1000 '(C) COPYRIGHT'
S 300 L 200 4D 5A

## SAVE                                                    Save on a disk

### Syntax:

SAVE [filename]

### Description:

Saves to disk the area starting at CS:100, BX:CX bytes long with the name *filename*. If filename is a file that you have just loaded in memory and that you have modified, it isn't necessary to specify a filename during SAVE.

You cannot make any changes to an .EXE file. To get around this, you can change the name of the extension before loading it in memory. After that, you can do any changes and then save the file. You just have to give an .EXE extension to the modified file.

If this were a new file and BX:CX were equal to 0000:00FF (255 decimal), TEST.COM would contain 255 bytes starting at CS:100.

### Example:

SAVE TEST.COM

## SET                                                          Set flag

### Syntax:

SET flag

### Description:

Sets the *flag* (to binary value 1). Valid flags are T  Z  O.

### Example:

SET T

## SIM                                            Starts an 80x86 simulation

### Syntax:

SIM [word]

### Description:

Start a simulation for the instruction or instructions starting at *word* which specifies the memory area to simulate. If you omit *word* only one instruction is simulated. If the processor window is reduced, SIM automatically enlarges it for needs of the simulation.

Here are the active instructions during simulation:

| | |
|---|---|
| **Spacebar** | To request or cancel pause. |
| **1** - **9** | Establishes SIM execution speed of the simulation. Press <1> for the fastest execution speed and <9> for the slowest execution speed. |
| **N** **I** **T** | Press these keys to change the status of the corresponding input pin: <br> <N>=NMI      <I>=INTR      <T>=TEST |
| **C** | Press this key to use the calculator (during a pause). Press <Esc> to return to the pause. |
| **Ctrl** **P** | Sets and resets the printer. When the printer is set, PR is displayed on the status line. The status of the processor is printed at the end of each instruction SIM executes. This includes the next disassembled instruction. |
| **Esc** or <br> **Ctrl** **C** | Ends simulation and returns to the Command Management Window. |

Refer to Appendix A for more information concerning the SIM instruction.

**Example:**

```
SIM  F00
```

## SKIP                                                            Set breakpoint

**Syntax:**

```
SKIP
```

**Description:**

The SKIP instruction establishes a breakpoint immediately following the instruction in progress and turns control to your program. For privileged mode users only.

Control is returned to SIM as soon as CS:IP is equal to the address of the next instruction. The message "80x86 Control" appears on the line reserved for error messages.

**Example:**

    SKIP

## STEP                                              Simulation mode

**Syntax:**

    STEP n

where n is a whole number from 0 to 4.

**Description:**

STEP specifies the number of waits during the execution of an instruction.

| STEP= | Effects |
|-------|---------|
| 4 | Waits after each instruction, each macro and microstep, each read/write and between each phase of verifying interrupts. |
| 3 | Waits between instructions, macro and micro stages. |
| 2 | Waits between instructions and macro stages (best mode for learning). |
| 1 | Waits only between instructions. |
| 0 | No waiting. |

**Example:**

    STEP 2

## T                                        Trace the instruction in CS:IP

**Syntax:**

    T [value]

**Description:**

Use the 80x86 Trap Flag to execute step by step a single instruction. If *value* is greater than 1, the <Enter> key lets you execute rapidly this step-by-step process. The <Spacebar> lets you execute the instruction step by step.

**Example:**

    T  FFFF

## U                                                           Disassemble memory

### Syntax #1:

```
U [addr]
```

### Description:

Disassembles memory beginning at *addr*. Either 18 or 6 bytes (depending on the screen size) are disassembled.

### Syntax #2:

```
U area
```

Disassembles all the instructions in an area.

### Example (applies to either syntax):

- INT 3 gives BRK.

- LOOPNE gives LOOPN.

- The disassembly window cuts off the instructions greater than 33 characters and then enters a "( )" in the column at the extreme right.

# Appendix E: Information and Instructions

Appendix E lists and describes the complete assembly language instruction set for the 8088 and 8086 with additional instructions for the 80286 and 80386.

## Calculating Effective Address Times   (8086 and 8088 only)

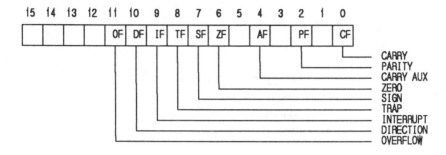

| Effective Address component | Cycles required |
|---|---|
| Displacement only | 6 |
| Base or Index only (BX, BP, SI, DI) | 5 |
| Displacement<br>+<br>Base or Index (BX, BP, SI, DI) | 9 |
| Base        BP,+DI, BX+SI<br>+<br>Index        BP+SI, BX+DI | 7<br>8 |
| Displacement    BP+DI+DISP<br>                 BX+SI+DISP<br>Base<br>+                BP+SI+DISP<br>Index            BX+DI+DISP | 11<br><br><br><br>12 |

*\* Add two cycles for the segment override*

Note that the hardware calculates the Effective Address of the 186/188. The time necessary for calculating is included in the time specified for each instruction.

## Operand Notation

| | |
|---|---|
| + | addition |
| - | subtraction |
| * | multiplication |
| / | division |
| % | modulo division |
| : | concatenation |
| & | anding |
| <- | assignment |

# Assembly Language Instruction Set

Each new generation of the 80x86 microprocessor has been designed upon the existing 80x86 microprocessors. For example, the first Intel microprocessors, 8086 and 8088, share a common instruction set for later generations.

Your PC may use an 8086, an 8088 (used in the IBM-PC/XT), an 80186, 80286 (used in the IBM-AT), 80386 or even an 80486. The later processors (80286 and 80386) use the same 8086/8088 instruction set.

The differences between the Intel 80386 processor and the 8088 and 8086 processors are mainly with registers, flags and several additional instructions.

### 80386 extended registers

The 80386 is a 32-bit processor. Several additional registers are able to handle the 32-bit operands. Although the 80386 uses the same general-purpose registers (AX, BX, CX and DX) as the 8088, 8086 and 80286, the 80386 registers are identified with an E prefix. These registers are *extended* registers: EAX, EBX, ECX and EDX. These are considered extended because they are 32-bit registers. If they're not indicated by the E prefix, only the lower 16 bits of each register are used.

In addition to the four general purpose registers, there are 32-bit registers for other purposes. For example, BP, SI, DI and SP are called EBP, ESI, EDI and ESP registers for the 80386.

There are six segment registers in the 80386 processor. The CS, DS, SS and ES segment registers remain the same for the 80386 because they are only 16-bits wide. However, the 80386 processors have two new registers (the FS and GS registers).

### 80386 Processor control flags

Although the 80386 uses 32-bit wide flag registers, the upper 14 bits are not available to programmers. In the following section we'll describe how the other 18 bits are affected by the execution of the instruction.

There are four flags in addition to the standard 8088, 8086 and 80286 flags:

- VM (virtual 8086 mode) determines if the 80386 operates in 8086 mode or in normal protected mode. If set, the 80386 executes in virtual 8086 mode. If clear, the 80386 operates in normal protected mode.

- RF (resume or restart flag) determines if debug faults are accepted or ignored. If RF is clear, debug faults are accepted. If RF is set, debug faults are ignored.

- NT (nested task) controls the operation of the IRET instruction.

- IOPL (I/O privilege level) specifies the privilege level required to perform I/O instructions.

In this section we'll list each instruction in alphabetical order and provide a description for each instruction. Remember, these instructions are valid for 8088/80x86 processors. The additional instructions for the 80286 and 80386 processors are indicated with a 286/386 or 386 listed above the description.

We'll also show which, if any, flags are affected by the following table:

| $\underset{=}{X}$ | Flag is changed by the instruction |
|---|---|
| X̶ | Flag is undefined after instruction |
| X | Flag not affected |

For example, you'll see that the AAA instruction lists the following under **Flag Indicators affected**:

$\underline{O}$ D I T $\underline{S}$ $\underline{Z}$ $\underline{\underline{A}}$ $\underline{P}$ $\underline{\underline{C}}$

This means that the O, S, Z and P flags are undefined after the instruction and the A and C flags are changed by the instruction. The remaining flags are not affected by this instruction.

---

## AAA                                                          ASCII Adjust After Addition

**Description:**

AAA adjusts the sum of the two unpacked decimal numbers contained in the AL register to two unpacked decimal numbers of the AX register. The contents of the AX register can then be converted to ASCII characters.

**Flag Indicators affected:**            **Operands:**

$\underline{O}$ D I T $\underline{S}$ $\underline{Z}$ $\underline{\underline{A}}$ $\underline{P}$ $\underline{\underline{C}}$            AAA no operands

## AAD — ASCII Adjust Before Division

**Description:**

AAD converts the two unpacked decimal numbers in the AX register to a binary number also in the AX register. AAD updates PF, SF and ZF. The contents of AF, CF and OF are not defined after an AAD instruction.

**Flag Indicators affected:**

O D I T S̲ Z̲ A P̲ C

**Operands:**

AAD no operands

## AAM — ASCII Adjust After Multiply

**Description:**

AAM converts the binary number in the AX register to two unpacked decimal numbers also in the AX register. AAM updates PF, SF and ZF. The contents of AF, CF and OF are undefined.

**Flag Indicators affected:**

O D I T S̲ Z̲ A P̲ C

**Operands:**

AAM no operands

## AAS — ASCII Adjust After Subtraction

**Description:**

AAS adjusts the difference of two unpacked decimal numbers contained in the AX register to a valid unpacked decimal number also in the AX register. The contents of the AX register can then be converted to two ASCII characters.

**Flag Indicators affected:**

O D I T S Z̲ A P C̲

**Operands:**

AAS no operands

## ADC — Add with Carry

**Description:**

ADC adds bytes, words or doublewords (80386 or 80486) and the carry flag. The result is in *dest*.

If CF is set, the result is incremented by one. The result is placed in *dest*. ADC updates AF, CF, OF, PF, SF and ZF.

**Flag Indicators affected:**                    **Operands:**

O̲ D I T S̲̲ Z̲̲ A̲̲ P C̲̲                    ADD dest,source

| **ADD** | Addition |

**Description:**

ADD adds source to dest which may be bytes, words or doublewords (80386 or 80486). The result is in *dest* (see AAA and DAA). ADD updates AF, CF, OF, PF, SF and ZF.

**Flag Indicators affected:**                    **Operands:**

O̲ D I T S̲̲ Z̲̲ A̲̲ P̲̲ C̲̲                    ADD dest,source

| **AND** | Logical AND |

**Description:**

AND logically ANDs the bits of *dest* with *source* and stores the results in *dest. Dest* and *source* may be bytes, words or doublewords (80386 or 80486). In the result, a bit is set if the corresponding bits in both operands were set prior to the operation.

**Flag Indicators affected:**                    **Operands:**

O̲ D I T S̲̲ Z̲̲ A P C̲̲                    AND dest,source

| **BOUND** | Check Array Index against Bounds |

*286/386*

**Description:**

BOUND compares the signed array index in *op1* with the low and high bound data structures in *op2*.

**Flag Indicators affected:**                    **Operands:**

O D I T S Z A P C                    BOUND op1, op2

## BSF — Bit Scan Forward

*386*

### Description:

BSF scans bits in *source* starting from least significant bit to most significant bit. If all bits in *source* are 0, the ZF is set to 1. If a 1 bit is found, the ZF is set to 0 and *dest* is set to the bit number. *Dest* and *source* may be either a byte, word, doubleword (80386 or 80486) value.

**Flag Indicators affected:**

O D I T S $\underline{\underline{Z}}$ A P C

**Operands:**

BSF dest source

## BSR — Bit Scan Reverse

*386*

### Description:

BSR scans bits in *source* starting from most significant bit to least significant bit. If all bits in *source* are 0, the ZF is set to 1. If a 1 bit is found, the ZF is set to 0 and *dest* is set to the bit number. *Dest* and *source* may be either a byte, word, doubleword (80386 or 80486) value.

**Flag Indicators affected:**

O D I T S $\underline{\underline{Z}}$ A P C

**Operands:**

BSR dest source

## BT — Bit test

*386*

### Description:

BT copies a bit from *source* at the position specified by *bitpos* to CF. *Source* may be a word or doubleword (80386 or 80486) register or memory location. *Bitpos* may be a byte or word register or immediate value.

**Flag Indicators affected:**

O D I T S $\underline{\underline{Z}}$ A P C

**Operands:**

BT source, bitpos

## BTC — Bit Test and Complement

*386*

**Description:**

BTC copies a bit from *source* at the position specified by *bitpos* to CF and then complements the original bit in *source*. *Source* may be a word or doubleword (80386 or 80486) register or memory location. *Bitpos* may be a byte or word register or immediate value.

**Flag Indicators affected:**

O D I T S $\underline{Z}$ A P C

**Operands:**

BTC source, bitpos

## BTR — Bit Test and Reset

*386*

**Description:**

BTR copies a bit from *source* at the position specified by *bitpos* to CF and then resets the original bit in *source*. *Source* may be a word or doubleword (80386 or 80486) register or memory location. *Bitpos* may be a byte or word register or immediate value.

**Flag Indicators affected:**

O D I T S $\underline{Z}$ A P C

**Operands:**

BTR source, bitpos

## BTS — Bit Test and Set

*386*

**Description:**

BTR copies a bit from *source* at the position specified by *bitpos* to CF and then sets the original bit in *source*. *Source* may be a word or doubleword (80386 or 80486) register or memory location. *Bitpos* may be a byte or word register or immediate value.

**Flag Indicators affected:**

O D I T S $\underline{Z}$ A P C

**Operands:**

BTS source, bitpos

---

## CALL
Call and perform subroutine

### Description:

CALL calls a subroutine. The offset address of the following instruction is pushed on the stack and the IP is loaded with the offset address of the subname. If subroutine subname is a FAR label, CALL pushes the segment address of the next instruction on the stack and loads CS with the segment address of the subname.

**Flag Indicators affected:**          **Operands:**

O D I T S Z A P C                     CALL subname

---

## CBW
Convert Byte to Word

### Description:

CBW converts the byte value in AL to a word value in AX. This has the effect of extending the sign of the 8-bit value.

**Flag Indicators affected:**          **Operands:**

O D I T S Z A P C                     CBW no operands

---

## CDQ
Convert doubleword to quadword

*386*

### Description:

CDQ converts the doubleword in EAX to a quadword in EDX:EAX by extending the sign bit to EDX.

**Flag Indicators affected:**          **Operands:**

O D I T S Z A P C                     CDQ no operands

---

## CLC
Clear Carry Flag

### Description:

CLC clears the carry flag (CF) by resetting it to zero.

**Flag Indicators affected:**          **Operands:**

O D I T S Z A P $\underline{C}$                     CLC no operands

## CLD — Clear Direction Flag

**Description:**

CLD clears the direction flag (DF) by setting it to zero.

**Flag Indicators affected:**

O D̲ I T S Z A P C

**Operands:**

CLD no operands

## CLI — Clear Interrupt Flag

**Description:**

CLI clears the interrupt flag (IF) by resetting it to zero. When the interrupt flag is cleared, the CPU does not recognize any maskable interrupts.

**Flag Indicators affected:**

O D I̲ T S Z A P C

**Operands:**

CLI no operands

## CMC — Complement Carry Flag

**Description:**

CMC reverses the setting of the carry flag (CF).

**Flag Indicators affected:**

O D I T S Z A P C̲

**Operands:**

CMC no operands

## CMP — Compare

**Description:**

CMP compares OP1 with OP2 which may be bytes, words or doublewords (80386 or 80486). The flags are set as if a subtraction between OP1 and OP2 occurred.

**Flag Indicators affected:**

O̲ D I T S̲ Z̲ A̲ P̲ C̲

**Operands:**

CMP op1,op2

| CMPS | Compare Strings (Byte or Word) |

## Description:

CMPS, CMPSB, CMBSW and CMPSD compare two strings. CMPS compares the strings OP1 and OP2, byte-by-byte. CMPSB, CMBSW and CMPSD compares the strings byte-by-byte and word-by-word and doubleword-by-doubleword, respectively.

One operand is pointed to by DS:SI or ES:SI. The other operand is pointed to by ES:DI. If DF=0, the SI and DI registers are incremented by the number of bytes being compared (1,2 or 4). If DI=1, the SI and DI registers are decremented by the number of bytes being compared.

Following execution, the flags are set as if a subtraction between the two operands was performed.

**Flag Indicators affected:**

O̲ D I T S̲ Z̲ A̲ P̲ C̲

**Operands:**

CMPS op1,op2

CMPSB no operands

CMBSW no operands

CMPSD no operands

| CWD | Convert Word to Doubleword |

## Description:

CWD converts the word value (16-bits) in AX to a double word value (32-bits) in DX:AX. This has the effect of extending the sign of the 16-bit value.

**Flag Indicators affected:**

O D I T S Z A P C

**Operands:**

CWD no operands

| CWDE | Convert Word Extended Doubleword |

*386*

## Description:

CWD converts the word value in AX to a doubleword in EAX by extending the sign bit to EAX.

355

**Flag Indicators affected:**

O D I T S Z A P C

**Operands:**

CWDE no operands

## DAA                                           Decimal Adjust After Addition

**Description:**

DAA adjust the sum of two packed numbers contained in the AL register to packed decimal format.

**Flag Indicators affected:**

<u>O</u> D I T <u>S</u> <u>Z</u> <u>A</u> <u>P</u> <u>C</u>

**Operands:**

DAA no operands

## DAS                                       Decimal Adjust After Subtraction

**Description:**

DAS adjusts the differences of two packed decimal numbers contained in the AL register to packed decimal format.

**Flag Indicators affected:**

<u>O</u> D I T <u>S</u> <u>Z</u> <u>A</u> <u>P</u> <u>C</u>

**Operands:**

DAS no operands

## DEC                                                           Decrement

**Description:**

DEC decrements by 1 the contents of *dest*. *Dest* is an unsigned binary value and may be a byte, word, doubleword (80386 or 80486), register or memory location.

**Flag Indicators affected:**

<u>O</u> D I T <u>S</u> <u>Z</u> <u>A</u> <u>P</u> C

**Operands:**

DEC dest

## DIV                                                                    Divide

### Description:

DIV divides the contents of the AX, DX:AX or EDX:EAX registers by divisor.

For 8-bit division, the AX register contains the dividend. After division, AL contains the quotient and AH contains the remainder.

For 16-bit division, the DX:AX register pair contains the dividend. After division, AX contains the quotient and DX contains the remainder.

For 32-bit division (80386 and 80486) the EDX:EAX register pair contains the dividend. After division, EAX contains the quotient and EDX contains the remainder.

All numbers are treated as unsigned binary values.

**Flag Indicators affected:**          **Operands:**

O D I T S Z A P C                          DIV divisor

## ENTER                                                          Create stack frame

*286/386*

### Description:

ENTER creates a stack frame. *Op1* is the amount of local variables (specified as bytes) for which stack space is allocated.

*Op2* is the nesting depth of the routine.

**Flag Indicators affected:**          **Operands:**

O D I T S Z A P C                          ENTER op1, op2

## ESC                                                                  Escape

### Description:

ESC gives the co-processor an *instr* instruction and *source* operand to execute. In a system without an 8087, ESC is identical to NOP (No Operation) but takes longer to execute.

**Flag Indicators affected:**          **Operands:**

O D I T S Z A P C                          ESC instr, source

## HLT
Halt

### Description:

HLT causes the processor to pause and wait with CS:IP pointing to the next instruction. The HLT is paused until it receives a hardware interrupt or when RESET is activated.

**Flag Indicators affected:**

O D I T S Z A P C

**Operands:**

HLT no operands

## IDIV
Integer Divide

### Description:

Same as DIV except the numbers are treated as signed binary values. All remainders have the same sign as the dividend.

If the divisor is 0 or the result of the division is greater than the capacity of the quotient, then interrupt 0 is generated.

**Flag Indicators affected:**

O̲ D I T S̲ Z̲ A̲ P̲ C̲

**Operands:**

IDIV divisor

## IMUL
Integer Multiply

### Description:

IMUL multiplies the contents of the AL,AX register by *multiplier*.

For 8-bit multiplication, AL contains the AX multiplicand. After multiplication, the result is in AX.

For 16-bit multiplication, AX contains the multiplicand. After multiplication, the result is in the DX:AX register pair.

For 32-bit multiplication (80386 and 80486), EAX contains the multiplicand. After multiplication, the result is in the EDX:EAX register pair.

All numbers are treated as signed binary values.

**Flag Indicators affected:**

O̲ D I T S̲ Z̲ A̲ P̲ C̲

**Operands:**

IMUL multiplier

## IN — Input from Port

### Description:

IN reads the value of an I/O port at *addr* into register *reg*, which may be AL, AX or EAX (80386 or 80486). The value is either 8-bit, 16-bit or 32-bit depending on the register used.

**Flag Indicators affected:**

O D I T S Z A P C

**Operands:**

IN reg, addr

## INC — Increment

### Description:

INC increments by 1 the contents of the *dest*. The *dest* is an unsigned binary value and may be bytes, words, doublewords (80386 or 80486), register or memory location.

**Flag Indicators affected:**

O D I T S Z A P C

**Operands:**

INC dest

## INS — Input String from Port

*286/386*

### Description:

INS transfers strings from an I/O port.

INS transfers byte, word or doubleword strings from port to *source* specified in register DX.

If DF=0, then SI is incremented by the number of bytes being transferred. If DF=1, then SI is decremented by the number of bytes being transferred.

**Flag Indicators affected:**

O D I T S Z A P C

**Operands:**

INS DX, portaddr

## INSB
Input Byte from Port

*286/386*

**Description:**

INSB transfers strings from an I/O port.

INSB transfers byte strings from the memory location specified by register pair DS:DI to the port specified in register DX.

If DF=0, then SI is incremented by the number of bytes being transferred. If DF=1, then SI is decremented by the number of bytes being transferred.

**Flag Indicators affected:**

O D I T S Z A P C

**Operands:**

INSB no operands

## INSB
Input String from Port

*286/386*

**Description:**

INSB transfers strings to an I/O port.

INSB transfers doubleword strings from the memory location specified by register pair DS:DI from the port specified in register DX.

If DF=0, then SI is incremented by the number of bytes being transferred. If DF=1, then SI is decremented by the number of bytes being transferred.

**Flag Indicators affected:**

O D I T S Z A P C

**Operands:**

INSB no operands

## INSW
Input Word from Port

*286/386*

**Description:**

INSW transfers strings to an I/O port.

INSW transfers word strings from the memory location specified by register pair DS:DI from the port specified in register DX.

If DF=0, then SI is incremented by the number of bytes being transferred. If DF=1, then SI is decremented by the number of bytes being transferred.

**Flag Indicators affected:**

O D I T S Z A P C

**Operands:**

INSW no operands

## INT                                                              Interrupt

**Description:**

INT generates a software interrupt to the processor. The CPU saves the IP and CS registers on the stack and loads the IP and CS with the values contained in the interrupt vector table corresponding to interrupt *intrup*.

The flags are also pushed on the stack and the TF and IF flags are cleared. The program continues at the new CS:IP address until a IRET instruction returns execution to the instruction following the INT instruction.

**Flag Indicators affected:**

O D I T S Z A P C
    = =

**Operands:**

INT intrup

## INTO                                                   Interrupt on Overflow

**Description:**

INTO generates interrupt 4 (INT 4) if the overflow flag (OF) is set.

**Flag Indicators affected:**

O D I T S Z A P C

**Operands:**

INTO no operands

## IRET
Interrupt Return

### Description:

IRET marks the end of an interrupt service routine. It pops the value of CS:IP and flags from the stack and resumes execution at the instruction following the original INT instruction.

**Flag Indicators affected:**

O D I T S Z A P C

**Operands:**

IRET no operands

## JA
Jump if Above

### Description:

JA causes the program to branch to *dest* if both the carry flag (CF) and zero flag (ZF) are clear.

**Flag Indicators affected:**

O D I T S Z A P C

**Operands:**

JA dest

## JAE
Jump if Above or Equal

### Description:

JAE causes the program to branch to *dest* if the carry flag (CF) is clear. The JNC instruction also works in a similar way.

**Flag Indicators affected:**

O D I T S Z A P C

**Operands:**

JAE dest

## JB
Jump if Below

### Description:

JB causes the program to branch to *dest* if the carry flag (CF) is set. The JC instruction also works in a similar way.

**Flag Indicators affected:**

O D I T S Z A P C

**Operands:**

JB dest

## JBE — Jump if Below or Equal

### Description:

JBE causes the program to branch to *dest* if either the carry flag (CF) or zero flag (ZF) is set.

**Flag Indicators affected:**

O D I T S Z A P C

**Operands:**

JBE dest

## JC — Jump on Carry

### Description:

JC causes the program to branch to *dest* if the carry flag (CF) is set. The JB and JNAE instructions also work in a similar way.

**Flag Indicators affected:**

O D I T S Z A P C

**Operands:**

JC dest

## JCXZ — Jump if CX is Zero

### Description:

JCXZ causes the program to branch to *dest* if the value of the CX register is zero.

**Flag Indicators affected:**

O D I T S Z A P C

**Operands:**

JCXZ dest

## JE — Jump if Equal

### Description:

JE causes the program to branch to *dest* if the zero flag (ZF) is set.

**Flag Indicators affected:**

O D I T S Z A P C

**Operands:**

JE dest

## JECXZ — Jump if ECX is Zero

*386*

### Description:

JECXZ branches to *target* if the value of ECX equals zero. *Target* is in the range -127 to +126 bytes from this instruction.

**Flag Indicators affected:**

O D I T S Z A P C

**Operands:**

JECXZ no operands

## JG — Jump if Greater

### Description:

JG causes the program to branch to *dest* if the sign flag (SF) equals the overflow flag (OF) or the zero flag (ZF) is clear.

**Flag Indicators affected:**

O D I T S Z A P C

**Operands:**

JG dest

## JGE — Jump if Greater or Equal

### Description:

JGE causes the program to branch to *dest* if the sign flag (SF) equals the overflow flag (OF).

**Flag Indicators affected:**

O D I T S Z A P C

**Operands:**

JGE dest

## JL — Jump if Less Than

### Description:

JL causes the program to branch to *dest* if the sign flag (SF) does not equal the overflow flag (OF).

**Flag Indicators affected:**

O D I T S Z A P C

**Operands:**

JL dest

## JLE — Jump if Less Than or Equal

### Description:

JLE causes the program to branch to *dest* if the sign flag (SF) does not equal the overflow flag (OF) or if the zero flag (ZF) is set.

**Flag Indicators affected:**

O D I T S Z A P C

**Operands:**

JLE dest

## JMP — Jump

### Description:

JMP causes the program to unconditionally branch to *dest*.

**Flag Indicators affected:**

O D I T S Z A P C

**Operands:**

JMP dest

## JNA — Jump if Not Above

### Description:

JNA causes the program to branch to *dest* if either the carry flag (CF) or zero flag (ZF) is set.

**Flag Indicators affected:**

O D I T S Z A P C

**Operands:**

JNA dest

## JNAE — Jump if Not Above or Equal

### Description:

JNAE causes the program to branch to *dest* if the carry flag (CF) is set. The JC instruction also works in a similar way.

**Flag Indicators affected:**

O D I T S Z A P C

**Operands:**

JNAE dest

---

## JNB — Jump if Not Below

### Description:

JNB causes the program to branch to *dest* if the carry flag (CF) is clear. The JNC instruction also works in a similar way.

**Flag Indicators affected:**

O D I T S Z A P C

**Operands:**

JNB dest

---

## JNBE — Jump if Not Below or Equal

### Description:

JNBE causes the program to branch to *dest* if both the carry flag (CF) and zero flag (ZF) are clear.

**Flag Indicators affected:**

O D I T S Z A P C

**Operands:**

JNBE dest

---

## JNC — Jump on No Carry

### Description:

JNC causes the program to branch to *dest* if the carry flag (CF) is clear. The JAE and JNB instructions also work in a similar way.

**Flag Indicators affected:**

O D I T S Z A P C

**Operands:**

JNC dest

---

## JNE — Jump if Not Equal

### Description:

JNE causes the program to branch to *dest* if the zero flag (ZF) is clear.

**Flag Indicators affected:**

O D I T S Z A P C

**Operands:**

JNE dest

## JNG — Jump if Not Greater

### Description:

JNG causes the program to branch to *dest* if the sign flag (SF) does not equal the overflow flag (OF) or if the zero flag (ZF) is set.

**Flag Indicators affected:**

O D I T S Z A P C

**Operands:**

JNG dest

## JNGE — Jump if Not Greater or Equal

### Description:

JNGE causes the program to branch to *dest* if the sign flag (SF) does not equal the overflow flag (OF).

**Flag Indicators affected:**

O D I T S Z A P C

**Operands:**

JNGE dest

## JNL — Jump if Not Less Than

### Description:

JNL causes the program to branch to *dest* if the sign flag (SF) equals the overflow flag (OF).

**Flag Indicators affected:**

O D I T S Z A P C

**Operands:**

JNL dest

## JNLE — Jump if Not Less Than or Equal

### Description:

JNLE causes the program to branch to *dest* if the sign flag (SF) equals the overflow flag (OF) or the zero flag (ZF) is clear.

**Flag Indicators affected:**

O D I T S Z A P C

**Operands:**

JNLE dest

## JNO
Jump on No Overflow

**Description:**

JNO causes the program to branch to *dest* if the overflow flag (OF) is set.

**Flag Indicators affected:**          **Operands:**

O D I T S Z A P C                      JNO dest

## JNP
Jump on No Parity

**Description:**

JNP causes the program to branch to *dest* if the parity flag (PF) is clear.

**Flag Indicators affected:**          **Operands:**

O D I T S Z A P C                      JNP dest

## JNS
Jump on No Sign

**Description:**

JNS causes the program to branch to *dest* if the sign flag (SF) is clear.

**Flag Indicators affected:**          **Operands:**

O D I T S Z A P C                      JNS dest

## JNZ
Jump on Not Zero

**Description:**

JNZ causes the program to branch to *dest* if the zero flag (ZF) is clear.

**Flag Indicators affected:**          **Operands:**

O D I T S Z A P C                      JNZ dest

## JO — Jump on Overflow

**Description:**

JO causes the program to branch to *dest* if the overflow flag (OF) is set.

**Flag Indicators affected:**

O D I T S Z A P C

**Operands:**

JO dest

## JP — Jump on Parity

**Description:**

JP causes the program to branch to *dest* if the parity flag (PF) is set.

**Flag Indicators affected:**

O D I T S Z A P C

**Operands:**

JP dest

## JPE — Jump on Parity Even

**Description:**

JPE causes the program to branch to *dest* if the parity flag (PF) is set.

**Flag Indicators affected:**

O D I T S Z A P C

**Operands:**

JPE dest

## JPO — Jump on Parity Odd

**Description:**

JPO causes the program to branch to *dest* if the parity flag (PF) is clear.

**Flag Indicators affected:**

O D I T S Z A P C

**Operands:**

JPO dest

## JS
Jump on Sign

### Description:

JS causes the program to branch to *dest* if the sign flag (SF) is set.

**Flag Indicators affected:**

O D I T S Z A P C

**Operands:**

JS dest

## JZ
Jump on Zero

### Description:

JZ causes the program to branch to *dest* if the zero flag (ZF) is set.

**Flag Indicators affected:**

O D I T S Z A P C

**Operands:**

JZ dest

## LAHF
Load AH with Flags

### Description:

LAHF copies the SF, ZF, AF, PF and CF flags into bits 7, 6, 4, 2 and 1 respectively of the AH register.

**Flag Indicators affected:**

O D I T S Z A P C

**Operands:**

LAHF no operands

## LDS
Load Pointer and DS Register

### Description:

LDS loads a 32-bit pointer from *source* into *register* DS (segment address) and register *reg* (offset address).

**Flag Indicators affected:**

O D I T S Z A P C

**Operands:**

LDS reg, source

370

## LEA — Load Effective Address

**Description:**

LEA calculates the effective address (offset) of *source* and places it into register *reg*. Reg must be a general 16-bit register. For 80386 and 80486, *reg1 DW*, *reg2 DW*, *source DW* and *dest DW* may be 32-bit operands.

**Flag Indicators affected:**

O D I T S Z A P C

**Operands:**

LEA reg, source

LEA reg1 DW, reg2 DW  (80386 and 80486)

LEA dest DW, source DW  (80386 and 80486)

## LES — Load Pointer and ES Register

**Description:**

LES loads a 32-bit pointer from source into register ES (segment address) and register *reg* (offset address).

**Flag Indicators affected:**

O D I T S Z A P C

**Operands:**

LES reg, source

## LFS — Load FS Register

*386*

**Description:**

LFS loads the *dest* with the offset address and segment address of *source* and loads the FS register with the segment address of *source*. *Dest* is a 16-bit or 32-bit register. *Source* is a 32-bit or 48-bit memory location.

**Flag Indicators affected:**

O D I T S Z A P C

**Operands:**

LFS dest source

**371**

## LGS
Load GS Register

*386*

### Description:

LGS loads the *dest* with the offset address and segment address of *source* and loads the FS register with the segment address of *source*. *Dest* is a 16-bit or 32-bit register. *Source* is a 32-bit or 48-bit memory location.

**Flag Indicators affected:**

O D I T S Z A P C

**Operands:**

LGS dest source

## LOCK
Lock Bus

### Description:

LOCK is a prefix for subsequent instructions to prevent other processors from interfering with that instruction. This instructions switches on the lock signal on the CPU bus.

**Flag Indicators affected:**

O D I T S Z A P C

**Operands:**

LOCK no operands

## LODS
Load String (Byte or Word)

### Description:

LODS, LODSB, LODSW and LODSD load string data into the accumulator. LODS loads either a byte into the AL register or a word into the AX register depending on *source*.

LODSB loads a byte pointed to by DS:SI into the AL register.

LODSW loads word pointed to by DS:SI into the AX register.

LODSD loads a doubleword pointed to by DS:SI into the EAX register (80386 and 80486).

If DF=0, the SI and DI registers are incremented by the number of bytes being loaded. If DF=1, the SI and DI registers are decremented by the number of bytes being loaded.

**Flag Indicators affected:**

O D I T S Z A P C

**Operands:**

LODS source
LODSB no operands
LODSW no operands
LODSD no operands

## LOOP                                                                    Loop

**Description:**

LOOP decrements the CX register and branches it to *target* if CX does not equal 0. If CX=0 the next instruction is executed. *Target* must be in the range -127 to +128 bytes from this instruction.

**Flag Indicators affected:**          **Operands:**

O D I T S Z A P C                      LOOP target

## LOOPE                                        Loop Using Register CX While Equal

**Description:**

LOOPE and LOOPZ decrement the CX register and branches to *target* if CX does not equal 0 and zero flag equals 0. *Target* must be in the range -127 to +128 bytes from this instruction.

**Flag Indicators affected:**          **Operands:**

O D I T S Z A P C                      LOOPE target

## LOOPNE                                  Loop Using Register CX While Not Equal

**Description:**

LOOPNE and LOOPNZ decrement the CX register and branches to *target* if CX does not equal 0 and zero flag equals 0. *Target* must be in the range -127 to +128 bytes from this instruction.

**Flag Indicators affected:**          **Operands:**

O D I T S Z A P C                      LOOPNE target

## LOOPNZ — Loop Using Register CX While Not Zero

**Description:**

LOOPNZ and LOOPNE decrement the CX register and branches to *target* if CX does not equal 0 and zero flag equals 0. *Target* must be in the range -127 to +128 bytes from this instruction.

**Flag Indicators affected:**

O D I T S Z A P C

**Operands:**

LOOPNZ target

## LOOPZ — Loop Using Register CX While Zero

**Description:**

LOOPZ and LOOPE decrement the CX register and branches to *target* if CX does not equal 0 and zero flag equals 0. *Target* must be in the range -127 to +128 bytes from this instruction.

**Flag Indicators affected:**

O D I T S Z A P C

**Operands:**

LOOPZ target

## LSS — Load SS Register

*386*

**Description:**

LSS loads the *dest* with the offset address and segment address of *source* and loads the FS register with the segment address of *source*. *Dest* is a 16-bit or 32-bit register. *Source* is a 32-bit or 48-bit memory location.

**Flag Indicators affected:**

O D I T S Z A P C

**Operands:**

LSS dest source

## MOV — Move

### Description:

MOV copies the contents of the *source* to the *dest*. The contents may be bytes, words or doublewords (80386 or 80486). One of the *source* or *dest* operands must represent a register.

**Flag Indicators affected:**

O D I T S Z A P C

**Operands:**

MOV dest, source

## MOVS — Move String

### Description:

MOVS, MOVSB, MOVSW and MOVSD move strings of data from one memory location to another.

MOVS moves byte, word or doubleword (80386 or 80486) strings from *source* to *dest*.

MOVSB moves byte data from the memory location pointed to by register pair ES:DI to the memory location pointed to by register pair DS:SI.

MOVSW moves word data from the memory location pointed to by register pair ES:DI to the memory location pointed to by the register pair DS:SI.

MOVSD moves doubleword data (80386 and 80486).

If DF=0, the SI and DI registers are incremented by the number of bytes being moved. If DF=1, the SI and DI registers are decremented by the number of bytes being moved.

**Flag Indicators affected:**

O D I T S Z A P C

**Operands:**

MOVS source, dest

MOVSB no operands

MOVSW no operands

MOVSD no operands

## MOVSX — Move with Sign Extended

*386*

### Description:

MOVSX transfers the contents of *source* to *dest* and extends the sign of *source* to fill the most significant bits in *dest*. *Dest* may be a word or doubleword register. *Source* may be a byte or word register or memory location and must be a smaller size than *dest*.

**Flag Indicators affected:**

O D I T S Z A P C

**Operands:**

MOVSX dest source

## MOVZX — Move with Zero Extended

*386*

### Description:

MOVZX transfers the contents of *source* to *dest* and zeros the most significant bits of *dest*. *Dest* may be a word or doubleword register. *Source* may be a byte or word register or memory location and must be a smaller size than *dest*.

**Flag Indicators affected:**

O D I T S Z A P C

**Operands:**

MOVZX dest source

## MUL — Multiply

### Description:

MUL multiplies the contents of the AL,AX register by *multiplier*.

For 8-bit multiplication, AL contains the AX multiplicand. After multiplication, the result is in AX.

For 16-bit multiplication, AX contains the multiplicand. After multiplication, the result is in the DX:AX register pair.

For 32-bit multiplication (80386 and 80486), EAX contains the multiplicand. After multiplication, the result is in the EDX:EAX register pair.

The difference between IMUL and MUL is that MUL treats all numbers as unsigned binary values.

**Flag Indicators affected:**          **Operands:**

O̲ D I T S̲ Z̲ A̲ P̲ C̲          MUL multiplier

## NEG                                                                 Negate

**Description:**

NEG produces the 2's complement of *dest* and stores the result there. *Dest* may be a byte, word, doubleword (80386 or 80486), register or memory location.

**Flag Indicators affected:**          **Operands:**

O̲ D I T S̲ Z̲ A̲ P̲ C̲          NEG dest

## NOP                                                           No Operation

**Description:**

NOP is a "do nothing" instruction. It takes up a normal processing cycle and one byte of code space.

**Flag Indicators affected:**          **Operands:**

O D I T S Z A P C          NOP no operands

## NOT                                                            Logical NOT

**Description:**

NOT inverts the bits of *dest* and stores the results there. *Dest* may be a byte, word, doubleword (80386 or 80486), register or memory location.

**Flag Indicators affected:**          **Operands:**

O D I T S Z A P C          NOT dest

---

## | OR | Logical OR |

### Description:

OR logically ORs the bits of *dest* with *source* and stores the results in *dest*. *Dest* and *source* may be bytes, words, doublewords (80386 or 80486), registers or memory locations.

**Flag Indicators affected:**          **Operands:**

O̲ D I T S̲ Z̲ A̲ P̲ C̲                    OR dest, source

---

## | OUT | Output to Port |

### Description:

OUT writes the value in *reg* to the I/O port at *addr*. *Reg* may be AL, AX or EAX (80386 or 80486). The value written to the port is an 8-bit, 16-bit or 32-bit depending on the register used.

**Flag Indicators affected:**          **Operands:**

O D I T S Z A P C                     OUT reg, addr

---

## | OUTS | Output String to Port |

*286/386*

### Description:

OUTS transfers strings to an I/O port.

OUTS transfers byte, word or doubleword strings from *source* to the port specified in register DX.

If DF=0, then SI is incremented by the number of bytes being transferred. If DF=1, then SI is decremented by the number of bytes being transferred.

**Flag Indicators affected:**          **Operands:**

O D I T S Z A P C                     OUTS DX, source

## OUTSB | Output Byte to Port

*286/386*

**Description:**

OUTSB transfers strings to an I/O port.

OUTSB transfers byte strings from the memory location specified by register pair DS:DI to the port specified in register DX.

If DF=0, then SI is incremented by the number of bytes being transferred. If DF=1, then SI is decremented by the number of bytes being transferred.

**Flag Indicators affected:**

O D I T S Z A P C

**Operands:**

OUTSB no operands

## OUTSW | Output Word to Port

*286/386*

**Description:**

OUTSW transfers strings to an I/O port.

OUTSW transfers word strings from the memory location specified by register pair DS:DI to the port specified in register DX.

If DF=0, then SI is incremented by the number of bytes being transferred. If DF=1, then SI is decremented by the number of bytes being transferred.

**Flag Indicators affected:**

O D I T S Z A P C

**Operands:**

OUTSW no operands

## POP | Pop Data from Stack

**Description:**

POP removes a word or doubleword (80386 and 80486) from the stack and places it in *dest*. *Dest* may be a byte, word, doubleword (80386 or 80486), register or memory location.

**Flag Indicators affected:**

O D I T S Z A P C

**Operands:**

POP dest

## POPAD — POP All general purpose Doubleword registers

*386*

### Description:

Reloads registers EDI, ESI, EBP, ESP (contents ignored), EBX, EDX, ECX and then EAX from the stack and reduces the stack pointer by 32.

**Flag Indicators affected:**

O D I T S Z A P C

**Operands:**

POPAD no operands

## POPF — Pop Flags from Stack

### Description:

POPF removes a word from the stack and places it in the flags register.

**Flag Indicators affected:**

O D I T S Z A P C

**Operands:**

POPF no operands

## POPFD — POP extended Flag register Doubleword from stack

*386*

### Description:

POPFD reloads the extended flag registers from the stack and reduces the stack pointer by 4.

**Flag Indicators affected:**

O D I T S Z A P C

**Operands:**

POPFD no operands

### Other Flag Indicators affected:

VM (virtual mode): R (resume); NT (nested task) and IOPL (I/O privilege level)

## PUSH — Push Data on Stack

### Description:

PUSH copies the word or doubleword (80386 and 80486) at *source* onto the stack.

**Flag Indicators affected:**

O D I T S Z A P C

**Operands:**

PUSH no operands

## PUSHAD                    PUSH All general purpose Doubleword registers

*386*

**Description:**

PUSHAD transfers the contents of registers EAX, ECX, EDX, EBX, ESP, EBP, ESI, and EDI to the stack and increments the stack pointer by 32.

**Flag Indicators affected:**

O D I T S Z A P C

**Operands:**

PUSHAD no operands

## PUSHF                                                        Push Flags

**Description:**

PUSHF places a copy of the flag register onto the stack.

**Flag Indicators affected:**

O D I T S Z A P C

**Operands:**

PUSH source

## PUSHFD                    PUSH extended Flag register Doubleword to stack

*386*

**Description:**

PUSHFD transfers the contents of the extended flag register to the stack and increments the stack pointer by 4.

**Flag Indicators affected:**

O D I T S Z A P C

**Operands:**

PUSHFD no operands

## RCL
Rotate through Carry Left

### Description:

RCL rotates the bits in *dest* to the left by the number specified by *numbits*. The most significant bit of *dest* is rotated to the carry flag and the carry flag is rotated to the least significant bit of *dest*.

**Flag Indicators affected:**

O D I T S Z A P C

**Operands:**

RCL dest, numbits

## RCR
Rotate through Carry Right

### Description:

RCR rotates the bits in *dest* to the right by the number specified by *numbits*. The least significant bit of *dest* is rotated to the carry flag, while the carry flag is rotated to the most significant bit of *dest*.

**Flag Indicators affected:**

O D I T S Z A P C

**Operands:**

RCR dest, numbits

## REP
Repeat

### Description:

REP is a prefix for repeating string-instructions the number of times specified in the CX register.

**Flag Indicators affected:**

O D I T S Z A P C

**Operands:**

REPE string-instruction

REPZ string-instruction

## REPE

**Description:**

REPE and REPZ are prefixes for conditionally repeating a string-instruction the number of times specified in the CX register. If CX is not zero and ZF=1, then the string-instruction is repeated.

**Flag Indicators affected:**

O D I T S Z A P C

**Operands:**

REPE string-instruction

## REPNE

**Description:**

REPNE and REPNZ are prefixes for conditionally repeating string-instructions the number of times specified in the CX register. If CX is not zero and ZF=1, then the string-instruction is repeated.

**Flag Indicators affected:**

O D I T S Z A P C

**Operands:**

REPNE string-instruction

## REPNZ

**Description:**

REPNZ and REPNE are prefixes for conditionally repeating string-instructions the number of times specified in the CX register. If CX is not zero and ZF=1, then the string-instruction is repeated.

**Flag Indicators affected:**

O D I T S Z A P C

**Operands:**

REPNZ string-instruction

## REPZ
Repeat if Zero

### Description:

REPZ and REPE are prefixes for conditionally repeating a string-instruction the number of times specified in the CX register. If CX is not zero and ZF=1, then the string-instruction is repeated.

**Flag Indicators affected:**

O D I T S Z A P C

**Operands:**

REPZ string-instruction

## RET
Return from Subroutine

### Description:

RET and RETN return from a CALL subroutine by popping IP from the stack.

RETF for returning from a FAR subroutine pops CS:IP from the stack. If an optional *ival* is used, their 16-bit immediate value is added to the stack pointer after the return address is popped to allow passing parameters by high level languages to be adjusted.

**Flag Indicators affected:**

O D I T S Z A P C

**Operands:**

RET no operands
RETN no operands
RETF no operands
RET [ival]
RETN [ival]
RETF [ival]

## ROL
Rotate Left

### Description:

ROL rotates the bits in *dest* to the left by the number specified by *numbits*. The most significant bit is rotated into the least significant bit in *dest*.

**Flag Indicators affected:**

O D I T S Z A P C

**Operands:**

ROL dest, numbits

## ROR — Rotate Right

### Description:

ROR rotates the bits in *dest* to the right by the number specified in the *source* operand. The least significant bit is rotated into the most significant bit in *dest*.

**Flag Indicators affected:**

O̲ D I T S Z A P C̲

**Operands:**

ROR dest, numbits

## SAHF — Store AH into Flags

### Description:

SAHF stores bits 7, 6, 4, 2 and 1 of the AH register respectively into the SF, ZF, AF, PF and CF flags.

**Flag Indicators affected:**

O D I T S̲ Z̲ A̲ P̲ C̲

**Operands:**

SAHF no operands

## SAL — Shift Arithmetic Left

### Description:

SAL and SHL shifts the contents of *dest* by the number specified by *numbits*. Any high order bits shifted out are lost. New low order fill bits are set to zero.

**Flag Indicators affected:**

O̲ D I T S̲ Z̲ A̲ P̲ C̲

**Operands:**

SAL dest, numbits

## SAR — Shift Arithmetic Right

### Description:

SAR shifts the bits in *dest* by the number specified by *numbits*. Any low order bits shifted out of *dest* are lost. New high order fill bits are filled with the original sign bit.

**Flag Indicators affected:**

O̲ D I T S̲ Z̲ A̲ P̲ C̲

**Operands:**

SAR dest, numbits

## SBB

Subtract with Borrow

### Description:

SBB subtracts *source* from *dest* and stores the result in *dest*. If the carry flag (CF) is set, the result is decremented by 1. *Dest* and *source* may be bytes, words, doubleword (80386 or 80486) values.

Both *dest* and *source* are treated as binary values.

**Flag Indicators affected:**
O D I T S Z A P C

**Operands:**
SBB dest source

## SCAS

Scan String (Byte or Word)

### Description:

SCAS, SCASB, SCASW and SCASD scan strings to search for a value.

SCAS scans byte strings, word strings or doubleword strings (80386 and 80486) looking for a match to the string identified by *val*.

SCASB scans strings looking for a match to the byte contained in register AL.

SCASW scans strings looking for a match to the word contained in register AX.

SCASD scans strings looking for a match to the doubleword contained in register EAX (80386 and 80486).

In all cases, the comparison string is pointed to by register pair ES:DI. If DF=0, then DI is incremented by the number of bytes being scanned. If DF=1, then DI is decremented by the number of bytes being scanned.

**Flag Indicators affected:**
O D I T S Z A P C

**Operands:**
SCAS val

SCASB no operands
SCASW no operands
SCASD no operands

## SETA | Set if Above

*386*

**Description:**

SETAE sets *dest* to 1 if CF=0 and ZF=0; otherwise it sets *dest* to 0. *Dest* is a byte register or memory location.

**Flag Indicators affected:**          **Operands:**

O D I T S Z A P C                       SETA dest

## SETAE | Set if Above or Equal

*386*

**Description:**

SETA sets *dest* to 1 if CF=0; otherwise it sets *dest* to 0. *Dest* is a byte register or memory location.

**Flag Indicators affected:**          **Operands:**

O D I T S Z A P C                       SETAE dest

## SETB | Set if Below

*386*

**Description:**

SETB sets *dest* to 1 if CF=1; otherwise it sets *dest* to 0. *Dest* is a byte register or memory location.

**Flag Indicators affected:**          **Operands:**

O D I T S Z A P C                       SETB dest

## SETBE
Set if Below or Equal

*386*

**Description:**

SETBE sets *dest* to 1 if CF=1 or ZF=1; otherwise it sets *dest* to 0. *Dest* is a byte register or memory location.

**Flag Indicators affected:**

O D I T S Z A P C

**Operands:**

SETBE dest

## SETC
Set if Carry

*386*

**Description:**

SETC sets *dest* to 1 if CF=1; otherwise it sets *dest* to 0. *Dest* is a byte register or memory location.

**Flag Indicators affected:**

O D I T S Z A P C

**Operands:**

SETC dest

## SETE
Set if Equal

*386*

**Description:**

SETE sets *dest* to 1 if ZF=1; otherwise it sets *dest* to 0. *Dest* is a byte register or memory location.

**Flag Indicators affected:**

O D I T S Z A P C

**Operands:**

SETE dest

## SETG · Set if Greater

*386*

**Description:**

SETG sets *dest* to 1 if SF=OF (overflow flag) and ZF=0; otherwise it sets *dest* to 0. *Dest* is a byte register or memory location.

**Flag Indicators affected:**     **Operands:**

O D I T S Z A P C     SETG dest

## SETGE · Set if Greater or Equal

*386*

**Description:**

SETGE sets *dest* to 1 if SF=OF (overflow flag); otherwise it sets *dest* to 0. *Dest* is a byte register or memory location.

**Flag Indicators affected:**     **Operands:**

O D I T S Z A P C     SETGE dest

## SETL · Set if Less

*386*

**Description:**

SETL sets *dest* to 1 if SF<>OF (overflow flag); otherwise it sets *dest* to 0. *Dest* is a byte register or memory location.

**Flag Indicators affected:**     **Operands:**

O D I T S Z A P C     SETL dest

## SETLE
Set if Less or Equal

*386*

**Description:**

SETLE sets *dest* to 1 if SF<>OF (overflow flag) or ZF=1; otherwise it sets *dest* to 0. *Dest* is a byte register or memory location.

**Flag Indicators affected:**

O D I T S Z A P C

**Operands:**

SETLE dest

## SETNA
Set if Not Above

*386*

**Description:**

SETNA sets *dest* to 1 if CF=1 or ZF=1; otherwise it sets *dest* to 0. *Dest* is a byte register or memory location.

**Flag Indicators affected:**

O D I T S Z A P C

**Operands:**

SETNA dest

## SETNAE
Set if Not Above or Equal

*386*

**Description:**

SETNAE sets *dest* to 1 if CF=1; otherwise it sets *dest* to 0. *Dest* is a byte register or memory location.

**Flag Indicators affected:**

O D I T S Z A P C

**Operands:**

SETNAE dest

## SETNB — Set if Not Below

*386*

**Description:**

SETNB sets *dest* to 1 if CF=0; otherwise it sets *dest* to 0. *Dest* is a byte register or memory location.

**Flag Indicators affected:**          **Operands:**

O D I T S Z A P C                      SETNB dest

## SETNBE — Set if Not Below or Equal

*386*

**Description:**

SETNBE sets *dest* to 1 if CF=0 and ZF=0; otherwise it sets *dest* to 0. *Dest* is a byte register or memory location.

**Flag Indicators affected:**          **Operands:**

O D I T S Z A P C                      SETNBE dest

## SETNC — SET if Not Carry

*386*

**Description:**

SETNC sets *dest* to 1 if CF=0; otherwise it sets *dest* to 0. *Dest* is a byte register or memory location.

**Flag Indicators affected:**          **Operands:**

O D I T S Z A P C                      SETNC dest

## SETNE
Set if Not Equal

*386*

**Description:**

SETNE sets *dest* to 1 if ZF=0; otherwise it sets *dest* to 0. *Dest* is a byte register or memory location.

**Flag Indicators affected:**

O D I T S Z A P C

**Operands:**

SETNE dest

## SETNG
Set if Not Greater

*386*

**Description:**

SETNG sets *dest* to 1 if SF<>OF or ZF=1; otherwise it sets *dest* to 0. *Dest* is a byte register or memory location.

**Flag Indicators affected:**

O D I T S Z A P C

**Operands:**

SETNG dest

## SETNGE
Set if Not Greater or Equal

*386*

**Description:**

SETNGE sets *dest* to 1 if SF<>OF; otherwise it sets *dest* to 0. *Dest* is a byte register or memory location.

**Flag Indicators affected:**

O D I T S Z A P C

**Operands:**

SETNGE dest

## SETNL                                                                 Set if Not Less

*386*

**Description:**

SETNL sets *dest* to 1 if SF=OF; otherwise it sets *dest* to 0. *Dest* is a byte register or memory location.

**Flag Indicators affected:**          **Operands:**

O D I T S Z A P C                      SETNL dest

## SETNLE                                                       Set if Not Less or Equal

*386*

**Description:**

SETNLE sets *dest* to 1 if ZF=OF; otherwise it sets *dest* to 0. *Dest* is a byte register or memory location.

**Flag Indicators affected:**          **Operands:**

O D I T S Z A P C                      SETNLE dest

## SETNO                                                               Set if Not Overflow

*386*

**Description:**

SETNO sets *dest* to 1 if OF=0; otherwise it sets *dest* to 0. *Dest* is a byte register or memory location.

**Flag Indicators affected:**          **Operands:**

O D I T S Z A P C                      SETNO dest

## SETNP                                                     Set if Not Parity

*386*

### Description:

SETNP sets *dest* to 1 if PF=0; otherwise it sets *dest* to 0. *Dest* is a byte register or memory location.

**Flag Indicators affected:**          **Operands:**

O D I T S Z A P C                       SETNP dest

## SETNS                                                       Set if Not Sign

*386*

### Description:

SETNS sets *dest* to 1 if SF=0; otherwise it sets *dest* to 0. *Dest* is a byte register or memory location.

**Flag Indicators affected:**          **Operands:**

O D I T S Z A P C                       SETNS dest

## SETNZ                                                       Set if Not Zero

*386*

### Description:

SETNLE sets *dest* to 1 if ZF=0; otherwise it sets *dest* to 0. *Dest* is a byte register or memory location.

**Flag Indicators affected:**          **Operands:**

O D I T S Z A P C                       SETNZ dest

## SETO
Set if Overflow

*386*

### Description:

SETO sets *dest* to 1 if OF=1; otherwise it sets *dest* to 0. *Dest* is a byte register or memory location.

**Flag Indicators affected:**      **Operands:**

O D I T S Z A P C      SETO dest

## SETP
Set if Parity

*386*

### Description:

SETP sets *dest* to 1 if PF=1; otherwise it sets *dest* to 0. *Dest* is a byte register or memory location.

**Flag Indicators affected:**      **Operands:**

O D I T S Z A P C      SETP dest

## SETPE
Set if Parity Even

*386*

### Description:

SETNLE sets *dest* to 1 if PF=1; otherwise it sets *dest* to 0. *Dest* is a byte register or memory location.

**Flag Indicators affected:**      **Operands:**

O D I T S Z A P C      SETPE dest

## SETPO                                                      Set if Parity Odd

*386*

### Description:

SETPO sets *dest* to 1 if PF=0; otherwise it sets *dest* to 0. *Dest* is a byte register or memory location.

**Flag Indicators affected:**          **Operands:**

O D I T S Z A P C                      SETPO dest

## SETS                                                          Set if Sign

*386*

### Description:

SETS sets *dest* to 1 if SF=1; otherwise it sets *dest* to 0. *Dest* is a byte register or memory location.

**Flag Indicators affected:**          **Operands:**

O D I T S Z A P C                      SETS dest

## SETZ                                                          Set if Zero

*386*

### Description:

SETZ sets *dest* to 1 if ZF=1; otherwise it sets *dest* to 0. *Dest* is a byte register or memory location.

**Flag Indicators affected:**          **Operands:**

O D I T S Z A P C                      SETZ dest

| SHLD | Shift Left, Double-precision |

*386*

**Description:**

SHLD shifts the contents of *dest* to the left by the number of bits specified by *numbits*. Any high order bits shifted out are lost. New low order bits are shifted in from *source*. *Dest* may be a byte, word, doubleword register or memory location. *Source* may be a word or doubleword register. *Numbits* is an immediate value or a value is register CL.

**Flag Indicators affected:**

O D I T S Z A P C

**Operands:**

SHLD dest, source, numbits

**Note:** The O and F flags are undefined.

| SHL | Shift Left |

**Description:**

SHL and SAL shifts the contents of *dest* by the number specified by *numbits*. Any high order bits shifted out of *dest* are lost. New low order fill bits are set to zero.

**Flag Indicators affected:**

O D I T S Z A P C

**Operands:**

SHL dest, numbits

| SHR | Shift Right |

**Description:**

SHR shifts the bits in *dest* bits by the number specified in *numbits* Any low order bits shifted out of *dest* are lost. New high order bits are filled with zero.

**Flag Indicators affected:**

O D I T S Z A P C

**Operands:**

SHR dest, numbits

## SHRD | Shift Right, Double-precision

*386*

**Description:**

SHRD shifts the contents of *dest* to the right by the number of bits specified by *numbits*. Any low order bits shifted out are lost. New high order bits are shifted in from *source*. *Dest* may be a byte, word, doubleword register or memory location. *Source* may be a word or doubleword register. *Numbits* is an immediate value or a value is register CL.

**Flag Indicators affected:**

O D I T S Z A P C

**Operands:**

SHRD dest, source, numbits

**Note:** The O and F flags are undefined.

## STC | Set Carry Flag

**Description:**

STC sets the carry flag (CF).

**Flag Indicators affected:**

O D I T S Z A P C

**Operands:**

STC no operands

## STD | Set Direction Flag

**Description:**

STD sets the direction flag (DF).

**Flag Indicators affected:**

O D I T S Z A P C

**Operands:**

STD no operands

## STI | Set Interrupt Flag

**Description:**

STI sets the interrupt flag (IF) regardless of its current condition. The CPU is then able to respond to maskable interrupts.

**Flag Indicators affected:**

O D I T S Z A P C

**Operands:**

No operands

## STOS                                          Store in String

**Description:**

STOS, STOSB, STOSW and STOSD store strings to memory locations.

STOS stores byte, word or doubleword (80386 and 80486) strings from the AL, AX or EAX registers respectively.

STOSB stores byte strings from the AL register.

STOSW stores word strings from the AX register.

STOSD stores doubleword strings from the EAX register (80386 and 80486).

In all four cases, the destination memory location is pointed to by register pair ES:DI. If DF=0, then DI is incremented by the number of bytes stored. If DF=1, then DI is decremented by the number of bytes stored.

**Flag Indicators affected:**

O D I T S Z A P C

**Operands:**

STOS dest

STOSB no operands

STOSW no operands

STOSD no operands

## SUB                                                Subtract

**Description:**

SUB subtracts *source* from *dest* and stores the result in *dest*. *Dest* and *source* may be bytes, words, doublewords (80386 or 80486), registers or memory locations. Both *dest* and *source* are treated as unsigned binary numbers. SUB updates AF, CF, OF, PF, SF and ZF.

**Flag Indicators affected:**

O D I T S Z A P C

**Operands:**

SUB dest, source

## TEST
Test Bits

### Description:

TEST performs a logical AND between *dest* and *mask* to set flags but does not retain the result. *Dest* and *mask* may be byte, word or doubleword (80386 or 80486) values.

**Flag Indicators affected:**

O̲ D I T S̲ Z̲ A̲ P̲ C̲

**Operands:**

TEST dest, mask

## WAIT
Wait

### Description:

WAIT puts the processor in a wait state until it detects a signal on the Test line.

**Flag Indicators affected:**

O D I T S Z A P C

**Operands:**

WAIT no operands

## XCHG
Exchange

### Description:

XCHG swaps or exchanges the values between *op1* and *op2*. *Op1* and *op2* may be byte, word or doubleword (80386 or 80486) operands. Either one of *op1* and *op2* must be a register.

**Flag Indicators affected:**

O D I T S Z A P C

**Operands:**

XCHG op1, op2

## XLAT
Translate

### Description:

XLAT translates an 8-bit value contained in AL to a corresponding value found in a table addressed by register pair DS:BX. AL is used as an index to the translation table beginning at DS:BX. The result is stored in AL.

**Flag Indicators affected:**

O D I T S Z A P C

**Operands:**

XLAT val

XLATB no operands

## XOR                                        Exclusive OR

**Description:**

XOR logically exclusive ORs the bits of *dest* and *source* and stores the results in *dest*. *Dest* and *source* may be bytes, words, doublewords (80386 or 80486), registers or memory locations.

**Flag Indicators affected:**              **Operands:**

O D I T S Z A P C                          XOR dest, source

# Appendix F: Chapter Exercise Answers

The following are the answers to the questions in the Chapter Exercises. Some of these questions may not have a specific "right or wrong" answer so don't be discouraged if your answer doesn't match our answers.

## Chapter 2

1)

```
 111111
 1111110
10000001
00101000
11111111
 0100010
```

2)

```
137
253
 31
 63
  4
  8
  3
131
```

3)

```
256  =   1 0000  0000
512  =  10 0000  0000
13   =           1101
347  =   1 0101  1011
1023 =  11 1111  1111
752  =  10 1111  0000
12   =           1100
21   =         1 0101
```

4)

```
FF   = 15 * 16 + 15 = 255
FE   = 15 * 16 + 14 = 254
F3E  = 15 * 256 + 3 * 16 + 14 = 3902
A2B  = 10 * 256 + 2 * 16 + 11 = 2603
```

```
221   = 2 * 256 + 2 * 16 + 1 = 545
34E   = 3 * 256 + 4 * 16 + 14 = 846
8000  = 8 * 4096 + 0 * 256 + 0 * 16 + 0 = 32768
44F   = 4 * 256 + 4 * 16 + 15 = 1103
```

5)

```
11    =                    1 0001
BA    =               1011 1010
CF3B  = 1100 1111    0011 1011
4E43  = 0100 1110    0100 0011
1234  =    1 0010    0011 0100
FF    =              1111 1111
F34E  = 1111 0011    0100 1110
```

6)

```
FFE + FEF   = 1FED
FA + A2     = 019C
A3B4 + F654 = 19A08
8987 + A567 = 12EEE
1 + 12      = 13
23 + A4E    = A71
```

7)

```
11011    OR     111001   =      111011
11101    AND    111001   =      011001
11101    AND    11101    =      11101   OR    11011   =      11111
111011   XOR    11011    =      100000

11011    AND
       (   11011   OR    110110   =    111111   )    =      011011

111011   AND
       (  NOT(1111001) = 110   OR   111100   =   111110   )
                                               =   111010

NOT    (   111001   XOR
                  (   11101   AND   101001   =   001001   )
                      =  110000   )
                                   =   001111
```

# Chapter 3

1)  The OR gate doesn't let the current pass except when one of the two inputs is in a high state (at 1). If both inputs are in a low state, the gate doesn't let the current pass. See Chapter 3.3.

2)    The AND gate only lets the current pass when both inputs are in a high state. If one of the inputs is in the low state, the current doesn't pass. See Chapter 3.3.

3)    The NOT gate reverses the state of the input. See Chapter 3.3.

4)    1964

5)    Reliability and speed

6)    Transistor-Transistor Logic

# Chapter 5

1)    The BIG command is a "toggle" command. When you use it the first time, it displays all the registers of the microprocessor. When you use it a second time, it only displays a selection of the registers. See Chapter 5.2.

2)    To enter the value 77h in the AX register, you must type:

```
>>AX77 <Enter>
```

3)    To load the BX register in binary base, type:

```
BASE BX BIN <Enter>
```

4)    To reconstruct the SIM display, type:

```
DSCRN <Enter>
```

See Chapter 5.3 or Appendix D.

5)

```
345h * FF5h      =      342C09
234h / 12h       =      1F
FF4h + 5FABh     =      6F9F
F6h - 6h         =      F0
```

6)

```
45    =    2D
457   =    1C9
255   =    FF
127   =    7F
78    =    4E
```

7)

```
45h   =      69
FF2   =    4082
6B    =     107
87h   =     135
8FF   =    2303
8890h =   34960
```

## Chapter 6

1)      A segment is a 64K memory block. Each segment begins and ends at a "paragraph boundary" (a multiple of 16 bytes). You can address all the memory within a segment using a single 16-bit register. See Chapter 6.1.

2)      The offset is the relative position of an address from the beginning of a segment. This position is given relatively to the first segment address. So by specifying the segment (which in fact, is the first address of the segment) and the offset, you can define the absolute address. See Chapter 6.1.2.

## Chapter 7

1)      Simply type "E" followed by the offset of the memory location you want to change and then press <Enter>. Next select the value indicated.

For the three examples given, enter the following in order:

```
E 212 21 <Enter>
E 215 30 <Enter>
E 217 4F <Enter>
```

2)      Type "E 217" then the <-> key (minus key). See Chapter 7.3.

3)      Type the "E" command, followed by the offset of the first memory location to be modified and the list of the data, separated by spaces:

```
E 212 15 13 1F FA 11 3A
```

See Chapter 7.3 or Appendix D.

4)      To display the contents of memory locations, use the DUMP command. The "D" command from SIM lets you do this. Between ssss:212 and ssss:217 there are six memory locations. So we'll display six memory locations beginning at offset 212:

```
D 212 L 6
```

See Appendix D.

5)      To display the contents of the 128 following bytes, type:

        D

See Appendix D.

6)      Display contents of memory location 0020:012B to 0020:02A0.

See Chapter 7.5 or Appendix D.

7)      Simply type the command:

        D 00A1:02F0 L 300

See Chapter 7.5 or Appendix D.

8)      Open a window using the DMEM command:

        DMEM 0212

See Chapter 7.5 or Appendix D.

9)      Open a memory window and specify that the data is to be displayed in word
        format:

        DMEM 0216 W

10)     Type the following:

        E 218 4B

Next type "E 218" again to observe the modification.

# Chapter 8

1)      Fill a memory area with the series of FF FE bytes. Use the "Fill" command.
        Suppose that you fill 3000 bytes from offset 100 of the present segment. Use the
        command:

        F 100 L 3000 FF FE

See Chapter 8 or Appendix D.

2)      Answer:

        D 100 L 3000

See Chapter 8 or Appendix D.

3) For example, put the value 45h at offset 200h of the user area:

```
E 200 45
```

4) For example, we'll do a search from offset 80h on an area of 300h bytes. We're looking for the value 45h:

```
S 80 L 300 45
```

See Chapter 8 or Appendix D.

5) To move 400h bytes, use the "Move" command. For example, let's move 400h bytes from offset 100h to offset 500h:

```
M 100 l 400 500
```

Now let's compare the 400h bytes starting at offset 100h with the 400h bytes beginning at offset 500h. Use the "C" command:

```
C 100 l 400 500
```

# Chapter 9

1) The data registers are usually used to store data. You have four 16-bit data registers which are each divided into two 8-bit data registers (or a total of eight 8-bit data registers). However, each one has a specific function:

AX = Accumulator
This register is often used to store an intermediate value to be used in an instruction. It's divided into AL and AH, two 8-bit accumulator registers.

BX = Base
This register is sometimes used as a base for calculations or operations on the memory. It is divided into two 8-bit registers of BL and BH.

CX = Counter
This register is used in some counter operations for decrementing. For example, this is used for loops. It is divided into CL and CH, two 8-bit registers.

DX = Data
This register sometimes contains data intended for processing by processor operations. It's divided into two 8-bit registers called DL and DH.

See Chapter 9.1.

2)      Indexing registers (DI = Destination Index and SI = Source Index) are used to specify a memory area with which to perform block copy operations for example. SP = Stack Pointer and BP = Base Pointer are similar to these registers in that they are also used to address a specific memory area called the stack. See Chapter 9.1 .

3)      A segment is a 64K memory area. A segment always begins at an address which is a multiple of 16 (a paragraph boundary). Segment registers are used to address these 64K blocks of memory. There is the code segment register (CS), the data segment register (DS), the source segment register (SS), and the extra segment register (ES). See Chapter 9.1 .

4)      The instruction pointer tells the microprocessor which instruction it will execute next. So it's a register that is incremented after each instruction is executed. See Chapter 9.1 .

5)      The flag register (FL) contains a certain number of "indicators" which give information about the status of the microprocessor. Thus, you can know whether the result of an operation on signed numbers is positive or negative. See Chapter 9.1.

6)      The Z register (data latch) is a kind of gate or mandatory passage by which all the data has to pass. It is divided into two 8-bit registers called ZH and ZL. See Chapter 9.1 .

7)      The abbreviation I L N I T represent certain control signals (pins) of the microprocessor. They represent the Input/Output pin, the Lock pin, the NMI pin (Non Maskable Interrupt), the Interrupt pin and the Test pin, respectively. See Chapter 9.2.

8)      CS:IP is the abbreviation of Code Segment:Instruction Pointer. This expression indicates the segment and offset of a memory address. It's the location where the instruction being executed is located. See Chapter 9.2.

9)      "Fetch Opcode" means "read the operation code". Here, the microprocessor loads the operation code in its internal registers so it can decode it and execute the instruction. See Chapter 9.2.

10)     To increment AX = INC AX.

        To increment DX = INC DX.

        See Chapter 9.3 or the 8088 instructions in Appendix E.

11)     Answer:

        `DEC BX`

See Chapter 9.4 or the 8088 instructions in Appendix E.

12)     Disassembling consists of reading the contents of the memory area and displaying the corresponding mnemonics. So the mnemonic of an instruction can correspond to each series of bytes. See Chapter 9.5.

13)     Use the "U" command followed by the memory area to be disassembled. See Chapter 9.5 or Appendix D.

14)     Use the "A" command followed by the offset from which you want to start assembling. See Chapter 9.5 or Appendix D.

15)     Press <A> and <Enter> to start assembling. Next enter the following instructions:

        `INC AX`
        `DEC AX`

To execute this program, stop the assembling process by pressing <Ctrl><C>, then go to the beginning of the program by setting the instruction pointer at the address of the beginning of the program (IP Address_beginning). Then start SIM in the STEP 4 mode.

16)     To set all the registers to display in binary mode, type:

        `BASE * BIN`

To start up SIM in STEP 4 mode, enter:

        `STEP 4`

Then:

        `SIM 2`

There are actually two instructions to execute. If you type "SIM" the simulator only executes one instruction. If you type "SIM 7", for example, it will execute seven instructions, etc. See Chapter 9.6 or Appendix D.

# Chapter 10

1)      Use the NEW command. See Chapter 10.1 or Appendix D.

2)      The MOV mnemonic is used to transfer values from a memory location or a register to another register or memory location. See the beginning of Chapter 10 or Appendix E.

3)      Answer:

```
MOV AX, 6787
```

4)      Answer:

```
MOV SI, 76
```

5)      Type <A> to assemble a program. Next, enter this instruction:

```
MOV CX, F004
```

Then press <Ctrl><C> to return to the SIM commands. Start the program by typing "SIM."

6)      Type the "A" command to assemble. Then select the following commands:

```
MOV AL, 64
DEC AL
```

Next press <Ctrl><C> to return to the SIM commands. Move into STEP 4 mode to see how the program is functioning. Then type "SIM 2" to simulate the two instructions that you have chosen.

7)      This is the program:

```
MOV AL, F5
MOV AH, 55
```

Start this program as you did the previous one.

# Chapter 11

1)      The Effective Address byte (EA) represents certain characteristics of the instruction to execute. These characteristics are coded in bit form. Each characteristic is represented by a "field" or series of several bits. The EA byte may contain these fields: D, W, MOD, REG and R/M fields. When the microprocessor reads the instruction, it decodes the EA byte. You usually don't need to be concerned with the status of the EA byte. The mnemonic of the instruction is explicit enough for you to know what the characteristics are of the EA byte.

2) "R/M" is the abbreviation for Register/Memory. This field specifies whether the operation executed concerns a register or the memory. In the case of a MOV, it indicates whether the value to transfer is in a register or whether it's a question of a memory location. See the section on REG and R/M fields in Chapter 11.

3) "D" means Destination. This field lets you know where the destination and source are located in a data transfer operation into the memory. In concrete terms, when "D" is set, it means that REG specifies the destination. If "D" is clear, R/M represents the destination. See the section on REG and R/M fields in Chapter 11.

4) "W" represents Word. This field lets you know if the operations are being executed on a byte (W is set) or a word (W is set). See the section on REG and R/M fields in Chapter 11.

5) It's the mnemonic MOV AL, BL.

6) It's the mnemonic XCHG SI, CX.

7) You have to use the MOV mnemonic with AX as the source register and BX as the target register:

```
MOV BX, AX
```

8) Use the XCHG instruction:

```
XCHG AX,CX
```

9) The DEC instruction lets you execute this operation:

```
DEC CX
```

# Chapter 12

1) The overflow flag is the O flag. See the first part of Chapter 12.

2) The sign flag is the S flag. See Chapter 12.2.

3) The CLC instruction is used to clear the carry flag. You generally clear the carry flag before an operation so you can then know if an operation resulted in setting or clearing the carry flag.

4) The zero flag lets you know if the result of an operation is equal to zero (zero flag set). See Chapter 12.1.

5)      To clear the Zero flag, you have to execute an operation whose result is different from zero. For example, you can put the value "0" in AX, then increment AX:

```
MOV AX, 0
INC AX
```

In this case, after executing both instructions, AX contains the value 01h. Then you just have to decrement AX with the DEC instruction:

```
DEC AX
```

6)      This is the program:

```
MOV AX, FFFC
INC AX
INC AX
INC AX
INC AX
```

At the end of this program, AX has a value of 0. Notice the status of the Z flag.

7)      This is the program:

```
MOV CL, 88
DEC CL
```

# Chapter 13

1)      The answer is the JZ mnemonic (Jump If Zero). See Chapter 13.1.

2)      The JNZ mnemonic (Jump if Not Zero). See Chapter 13.1.

3)      The JS mnemonic (Jump if Sign). See Chapter 13.1.

4)      The JCXZ mnemonic (Jump if CX is Zero). See Chapter 13.1.

5)      This is the program. Start your selection with IP=100h.

```
MOV BX, AX
DEC AX
JNZ 100
```

6)      This is the program. Start your selection with IP=100h.

```
MOV AX, 80
INC AX
JNP 103
```

7) This is the program. Start with IP=100h.

```
MOV AX,00
MOV DX,AX
INC AX
JNZ 103
MOV AX,DX
```

# Chapter 14

1) It's the LOOP mnemonic. As long as CX is different from zero, this instruction jumps to the memory location specified. For example, LOOP 103 jumps to offset 103 as long is CX is different from zero. See the beginning of Chapter 14.

2) It's the JNZ 150 instruction.

3) It's the JMP 130 instruction. See Chapter 14.1.

4) Here's the program:

```
MOV AX,04
MOV CX,FF
DEC CX
JNZ 106
```

You can also write it like this:

```
MOV AX,04
MOV CX,FF
LOOP 106
```

The LOOP instruction tests whether CX=0. If not, it jumps to address 103h.

5) Here is the continuation of the program:

```
INC AX
MOV DX,AX
DEC DX
INC DX
JNZ 106
```

What are operations DEC DX, INC DX used for? Well, since we haven't yet seen a mnemonic for testing the DX register, we have to use a trick. To do it, we execute a null operation (increment, then decrement of the DX register). If the result is not zero (or it's equivalent to DX is different from zero), jump to offset 106h where either the LOOP 106 instruction or the DEC CX instruction is, depending on the solution that you chose in the first part of the program.

# Chapter 15

1) It's the mnemonic ADD AX. BX. The result is placed in AX. See the beginning of Chapter 15.

2) The ADC instruction uses the carry flag for operations with results greater than 16 bits. See Chapter 15.1.

3) It's the mnemonic CMP BL, 23. See Chapter 15.2.

4) This is the program:

```
MOV AH, 77
MOV BX, 76
ADD AX, BX
```

Be careful with this type of program. In fact, when you perform addition between an 8-bit register and a 16-bit one, there are two solutions:

- First clear the high order part of the register (AH in this case) and then add the two 16-bit registers (AX and BX).

- Or save the contents of the 16-bit register (AX, in our case) which contains the 8-bit register to add (here it's AH) and you clear the second 8-bit register (AL). Then perform a 16-bit addition and eventually restore the previous contents of the 16-bit register.

5) This is the program:

```
MOV AL, 55
MOV BL, 55
ADD AL, BL
MOV CX, AL
```

The carry flag is set after you add AL and BL.

6) Here's the program:

```
MOV AX, 77
DEC AX
CMP AX, 50
JNE 103
```

Remember that JNE means "Jump if Not Equal".

7)      Here is the continuation of the program:

```
MOV CX,96
MOV CX,AX
ADC CX,BX
MOV BX,0
```

We enter the contents of the AX register in CX and perform an addition with a remainder between CX and BX and a result in CX. BX still contains the same value as before. Next, we can clear BX so the value of BX:CX with the remainder is the addition of AX and BX.

## Chapter 16

1)      It's the mnemonic MOV BL,CS:[5C8]. See the beginning of Chapter 16.

2)      The segment prefix is used to specify in which segment the operation concerned is executed. So in the first exercise of this chapter, we specified that the value should be read in the code segment. See Chapter 16.1.

3)      It's the mnemonic DEC [36]. See Chapter 16.2.

4)      This is the program. Start with IP=100h.

```
MOV AX,DS:[F8]
DEC DS:[F8]
JNZ 103
MOV DS:[F8],AX
JMP 100
```

## Chapter 17

1)      It's the mnemonic MUL AX. See Chapter 17.1.

2)      AX is the base register for the division. The DIV instruction lets you divide AX by a register that is specified in the DIV instruction. Therefore, DIV BX divides the contents of the AX register by the contents of the BX register. To put the result in BX, you have to transfer the AX register into the BX register:

```
MOV BX,AX
```

3)      Here is the program with the offsets:

```
CS:0100 MOV BX,04
CS:0103 MOV AX,BX
CS:0105 DEC BX
CS:0106 MUL BX
CS:108 CMP BX,0001
CS:10B JNZ 105
```

This program calculates the factorial of a number entered in BX.

4)      Here is the program with n=3 and AL=05. We're going to calculate $5^3$:

```
CS:0100 MOV AL,05
CS:0102 MOV BL,03
CS:0104 MOV DL,AL
CS:0106 MUL DL
CS:0108 DEC BL
CS:010A CMP BL,01
CS:010D JNZ 0106
```

The result at the end of the operation is in AL. You begin by entering the contents of AL in DL. Then multiply DL by AL until BL equals 1.

5)      Here's the program:

```
CS:0100 MOV AX,23
CS:0103 MOV BX,24
CS:0106 MUL AX
CS:0108 MOV CX,AX
CS:010A MOV AX,BX
CS:010C MUL BX
CS:010E ADD AX,CX
```

Start by specifying the length of the two sides (for example, 23 and 24). Multiply the first side by itself. Save the contents of the AX register which contains this value in the CX register. Transfer the length of the second side into AX. Then multiply AX by BX (you could also multiply it by itself). Finally, add the square of the length of the two sides.

# Chapter 18

1)      Here's the program:

```
MOV AX,33
SHL AX,1
```

See Chapter 18.1.

2)      Here's the program:

```
MOV BX,44
RCL BX,1
```

3)      Here's the program:

```
MOV BX,44
ROR BX,1
```

See Chapter 18.2.

4)    Here's the program:

```
MOV DX, 67
MOV CL, 3
SHL DX, CL
```

# Chapter 19

1)    Here's the program:

```
MOV   AL, 37
AND   AL, 17
```

2)    Here's the program:

```
MOV   BL, 22
OR BL, 14
```

3)    Here's the program:

```
MOV   AX, F80A
XOR   AX, 2600
```

4)    One way to clear the CX register is to set all the bits at zero with the AND instruction:

```
AND  CX, 0
```

See the beginning of Chapter 19.

5)    Here's the program:

```
MOV BL, 89
TEST BL, 80
JNZ  010A
SHL BL, 1
BRK
SHR BL, 1
BRK
```

The value 40h is represented in binary by 10000000. This explains the instruction TEST BX,80.

6)    Here's the program:

```
CS:0100 MOV BX, F7
CS:0103 INC BX
CS:0104 TEST BX, 04
CS:0108 JNZ 103
CS:010A ROL BX, 1
CS:010B MOV AX, BX
```

Remember that rotating a value to the left by one bit is equivalent to multiplying it by 2.

# Chapter 20

1)

```
 -12    = 1111 1111 1111 0100
 -15    = 1111 1111 1111 0001
 -22    = 1111 1111 1110 1010
 -27    = 1111 1111 1110 0101
 -38    = 1111 1111 1101 1010
-553    = 1111 1101 1101 0111
```

2)      Multiplying two negative numbers is equal to multiplying the absolute value of these same two numbers. For example, you can use the following program:

```
MOV AX,22
MOV BX,34
MUL BX
```

and the result is in AX.

3)      Here's the program:

```
MOV AX,5
SUB AX,11        (17 dec = 11h)
CBW
```

Remember that CBW means "Convert Byte to Word". See Chapter 20.1.

# Chapter 21

1)      First convert the string of characters HELLO to hexadecimal. (See the ASCII table.)

```
 H     E     L     L     O
48h   45h   4Ch   4Ch   4F
```

Now calculate the address of the position line 7, column 5:

Assuming that each line has 80 columns, the offset you're looking for is at (80*6)+5=484 (line 7 = 0 at 6, column 5 = 0 at 4) from the beginning of the video RAM. However, be careful, since you're working with words. You have to multiply the value by 2:

```
485 * 2 = 968
```

Convert this to hexadecimal:

3C8h

To write HELLO on line 7, column 5 of the screen, enter:

E B000:3CA 48 48 45 45 4C 4C 4C 4C 4F 4F

Repeat the letter twice because they're words and not bytes. The second byte is used to specify certain attributes of the text. For example, try:

E B000:3CA 48 FF 45 FF 4C FF 4C FF 4F FF

If you have a color card, the segment address is B800.

# Chapter 22

1)      It's the mnemonic MOV AX,DI.

2)      It's the mnemonic MOV [SI+36],AX. See Chapter 22.1.

# Chapter 23

1)      Use the mnemonic MOV SP,B800.

2)      First you have to enter this value in a register, for example:

```
MOV AX,55
```

Then put the register on the stack:

```
PUSH AX
```

3)      This works the same as the last problem:

```
MOV AX,67
PUSH AX
```

4)      Use the POP command:

```
POP CX
```

See Chapter 23.3.

## Chapter 24

1)      This is the program:

```
CS:0100 MOV SI,200
CS:0103 CALL [SI]
...
CS:0200 MOV AX,30
CS:0203 RET
```

## Chapter 25

1)      It's the following sequence:

```
MOV CX,100
MOV SI,100
MOV DI,400
REP MOVSB
```

See Chapter 25.2.

2)      It's the following sequence:

```
MOV CX,200
MOV SI,300
MOV DI,350
STD
REP MOVSB
```

3)      Here's a program that lets you execute it:

```
MOV SI,100    (Destination string)
MOV AX,41     (character "A")
MOV CX,FF     (FF tests)
REPNE SCAS
```

See Chapter 25.5.

## Chapter 26

1)      Here's the program:

```
TEST PROC NEAR
            mov ax, 0000
            mov si, ax
            mov cx, B000
            mov ds, cx
```

```
loop:      add ax, [si]
           inc si
           loop
           mov bl, 0ffh
           div bl
```

2)

```
           mov cx, 0ffh
loop2:     mov [si],ax
           dec si
           loop2
           ret
test endp
code ENDS
end
```

# Chapter 27

1) The input/output ports are the connections of the processor which link it to its peripherals. A memory address corresponds to each port. When you store a value in this memory address, it is transferred to the peripheral.

2) It's the mnemonic IN 60 (example: IN AX,60). See Chapter 27.1.

3) It's the mnemonic OUT 61 (example: OUT 61,AL). See Chapter 27.3.

# Chapter 29

1) An interrupt is a signal sent to an interrupt pin of the microprocessor. When such a pin is set, the processor stops its work in progress to take care of another task.

2) Here's the program:

```
MOV AH, 02          ;set up function 02h
INT 16h             ;call keyboard status interrupt
AND AL,20h          ;test bit 5 only, others = 0
CMP AL,20h          ; Is <NumLock> on?
```

# Chapter 30

1) Here's the program:

```
MOV  AH,02h         ;set up function 02h
INT 16h             ;call keyboard status interrupt
PUSH AX             ;store AL
AND AL,20h          ;test bit 5 only
CMP AL,20h          ;<NumLock> key on?
```

```
              JNX CAP              ;If no, test <CapsLock>
              MOV AH,02h           ;If yes, set up to display
              MOV DL,4Eh           ; move "N" to DL
              INT 21h              ;display
      CAP     POP AX               ;use original value of AL
              AND AL,40h           ;<CapsLock> on
              JNZ EXIT             ;If no exit or BRK
              MOV AH,o2h           ;If yes display
              MOV DL,43h
              INT 21h

      EXIT:                        ;end
```

# Chapter 31

1)      This should be easy:

```
        NOP
        NOP
        NOP
```

See the beginning of Chapter 31.

2)      A routine like this is only made up of one mnemonic:

```
        NEG AX
```

Return the negative equivalent of the value contained in AX.

# Appendix G: Modifying SIM Screen

1.  Make a copy of SIM.EXE but use a different extension (for example, TMP):

    ```
    C>COPY SIM.EXE TMP <Enter>
    ```

2.  Start SIM and then load the copy of SIM:

    ```
    C>SIM TMP <Enter>
    ```

3.  Use the SEARCH instruction to find the DEFAULT: string. The area to modify should be about 76K from the top of the program or from the end of the program. Since by default you can't search through more than 64K (from the data segment), you have to specify a greater value in the SEARCH instruction. If the beginning of the user area in your computer starts at 1234h (or the "ssss" value displayed in the four segment registers starting SIM), search for the next 64K segment:

    ```
    >>S 2234:0 L FF00 'DEFAULT:'
    ```

4.  Then perform a DUMP of the area surrounding this string. The two bytes immediately following the colon (:) (at an address 8 bytes farther than provided by our search) should be 07 00. These values are the current foreground and background colors of SIM (white on a black background). SIM uses these display values every time it writes in the video memory.

    These values represent the Red, Green and Blue variables which control the signals of the video card. Set the three values to produce a white screen or clear them to produce a black screen. Combine them to produce secondary colors.

5.  Enter the values. For example, for the bytes at 2234:2CAE:

    ```
    >>E 2234:2CAE 1 0     ' blue on black background
    >>E 2234:2CAE 2 0     ' green on black background
    >>E 2234:2CAE 1 2     ' blue on green background
    >>E 2234:2CAE 0 7     ' inverted video; black on white
    >>E 2234:2CAE 0 0     ' black on black;  NOT ADVISABLE!
    ```

6.  Save the file and exit SIM.

    ```
    >>SAVE <Enter>
    >>Q <Enter>
    ```

7.  Rename the file with the .EXE extension and load it:.

    ```
    A>REN TMP SIMVERT.EXE <Enter>
    ```

# Index

# C

# D

# E-F

# M

# N-O

# P-Q

# T - Z

# Abacus pc catalog

## Order Toll Free 1-800-451-4319

**5370 52nd Street SE • Grand Rapids, MI 49512**
**Phone: (616) 698-0330 • Fax: (616) 698-0325**

# Programming VGA Graphics

VGA is now the standard display mode among the top selling PC software packages. If you develop software and want to support VGA mode, Programming VGA Graphics will help you write for almost any VGA video card. Programming VGA Graphics is a collection of language extensions for the Turbo Pascal and Turbo BASIC programmer.

Here's a look at what Programming VGA Graphics contains:

- Introduction to VGA, including system requirements (hardware and configuration, essential software, operating system, display adapter, monitors)
- Complete documentation to the routines included in the VGA Toolbox, featuring example programs
- DOS command extensions using Turbo Pascal (color changes in text modes, flipping between text and graphic modes and 256-color video show)
- Demonstrations of all video modes: Hercules, MDA, CGA, EGA, VGA. Introduction to small font sizes, graphic demos of all video modes (including EGA mode 13 and VGA/MGCA mode 19-inaccessible from BASIC or Pascal until now)
- Important tables and register usage (VGA, BIOS registers, video mode tables, new Pascal and DOS commands, etc.)

Still reluctant to make the investment? Programming VGA Graphics also includes real world applications - a game called "The search for alien planet Earth" and a multicolor fractal demonstration for video mode 19. Beginning programmers and professional developers alike can profit from Programming VGA Graphics. What can YOU do with VGA? Find out with our Programming VGA Graphics. w/2 companion disks.
ISBN 1-55755-099-9. $39.95

### Word 5.0 Know-How

This new book is written for users who demand professional results. Here you'll find dozens of in-depth techniques for producing high quality documents with the least amount of effort. You'll see how to easily select special purpose fonts, combine graphics into your text, work with multiple columns and use Word 5.0 for desktop publishing. 550 pp. w/ companion disk.
ISBN 1-55755-088-3. $24.95
Canada: 54385 $33.95

### Word for Windows Know-How

Microsoft Word for Windows is considered the premier wordprocessor among Windows users. This book is not only a guide to using Word for Windows, but presents many important techniques for exploiting all of the powerful features in this package. Working with macros; complete details on the new Word BASIC; handling graphics; printer formatting and more. Includes companion disk containing style sheets, Word BASIC examples, macros and more.
ISBN 1-55755-093-X. $34.95
Canada: 53924 $45.95

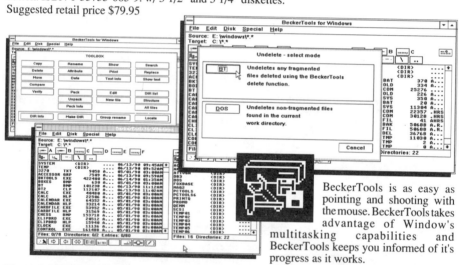